The Bedford Guide to
Teaching Writing in the Disciplines

The Bedford Guide to Teaching Writing in the Disciplines

AN INSTRUCTOR'S DESK REFERENCE

Rebecca Moore Howard
Colgate University

Sandra Jamieson
Drew University

Bedford Books *of* St. Martin's Press • Boston

For information, write: St. Martin's Press, Inc.
175 Fifth Avenue, New York, NY 10010
Editorial Offices: Bedford Books *of* St. Martin's Press
29 Winchester Street, Boston, MA 02116

ISBN: 0–312–106661

Cover design: Hannus Design Associates

Acknowledgments

Sample paper outline in Chapter 4 from *The Bedford Handbook for Writers*, Fourth Edition, by Diana Hacker, pages 516-517. Copyright © 1994 by St. Martin's Press Incorporated. Reproduced by permission of St. Martin's Press.

List of suggestions for avoiding sexist language in Chapter 5 from "Hearing is Believing: The Effect of Sexist Language on Language Skills" by Alice F. Freed, in *Teaching Writing: Pedagogy, Gender, and Equity*, Cynthia L. Caywood and Gillian R. Overing (eds.). Copyright © 1987 by State University of New York Press. Reprinted with permission.

Sample dichotomous scale grading sheet in Chapter 11 from "Responding to Student Writing" by Joyce MacAllister, in *Teaching Writing in All Disciplines*, C. W. Griffin (ed.), page 63. New Directions for Teaching and Learning, no. 12. Copyright © 1982 by Jossey-Bass Inc., Publishers. Reprinted with permission.

Summary writing assignment in Chapter 12 adapted from "A Six-Step Process for Writing Summaries" in *Writing and Reading Across the Curriculum* by Laurence Behrens and Leonard J. Rosen. Copyright © 1982. Reprinted by permission of HarperCollins College Publishers.

Preface

More and more instructors in a variety of disciplines—from history to chemistry, from anthropology to mathematics—are including writing in their courses, whether out of their own initiative or as part of a university requirement. Such efforts not only enhance students' learning and improve their general writing skills, but also introduce students to conventions of writing in particular fields, helping them become confident participants in those fields.

Though instructors in various disciplines may see the value of including writing in their courses, many have questions about how to do so: What kinds of assignments should I give and when? How do I evaluate students' writing, and how much attention should I pay to grammar and punctuation? How can I help students improve their writing without taking up a lot of class time? Are there ways to get students to really *use* their handbooks? How can I get students to understand what a college research paper requires?

This guide answers those questions and more. It includes practical advice on preparing a syllabus, designing writing assignments and essay exams, helping students use handbooks and other writers' resources, guiding them through research and writing processes, and grading and responding to papers. Abundant samples of assignments, handouts, and other materials from instructors in a variety of disciplines appear throughout the guide, and the samples are annotated to point out helpful features.

The Bedford Guide to Teaching Writing in the Disciplines can be read from start to finish as a self-contained course in teaching writing in the disciplines, but it is primarily intended to be a handy reference. Discrete, focused chapters and sub-sections help instructors find advice for specific problems and questions. Though the guide is firmly grounded in writing across the curriculum theory and research, it is designed and written to be accessible to instructors who may be unfamiliar with that research. Instructors who want a greater understanding of writing across the curriculum issues and theories can refer to sources listed in the extensive bibliographies that conclude each chapter. (A bibliography of discipline-specific sources for teaching writing appears at the end of the book.)

This guide draws on our experiences as rhetoricians at Colgate University, where writing faculty come from a variety of disciplines.

In addition to teaching regular courses in their disciplines, the writing instructors at Colgate teach writing-intensive disciplinary and interdisciplinary courses and composition courses. Many of the suggestions and samples in this book were drawn from those instructors. After we started work on this book, Sandra Jamieson took a position at Drew University, where writing is also a significant vehicle of instruction and evaluation. Our good fortune in teaching in these environments has allowed us to observe and participate in the myriad ways in which writing and pedagogy interact. We have been witness and party to a variety of problems, successess, resistances, and innovations from both faculty and students.

Throughout this book we have credited the specific contributions of colleagues who have generously shared course materials. But there are many others who have helped us write this book. We would like to thank Tom Howard for hours of patience and editing; Walter Jacobsohn for his enduring faith in the project; Peter Jorgensen, whose computer wizardry made long-distance collaboration not only possible but fun; and the reviewers who responded to early drafts and helped us shape the final manuscript: Abby Attias of Rutgers University; Mark Birchette of Long Island University; Monys A. Hagen of Metropolitan State College of Denver; Keith Hjortshoj of Cornell University; Kevin Santiago-Valles of the State University of New York at Binghamton; Mary Jane Schenck of the University of Tampa; and David Strang of Cornell University. We would also like to thank Liz Hamp-Lyons and Ulla Grapard for their improvements on early drafts, Beth Degen for her tireless help with research, and Stacey Halloran for keeping the mail flowing.

At Bedford Books, we would like to thank Joan Feinberg for her encouragement and support and Charles Christensen for imagining this book and imagining our writing it. Special thanks go to Beth Castrodale for her humor, encouragement, and inspired synthesis of editing suggestions. Thanks also to production editor Ann Sweeney, who ably guided the manuscript through production, and to Barbara Flanagan for her superb copyediting.

Finally, we would like to thank all of the students at Colgate, Drew, West Virginia University, and SUNY-Binghamton who have made pedagogy a source of intellectual excitement for us.

Rebecca Moore Howard
Colgate University

Sandra Jamieson
Drew University

Contents

Preface   v

Chapter 1

Including Writing in the Course Plan   **1**

Rationale for Teaching Writing in the Disciplines   1
An Explanation of Terminology   2
Approaches to Teaching Writing in the Disciplines   4
Checklist for Including Writing in the Course Plan   10
For Further Reading   11

Chapter 2

Preparing the Syllabus   **14**

Features of the Syllabus   14
Scheduling Writing Assignments and Instruction   21
Checklist of Potential Components of a Syllabus for a
   Course in Writing in the Disciplines   24
For Further Reading   25

Chapter 3

Integrating Writers' Resources   **26**

Choosing an Appropriate Handbook   26
Teaching Students How to Use a Handbook   28
Supplementing the Handbook with Handouts   33
Conferring with Students   35
Referring Students to Tutors   37
A Selected Bibliography of Writers' Handbooks and Guides   39
Checklist for Integrating Writers' Resources into the Course   43
For Further Reading   44

Chapter 4

Teaching the Writing Process   **45**

Why Teach the Writing Process?   45
Before Students Begin the Paper—Teaching Prewriting   46
As Students Begin the Paper—Teaching Drafting   58
Responding to Drafts   61
After Students Compose the First Draft—Teaching Rewriting   67
Handling Multiple Drafts   70
Checklist for Teaching the Writing Process   71
For Further Reading   72

Chapter 5

*Teaching and Responding to Style, Grammar,
and Punctuation*   **76**

The Place of Style, Grammar, and Punctuation in the
     Pedagogy of Writing in the Disciplines   76
Teaching and Responding to Style   81
Teaching and Responding to Grammar and Punctuation   88
*Checklist for Teaching and Responding to Style, Grammar,
     and Punctuation*   91
For Further Reading   92

Chapter 6

Designing Writing Assignments   **95**

Features of the Writing Assignment   95
Pedagogical Uses of Writing Assignments   101
Multistaged Assignments   110
Sequenced Assignments   111
Checklist for Designing Writing Assignments   115
For Further Reading   116

Chapter 7

*Assigning Research Papers Using Laboratory,
Field, and Library Data*   **119**

Helping Students Make the Transition to
     College-Level Research   119
Assigning Annotated Bibliographies   121
Assigning Reviews of the Literature   123
Assigning Research Proposals   124
Assigning Library Research Papers   127
Assigning Laboratory and Field Notebooks   132
Assigning Laboratory and Field Reports   135
Assigning Policy Analysis   141
Checklist for Assigning Research Papers   143
For Further Reading   144

Chapter 8

Designing and Evaluating Essay Exams   **146**

Choosing an Appropriate Type of Essay Exam   146
Designing Exams for Accurate Evaluation   150
Designing Exams for Effective Teaching   155
Responding to Essay Exams   156
Grading Essay Exams   159
Checklist for Designing and Evaluating Essay Exams   161
For Further Reading   162

Chapter 9

Assigning and Evaluating Collaboration   **164**

Creating an Environment for Collaboration   164
Leading Class Discussion   166
Small-Group Discussion   168
Assigning Collaborative Writing   172
Responding to Collaborative Work   178
Grading Collaborative Work   180
Collaborative Student Dialogues   180
Peer Response to Writing   184
Checklist for Collaborative Learning and Writing   190
For Further Reading   191

Chapter 10

Assigning and Evaluating Journals   **193**

The Purposes of Academic Journals   193
Assigning Journals   198
Responding to Journals   200
Grading Journals   204
Checklist for Assigning and Evaluating Journals   205
For Further Reading   206

Chapter 11

Grading Student Writing   **208**

Assigning Grades to Papers   208
Coping with Plagiarism   217
Dealing with Ideologically Objectionable Papers   221
Using Writing Portfolios for Evaluation   223
Checklist for Grading Student Writing   228
For Further Reading   229

Chapter 12

Teaching Advanced Reading Skills   **232**

The Reading-Writing Connection   232
Students' Alternatives to Reading   234

Reading Strategies for Students   236
Checklist for Teaching Advanced Reading Skills   241
For Further Reading   242

Appendix A
*A Bibliography of Discipline-Specific Sources for
Teaching Writing*   245

Appendix B
List of Samples Featured in Book, by Discipline   257

Index   269

The Bedford Guide to
Teaching Writing in the Disciplines

CHAPTER 1

Including Writing in the Course Plan

In this chapter:
❏   Rationale for teaching writing in the disciplines
❏   An explanation of terminology
❏   Approaches to teaching writing in the disciplines
❏   Checklist for including writing in the course plan
❏   For further reading

Rationale for Teaching Writing in the Disciplines

Each person who comes to the teaching of writing brings his or her own ideas and goals to the enterprise. Some instructors come to share what they themselves have learned about the joys of writing; some are determined to stop a perceived nationwide slide in advanced literacy skills—and most believe themselves unqualified to teach writing. Those who nevertheless undertake and stay with the task usually conclude that writing is best taught in context rather than as a set of discrete "skills" or universal principles. In the 1970s, so many people came to believe in the efficacy of contextualized writing instruction that a new movement, "writing across the curriculum" (often known by the infelicitous acronym WAC), arose in higher education pedagogy. As a result, writing is now widely taught not just in the English Department but also in the other academic disciplines. Writing across the curriculum has, over the last two decades, grown into an important field of literacy research and pedagogy, with a number of different and sometimes competing theories and goals.

Common to all writing across the curriculum is the idea that successful writing instruction engages students as active learners—active in a specific academic discipline and in their own intellectual development. Students who are actively engaged learn more and are more likely to enjoy that learning. Writing papers increases their sense of commitment to and participation in a course. This participation involves not just repeating the ideas of experts but also making contributions to and asserting some control over the discipline in which those experts prevail. Hence, writing instruction in the disciplines frequently focuses on and produces critical thinking skills, the ability not just to provide the "right" answers but also to ask one's own informed, reflective, even challenging questions and to apply information and processes from the course to try to answer those questions. Students who are asked to participate in the academic endeavor in the way their instructors do—through writing—are more apt to perceive themselves as part of the academy and thus perceive the course material as part of a learning process rather than part of an evaluative process in which they are simply graded on what they can repeat.

An Explanation of Terminology

Traditional models

Writing across the curriculum is a pedagogical movement focused on the writer in interaction with society—the "society" of the academic disciplines. Much of the pedagogy developed in the early stages of the writing-across-the-curriculum movement encouraged instructors to assign and evaluate writing but not necessarily to teach it. In this traditional model, which is often adopted today by instructors of large classes for whom any other approach to writing instruction would be too time-consuming, the act of writing is taken to be sufficient to enhance students' learning experiences and to make them participants in the disciplines. The instructor's role is to design good assignments and to evaluate them equitably, perhaps writing comments that might not only help students understand the effect of their efforts but also guide them to write even more effectively in the future. The traditional model has produced many useful types of writing assignments, including journals, response papers, and written dialogues between students. Some instructors have gone as far as to assign poetry or drama exercises based on class material—even in biology and geology courses. Many practitioners of traditional methods still adhere to the principles that informed most composition pedagogy in the first half of the twentieth century, a pedagogy that was derived from the philosophy of the Romantic movement in literature and that assumed that writing could not be taught. Students, according to those who practice traditional methods, can be provided with tasks and environments in which to do their best work and they can be drilled in the rules of punctuation and grammar; but they cannot actually be taught to write because good writing derives from an innate gift spurred by intangible inspiration.

Instructors following traditional models of writing instruction, assigning and evaluating but not teaching writing, perform an important role in the academy, for they emphasize the centrality of writing in academic life. According to most contemporary theorists, however, "teaching" writing means involving oneself in or guiding students' writing processes. From her extensive experience in writing across the curriculum, Susan McLeod argues in favor of this approach because it emphasizes *teaching* as distinct from assigning and evaluating. Most contemporary theorists and many practitioners believe that many or all writing skills can and should be taught and that the teaching is especially effective in the context of "real" writing in the disciplines rather than in assignments concocted in decontextualized composition courses.

Writing-across-the-curriculum programs of the 1970s and 1980s brought composition specialists together with their colleagues from other disciplines to address the question "How can we work together to improve our students' writing and thinking skills?" Responses to this essential question took writing across the curriculum in directions other than the traditional, activity-based model. While methods that departed from the old norm may seem to have been developed in discrete chronological stages, all are still in use and none is of recent invention. Describing them in terms of chronological stages is at most a convenience for identifying which "school" of writing across the curriculum has the greatest number of proponents (or the most influential ones) at any given time.

What is rather well established as a result of the writing-across-the-curriculum movement in American colleges is that a writing component to a course must involve more than an add-on assignment or two. It involves the instructor's reconsideration of the ways in which words and language are used in the discipline; of the ways in which that language uses not only communicates knowledge but constructs it; and of the ways in which classroom attention to discipline-specific language can help students enter that discipline as self-aware learners.

Write-to-learn and disciplinary genres

What Charles Bazerman terms "first-stage WAC" asserts that writing can serve as an aid to learning and as a tool of critical thinking. Adherents of this model call for all courses to include some writing component. They believe that because writing skills are generic, what is learned about writing in one course can be applied in the other disciplines and should be reinforced in all courses. Because this write-to-learn model emphasizes pan-disciplinary, generic writing and critical thinking skills, the preposition *across* is crucial in the label "writing across the curriculum." Also, because all courses are seen as a functioning whole for the transmission of such skills, the collective noun *curriculum* (rather than *disciplines*, which implies individuality) is equally important.

What Bazerman terms "second-stage WAC" proposes that each discipline has a specific discourse that is not readily accessible to students with "general" reading and writing skills and that must therefore be taught. Second-stage WAC theorists believe that because writing is an act of membership in a discourse community, it should always be taught in its social context, which means that it should be taught by members of the specific discourse communities. What an English instructor teaches about writing has limited value in a biology paper, these scholars argue. This school might rightly be termed "writing *in* the disciplines" (rather than *across*), because its adherents call for each instructor to teach the skills and conventions of his or her own discipline. Equally important is the choice of *disciplines* rather than *curriculum.*

Many theorists and most practitioners pursue a mix of objectives from both writing *across* the *curriculum* (which includes both the "traditional genres" that consider the assigning and grading of writing to be tantamount to teaching writing and the "write-to-learn" genres that emphasize acquisition of generic skills of writing and critical thinking) and writing *in* the *disciplines* (which embraces "disciplinary" genres of writing as a means of understanding, gaining entry to, and participating in the community of an academic discipline). Thus the terms *writing across the curriculum* and *writing in the disciplines* are often used interchangeably, and there is no umbrella term that embraces both. In this book we use the term *writing in the disciplines* to refer to both approaches, choosing it simply because it is the label applied to the model that is currently claiming the most attention from researchers in the field. To make further differentiations, we use the terms *traditional courses, write-to-learn courses,* and *disciplinary courses.*

Approaches to Teaching Writing in the Disciplines

Teaching writing by assigning writing

The intention of many early projects in writing in the disciplines was simply to increase the quantity of writing assigned in American colleges. The decline in writing standards was thought to be partially the result of the tendency of instructors not to assign papers in most lower-level and many upper-level classes. The discovery that students graduated with bachelor's degrees without ever having written a college paper prompted writing requirements and "writing-intensive" courses in the disciplines. Sometimes writing-intensive courses were new courses, but more commonly they were existing courses that began to require a certain number of pages of writing but that did not necessarily offer any writing instruction. Many writing-across-the-curriculum courses still follow this traditional model.

Writing-intensive courses in the disciplines benefit students in several ways. First, such courses introduce students to the importance of writing in the academy and give them incentive to learn how to write more effectively. Second, they allow students to apply skills learned in other courses to the intellectual purposes of the discipline. Third, the courses improve students' performance on essay exams. Fourth, they may encourage students to seek out resources for improving their writing—whether these be the writing center, peer tutors, teaching assistants, instructors, handbooks, or their roommates. Finally, simply going through the writing process, even without guidance, helps students become more effective writers.

Instructors working in traditional genres of writing in the disciplines will find chapters 5 ("Teaching and Responding to Style, Grammar, and Punctuation"), 6 ("Designing Writing Assignments"), and 11 ("Grading Student Writing") especially helpful.

Writing as means to and expression of personal commitment

Many students come to college inculcated with the idea of writing as performance. They believe that if they draw their own conclusions and write about them, the result is an "opinion" paper. Otherwise, they expect to write about received "facts"—the facts of a laboratory experiment or of Hawthorne's intentions when he wrote *The Scarlet Letter*. Because undergraduate students are not experts in chemistry or American literature, they may think that they can reach no authoritative conclusions; therefore, they view their academic writing as performance, in which they adopt and describe the beliefs and findings of others (regardless of whether the student writers actually subscribe to or even understand them) or in which they relate the facts immediately at hand (regardless of whether they see significance in them). They write to please the instructor, believing that this will help them get good grades.

What is new to many students is the idea that their writing, *including academic writing*, can be an expression of their own interpretations and conclusions based on research, experimentation, or reflection. Once students begin to understand this, their writing may improve dramatically, for they may now find themselves with something compelling to say. They begin to realize that statements made in academic papers are supposed to be expressions of their own opinions, derived from data selected and examined from a viewpoint—the epistemology of the discipline. They begin to view writing as part of their learning process and as a way of articulating it, rather than as a mere performance required by the instructor. Many instructors who teach writing therefore consider this realization a fundamental goal of pedagogy. Collaborative writing (Chapter 9) and journal-keeping (Chapter 10) are important means to that goal.

Writing as conversation

By perceiving writing as a conversation, students learn to see themselves as part of the ongoing process of making knowledge, and instructors are reminded not only to transmit the data of their discipline but also to teach their students about audience and rhetorical purpose in that discipline. Describing a variety of techniques for academic collaboration, composition theorist Kenneth Bruffee depicts writing as "displaced conversation."

Instructors adopting a "writing-as-conversation" approach might assign students to peer response groups in which they respond to and critique one another's papers. (See pages 184–189.) They might also assign dialogic notebooks in which students record class and research notes on one side of the page and reflections on, responses to, and connections among those notes on the other. The students thereby literally enter into a dialogue with the class material, which encourages them to bring a dialogic attitude to their formal writing assignments (see pages 196–197). Students can also be encouraged to understand the interactive nature of writing through electronic mail exchanges (see pages 183–184).

Writing as a form of critical thinking

C. H. Knoblauch and Lil Brannon, proponents of write-to-learn genres of writing in the disciplines, emphasize writing as a means of making learning an active process. Knoblauch and Brannon place a premium on collaborative work. Like journal-keeping and peer response workshops, collaborative assignments encourage students to develop a personal commitment to the topic and to recognize that commitment as deriving from social and intellectual interaction. (See Chapter 9.)

Collaborative assignments depict learning and critical thinking as exercises in community rather than as efforts of the isolated individual. Knoblauch and Brannon articulate common expectations for such pedagogy: "In this revised model of writing-to-learn-across-the-curriculum, the teacher's concern changes from dispensing knowledge to stimulating conceptual involvement and investigation in order to encourage the growth of students' intellectual capacities" (471).

Connections between writing and reading skills

Toby Fulwiler's *Teaching with Writing* makes explicit the connection between writing and reading, asserting both as essential skills. Fulwiler endorses James Britton's argument that "knowledge is a process of knowing rather than a storehouse of the known" (qtd. in Fulwiler 4), and he, too, emphasizes the role of conversation. If students learn to read critically and actively in a dialogic relationship with their texts, they will be both more engaged with the material and better editors of their own written work. (See Chapter 12.)

To emphasize the connections between reading and writing, some instructors discuss rhetorical strategies in assigned readings and invite students to imitate them. (See, for example, "Sample assignment: teaching style through imitation," on page 88.) Teaching students to take effective notes and to write summaries and analyses as they read helps them to understand how knowledge develops and how one writes and talks about it in the academy. (See Chapter 12.) It also improves their editing and revision skills and makes them aware that readers' needs affect the structure of papers.

The place of grammar and mechanics in writing instruction in the disciplines

In 1985 Otto Pflanze, outgoing editor of the *American Historical Review*, offered the following criticism of the work of scholars in his discipline:

> Careless English, incomplete and inaccurate footnotes, doubtful archival references, and statistics that do not add up—these blemishes cause editors to wonder at times about the solidity of the historical enterprise itself. Does sloppy workmanship on the surface mean sloppy workmanship underneath?

Reading Pflanze, one might conclude that discipline-specific writing courses, such as writing in history, should include coverage of grammar and mechanics. Certainly, many educators agree that students lacking an active command of Standard Written English will have difficulty advancing in academia and in many professions.

Kristine Hansen points out that helping students write well should not be the only or even the primary agenda for a writing course in the social sciences (168). Instead, she advocates a primary emphasis on epistemological and rhetorical training, with a secondary emphasis on grammar insofar as it relates to epistemology and rhetoric. Hansen does not ignore the importance of good writing, but she argues that writing skills are best taught as part of disciplinary instruction rather than as decontextualized, free-floating principles. The integration of purposes that Hansen advocates would emphasize the difficulty of gaining membership in the community of an academic discipline without first mastering the language of the larger community of higher education—the language that is commonly called "good" or "correct" English.

Hansen's point of view is widely shared among writing instructors. Students learn to write "correctly" when they learn to write meaningfully for a specific audience. The work of David A. Jolliffe and Ellen M. Brier in disciplinary genres has led them to conclude that "a person's participation in the intellectual activities of an academic discipline directly affects his or her acquisition, use, and awareness of these kinds of knowledge." For this reason they and many others teach "the kinds of knowledge that enable a writer in academia to execute processes and to produce written texts that experienced practitioners in an academic discipline deem successful and perhaps even distinctive" (35). Effective writing assignments aim to immerse students in the discourse of the discipline and help them think as its members do. Reading and responding to journal articles and reviews, analyzing and adopting the conventions demonstrated in specific journals, and engaging in the same kinds of open-ended research as do members of the discipline can encourage students' understanding of and entry into a discipline.

Because little correlation has been found between students' scores on decontextualized drills and their ability to write in correct, standard English, most instructors in the disciplines prefer to respond directly to the style and grammar in each student's paper, tailoring their instruction to each individual's needs. Or they teach students to use handbooks on their own to find answers to common problems with grammar and punctuation. Chapters 3 and 5 offer a variety of approaches to such instruction.

Entering the academic community

Anne Herrington and Charles Moran affirm the widely felt need to use writing as a way of teaching students how to become members of an academic discourse community:

> It may be . . . that we are readier now than we have been before to see the academy as a set of sites, each local, for the construction of knowledge. One of the received assumptions of writing in the disciplines is that there are differences among disciplinary discourses—an assumption that makes it more difficult to call for system-wide "good writing" as an undifferentiated absolute. [Writing in the disciplines] thus encourages us to see the academy as a cultural democracy, and the disciplines as localities—as cultures within the larger culture. (234)

Each discipline in the university can be regarded as a community—as can each department, the university, and higher education itself. *Community*, as Walter R. Fisher defines it, is "a set of values

. . . specifying norms of character, role performance, interaction, and ideal aspiration" (212). These values are embedded in the ways of talking—the dialect, the language—that are particular to each discipline. The language of each discipline, therefore, amounts to a way of approaching the world. Newcomers become members of a community through the acquisition and application of the language. To become members they must think in the same frameworks that the community does and ask questions that it deems meaningful.

Disciplinary genres strive to make the language and culture of the discipline explicit. A variety of means can accomplish this goal: teaching the language of the discipline (its vocabulary as well as its style); teaching the ways in which questions are asked and answered in the discipline (its epistemological framework); and teaching the acceptable ways in which ideas are communicated among members (the rhetoric of the discipline). Of course, language, epistemology, and rhetoric are inextricably intertwined and, as Hansen observes, epistemology is buried in rhetoric; to learn the rhetoric of a discipline is to learn something of its epistemology (167). Nevertheless, these three categories can be considered separately for the purpose of setting and pursuing goals for a writing course aimed at helping students enter a particular discipline. Nearly every section of this book offers pedagogical possibilities that can be applied to this purpose, but of particular interest to practitioners of disciplinary genres will be Chapters 6 ("Designing Writing Assignments") and 7 ("Assigning Research Papers Using Laboratory, Field, and Library Data").

Checklist for including writing in the course plan

_____ Refer to Chapter 3 for guidance on selecting an appropriate handbook or reference book and the use of other resources.

_____ Refer to Chapter 6 for a discussion of different types of writing assignments and ways to incorporate them into the course and Chapter 11 for a discussion of the role of evaluative methods in assignment design. This section includes the use of writing portfolios.

_____ If assigned writing is to include field or library research or laboratory reports, refer to Chapter 7 for models and suggestions.

_____ For alternatives to traditional assignments, turn to Chapter 9 (collaboration) and Chapter 10 (journal-keeping).

_____ Consult Chapter 8 if you plan to give written examinations.

_____ If you plan to teach style and usage or respond to them in papers, refer to Chapter 5.

_____ Refer to Chapter 12 for advice on teaching advanced reading skills.

_____ If you plan to teach or discuss the writing process, refer to Chapter 4 for strategies and models.

_____ Finally, once you have considered these elements, turn to Chapter 2 for suggestions about how to outline and explain your course plans in the syllabus.

For Further Reading

Histories and surveys of writing in the disciplines

Bazerman, Charles. "The Second Stage in Writing Across the Curriculum." *College English* 53 (1991): 209–22.

Fulwiler, Toby. "How Well Does Writing Across the Curriculum Work?" *College English* 46 (1984): 113–25. Fulwiler offers case-study advice on the politics of WAC: how to avoid territorial battles and eschew the urge to proselytize.

Fulwiler, Toby, and Art Young, eds. *Programs That Work: Models and Methods for Writing Across the Curriculum.* Portsmouth, NH: Boynton/Cook, 1990. Addressed to WAC administrators and program developers, this volume describes fourteen WAC programs—at research universities, community colleges, liberal arts colleges, and business colleges—and includes an annotated bibliography prepared by WAC historian C. W. Griffin.

———, eds. *Writing Across the Disciplines: Research into Practice.* Portsmouth, NH: Boynton/Cook, 1986.

Griffin, C. W. "Programs for Writing Across the Curriculum: A Report." *College Composition and Communication* 36 (1985): 398–403. "To write is to learn" (403). Griffin offers this as one of three premises of writing in the disciplines; the other two involve university-wide responsibility for student writing.

McLeod, Susan H., ed. *Strengthening Programs for Writing Across the Curriculum.* San Francisco: Jossey-Bass, 1988.

———. "Writing in the Disciplines: The Second Stage and Beyond." *College Composition and Communication* 40 (1989): 337–42. Noting the widespread success of WAC programs as attested by their continuation beyond the lives of their founding grants, McLeod proposes agendas for the WAC programs of the future: expanding the established notions of faculty workshops and development; expanding the role of WAC in the curriculum; grounding WAC either in critical thinking and writing or in entering the disciplines; and defining what is meant by the term "writing in the disciplines."

Parker, Robert, and Vera Goodkin. *The Consequences of Writing: Enhancing Learning in the Disciplines.* Portsmouth, NH: Boynton/Cook, 1987.

Russell, David R. "Vygotsky, Dewey, and Externalism: Beyond the Student/Discipline Dichotomy." *Journal of Advanced Composition* 13.1 (1993): 173–98.

———. *Writing in the Academic Disciplines, 1870–1990: A Curricular History.* Carbondale: Southern Illinois UP, 1991.

———. "Writing Across the Curriculum in Historical Perspective: Toward a Social Interpretation." *College English* 52 (1990): 52-73.

Stanley, Linda C., and Joanna Ambron, eds. *Writing in the Curriculum in Community Colleges.* San Francisco: Jossey-Bass, 1991.

Tchudi, Stephen N. "The Hidden Agendas in Writing in the Disciplines." *English Journal* 75 (1986): 22–25.

Purposes and applications of writing in the disciplines

Britton, James. *Language and Learning.* New York: Penguin, 1970. Britton's work is the foundation of many write-to-learn genres of WAC. In this book he explores the relationships among experience, thought, language, and learning.

Bruffee, Kenneth A. "Thinking and Writing as Social Acts." *Thinking, Reasoning, and Writing.* Ed. Elaine P. Maimon, Barbara F. Nodine, and Finbarr W. O'Connor. New York: Longman, 1989. 213–22. While Bruffee describes writing in terms of community, he is not speaking to the communities of academic disciplines, but rather to a "felt sense" of community on the part of the writer. Bruffee advocates various forms of collaboration as a means of teaching students how to internalize conversation and then to "displace" it in writing (218). Applied to writing in the disciplines, this article would support write-to-learn genres.

Emig, Janet. "Writing as a Mode of Learning." *College Composition and Communication* 28 (1977): 122–28. A foundational source for write-to-learn genres.

Faery, Rebecca Blevins. "Women and Writing Across the Curriculum: Learning and Liberation." *Teaching Writing: Pedagogy, Gender, and Equity.* Ed. Cynthia L. Caywood and Gillian R. Overing. Albany: SUNY UP, 1987. 201–14. The authors contend that writing helps students learn and that they will learn more about a subject if they write about it frequently.

Hedley, Jane, and Jo Ellen Parker. "Writing Across the Curriculum: The Vantage of the Liberal Arts." *ADE Bulletin* 98 (Spring 1991): 22-28. This article argues that disciplinary genres reinforce what students perceive as the arbitrariness of writing conventions and contribute to the rigidity of disciplinary boundaries. Instead, Hedley and Parker propose that "the purpose of higher education is best expressed in general terms" (24), which is also where students' interests lie (25).

Herrington, Anne, and Charles Moran. "Writing in the Disciplines: A Prospect." *Writing, Teaching, and Learning in the Disciplines.* Ed. Anne Herrington and Charles Moran. New York: MLA, 1992. 231–44. The authors observe that WAC has come to focus on disciplinary genres.

Jolliffe, David A., and Ellen M. Brier. "Studying Writers' Knowledge in Academic Disciplines." *Writing in Academic Disciplines..* Ed. David A. Jolliffe. Advances in Writing Research 2. Norwood, NJ: Ablex, 1988. 35–88. Quantitative analysis of stylistic features of students' prose suggests that style improves when the writer understands the discourse of the discipline.

Jones, Robert, and Joseph J. Comprone. "Where Do We Go Next in Writing Across the Curriculum?" *College Composition and Communication* 44 (1993): 59–68. The authors believe that the problem facing WAC is that "individuals locally involved in WAC programs often respond in oversimplifying and dichotomous ways to the question of whether WAC is a program fostering humanistic approaches to general educational reform (as embodied in the writing-to-learn and expressive-discourse movements) or a program for approaching the teaching of writing through the conventions of different discourse communities (as, for example, represented in the learning of laboratory report formats or the structure of the scientific article)" (61). The authors set four goals for programs of writing in the disciplines.

Knoblauch, C. H., and Lil Brannon. "Writing as Learning through the Curriculum." *College English* 45 (1983): 465–74. The authors advocate a program of writing in the disciplines that exploits "the potential for new learning implicit in the act of writing itself" (466). This view of learning as active and process-based contrasts with traditional passive models (467). "In this revised model of writing-to-learn-across-the-curriculum, the teacher's concern changes from dispensing knowledge to stimulating conceptual involvement and investigation in order to encourage the growth of students' intellectual capacities" (471).

McLeod, Susan H. "Defining Writing Across the Curriculum." *WPA: Writing Program Administration* 11.1–2 (1987): 19–24. McLeod explores the impact of writing in the disciplines on students and faculty, and she defines writing in the disciplines in terms of change—"change in the structure of writing programs, change in the university curriculum, change in faculty behavior in the classroom" (23).

Schmersahl, Carmen B., and Byron L. Stay. "Looking under the Table: The Shapes of Writing in College." *Constructing Rhetorical Education.* Ed. Marie Secor and Davida Charney. Carbondale: Southern Illinois UP, 1992. 140–49. A survey of twenty-two instructors at Mount Saint Mary's College suggests that before one makes recommendations about writing across the disciplines, one should ascertain whether instructors are actually teaching disciplinary genres (147–48). Only instructors in English and biology at Mount Saint Mary's were; the others gave assignments that were "tied at least as much to the types of thinking and learning that are valued as part of general education as to the habits and values of specific disciplines" (144). The twenty-two instructors' assignments suggest that the purposes of writing at liberal arts colleges might be different from those at research universities (148).

Guides for teachers of writing in the disciplines

Bogel, Fredric V., and Katherine K. Gottschalk, eds. *Teaching Prose: A Guide for Writing Instructors.* New York: Norton, 1984.

Bullock, Richard. *The St. Martin's Manual for Writing in the Disciplines: A Guide for Faculty.* New York: St. Martin's, 1994.

Fulwiler, Toby. *Teaching with Writing.* Portsmouth, NH: Boynton/Cook, 1987.

Hairston, Maxine. "On Not Being a Composition Slave." *Training the New Teacher of College Composition.* Ed. Charles W. Bridges. Urbana: NCTE, 1986. 117–24. Although Hairston's remarks are addressed to the instructor of a college composition class, they are readily applicable to teaching writing in the disciplines.

Martin, Nancy, et al. *Writing and Learning Across the Curriculum, 11–16.* London: Schools Council Publications, 1976.

Moss, Andrew, and Carol Holder. *Improving Student Writing: A Guidebook for Faculty in All Disciplines.* Pomona: California State Polytechnic U, 1988. Distr. Dubuque, IA; Kendall/Hunt.

Tchudi, Stephen N. *Teaching Writing in the Content Areas: College Level.* Washington: NEA, 1986.

Walvoord, Barbara E. Fassler. *Helping Students Write Well: A Guide for Teachers in All Disciplines.* 2nd ed. New York: MLA, 1986.

Other resources for teachers of writing in the disciplines

Two additional resources of great potential support to the instructor of writing in the disciplines are a new journal, *Language and Learning Across the Disciplines,* and a well-established electronic discussion group, WAC-L. Subscription rates to *Language and Learning* are $20 per year for individuals and $25 per year for institutions. (For subscriptions outside the United States, add $5.) Subscriptions should be sent to Michael Pemberton, Editor, *Language and Learning Across the Disciplines,* Department of English, University of Illinois, Urbana-Champaign, 608 S. Wright St., Urbana, IL 61801. Computer users with access to Internet or Bitnet can subscribe to WAC-L by sending the message SUB WAC-L to IN%"LISTSER-V@VMD.CSO.UIUC.EDU" or IN%"LISTSERV@UIUCVMD.BITNET."

Additional references

Fisher, Walter R. "Narration, Reason, and Community." *Writing the Social Text: Poetics and Politics in Social Science Discourse.* Ed. Richard Harvey Brown. New York: Aldine de Gruyter, 1992. 199–218.

Hansen, Kristine. "Rhetoric and Epistemology in the Social Sciences: A Contrast of Two Representative Texts." *Writing in Academic Disciplines.* Ed. David A. Jolliffe. Advances in Writing Research 2. Norwood, NJ: Ablex, 1988. 167–210.

Pflanze, Otto. "Report of the Editor, American Historical Review: A Parting Word." *Program of the One Hundredth Annual Meeting.* American Historical Association. New York, 27–30 Dec. 1985.

Summa, Hikka. "The Rhetoric of Efficiency: Applied Social Science as Depoliticization." *Writing the Social Text: Poetics and Politics in Social Science Discourse.* Ed. Richard Harvey Brown. New York: Aldine de Gruyter, 1992. 135–54.

CHAPTER 2

Preparing the Syllabus

In this chapter:

❏ Features of the syllabus

❏ Scheduling writing assignments and instruction

❏ Checklist of potential components of a syllabus for a course in writing in the disciplines

❏ For further reading

Features of the Syllabus

During the first week of class, most instructors hand out a syllabus that includes the course name and number; the instructor's name, office number, telephone number, and office hours; the course description; a list of textbooks for the course; and the attendance and grading policies. The syllabus for a course in writing in the disciplines might additionally explain the purposes of writing in the course; describe the types of writing assignments and writing instruction offered in the course; suggest guidelines for writing in the course; and provide a calendar of writing assignments (perhaps including one or more of the assignments themselves).

Explaining the purposes of writing in the course

To enable students to think of writing as part of the course, the syllabus should specify not only the general goals for the course but also the role of writing in it—whether writing assignments are for the purpose of evaluating learning, facilitating learning, promoting membership in the discipline, or some combination of these aims.

SAMPLE COURSE DESCRIPTION
Explaining the role of writing in the course (disciplinary genres)
Introduction to Political Science I: Michael Johnston

This is a course about democracy, freedom, liberty, legitimacy, and order. It is also an introduction to the framing and analysis of political questions. The course emphasizes writing, critical reading and thinking, and active participation in discussions. It is *not* an introduction to American government; many of our texts and examples will be drawn from places and times other than the contemporary US. Still, by the end of the course you will be able to think critically about the enduring issues, ideas, and conflicts that lie below the surface of current political events.

By introducing the writing component immediately after the statements about the course content, Professor Johnston suggests an integral role for writing in the course. He specifies that writing, reading, and speaking are the means to mastering disciplinary content, enabling students to think like professionals in the discipline.

The role of writing in the course can also be established indirectly through the layout of the syllabus and the description of writing assignments.

SAMPLE SYLLABUS (EXCERPTS)
Integrating writing into the course (write-to-learn genres)
Dinosaur Extinctions: Paul R. Pinet

ASSIGNMENTS THROUGH TERM
2 three-to-four-page papers
3 or 4 two-page papers
Several problem sets to promote critical thinking
Journal record on thinking

WEEK 1: THE LANGUAGE OF ARGUMENT
Ruggiero's Chs. 1–4; Raup's book in its entirety
Appendixes A, D

Arguments
What is thinking?
Why people don't think clearly
The nature of arguments
Deductive and inductive logic
Probability
Thinking on your feet

Extinctions
Evolution of oceans
Mountain building
Geologic time scale
Organic evolution
The nature of extinctions
The causes of extinctions

In his syllabus Professor Pinet shows how science, critical thinking, and writing are integrated in the course. His week-by-week schedule sets the science and the critical thinking materials side by side, demonstrating their complementarity. His list of writing tasks suggests how those activities support the critical thinking component of the course, and the journal assignment provides a place for students' further exploration of the arguments listed throughout the syllabus.

Providing a course calendar

Because many students rely on "pulling an all-nighter" when a paper is due, college courses serve an important role when they provide opportunities and methods for developing more orderly, reflective writing habits. By listing the number of papers that will be assigned, due dates, and estimated lengths, the syllabus can help students manage their time and work flow. Students may even decide that they have to drop or change a course if they see that they have too many writing-intensive classes in one term. Detailed syllabi also help students schedule sufficient time for study and for writing. If, for example, they know weeks in advance that major assignments will arise in two classes simultaneously, they can begin work on those assignments earlier than they otherwise might have begun.

Even though it may be revised as the semester goes along, a day-by-day calendar of reading and writing assignments is another useful type of syllabus design. By providing a sense of how the course will unfold, the calendar enables students to plan their reading and research as well as their writing. It also helps instructors keep the course on track.

The columns in Professor Nolen's syllabus allow students to see the various types of activities in any given week and also to see the development of topics and types of papers as the semester goes along. Elsewhere in the syllabus and course materials Professor Nolen provides explanations of the different types of writing assignments.

SAMPLE SYLLABUS (EXCERPT)
Calendar of assignments
Juggling Science and Judeo-Christian Thought: Ernest Nolen

WEEK	TOPIC	READINGS	PAPERS
Sept. 1	Prologue	Shapiro handout	Paradigm
Sept. 7	Miracles	Lewis 1–13	Analysis
Sept. 14	Genesis	Gen. 1–3 Hummel 8–10	Scientific method
	Archaeology	Dead Sea handout	
Sept. 21	Archaeology (cont.)	Video	Critique
	Definitions	McGowan 1 VanTill 10–12 Johnson 12 Hummel 13	

Describing types of writing assignments

The syllabus might also indicate the types of writing that the instructor expects to assign. As students learn more about their own writing processes, they will be better able to predict how long it will take them to complete various types of assignments and can schedule their time accordingly. In addition, knowing what kinds of writing assignments to expect during the semester can improve students' overall understanding of the course and allow them to take an active role. If, for example, they know they will be designing their own research projects at midterm, many students in the early part of the term will make a note of topics that interest them. Similarly, if students know they will be expected to collaborate, they may keep an eye out for classmates with whom they might have a good working relationship.

SAMPLE SYLLABUS (EXCERPT)
Types of writing assignments
Political Anthropology: Conflict and Cooperation: Mary Moran

Writing requirements are as follows: 2 take-home essay exams (due Feb. 19 and April 2), a 15-page research paper on a topic to be agreed upon by the student and the instructor (due April 16), and a final take-home exam, due April 30. All written work must be turned in on the date indicated. Unless arrangements have been made with the instructor in advance, *assignments which are handed in late will not be accepted.*

This part of the syllabus lets students know precisely what sorts of writing they will be doing in the course, how long the paper will be, and when the assignments are due. It also provides a late-paper policy.

These assignments are well timed: The first exam comes early in the semester, a month after its beginning, giving students a chance to improve their studying and test-taking skills for succeeding exams. The research paper is due three weeks before the end of the semester, allowing for its grading and return before semester's end.

Describing the writing instruction offered in the course

Many instructors find the syllabus a useful opportunity for discussing the kinds of writing instruction they intend to offer. Such a discussion reassures students that the course will teach them how to do what it requires them to do. It also explains the writing component, which might otherwise confuse students by its sudden appearance in a "non-English" course. The instructor can state whether students will receive handouts of the instructor's or the discipline's stylistic preferences; whether class time will be devoted to writing instruction; whether the instructor will schedule individual or small-group conferences with all the members of the class (see pages 35–37); whether the students will receive peer response to their work in progress (see pages 184–189); whether they will have an opportunity to revise their work after it has been graded (see pages 32–33); and whether tutoring is available for the course (see pages 37–39).

In this introduction to the syllabus for an upper-level anthropology course, Professor Hess describes the writing instruction in terms of developing skills with the characteristics of texts (e.g., thesis, antithesis). He also explains how students will use these skills and emphasizes that they will have models whose style, strategies, and interpretive techniques they can imitate. By assigning peer response, Professor Hess alerts students to the fact that their writing is for an audience as well as for a grade.

SAMPLE SYLLABUS (EXCERPT)
Types of writing instruction in the course (write-to-learn and disciplinary genres)
Ethnographic Writing: Describing and Interpreting Social Action: David Hess

This course is for social science and history majors who would like to improve their writing skills while at the same time learning more about the art and science of ethnography (descriptive social science). Writing instruction will include developing a thesis and an antithesis; using narrative techniques and symbolic interpretation; developing appropriate quotations, footnotes, and diagrams; and developing a narrator's voice and a personal style. Students will choose one aspect of local life (church services, dining, social life, studying in the library, etc.) and write descriptions and interpretations of what they observe and hear. Readings will provide models of ethnographic writers (e.g., Geertz, Lévi-Strauss) and strategies for describing and interpreting observations. Students will present their descriptions in class for commentary and constructive criticism.

Providing guidelines for writing

The syllabus is of further benefit if it details how writing will be evaluated. Will the instructor consider style, grammar, punctuation, and spelling? Is a particular style (such as MLA, APA, or CBE) required? In courses emphasizing disciplinary genres, an introduction to the style and language of the discipline should precede any assignments that require disciplinary discourse or method. Such sequencing will help students appropriate disciplinary voices, enabling them not just to talk but also to think like members of the discipline. Their papers will therefore have a more professional air and reflect a more thorough consideration of their audience. (See page 102.) Providing writing guidelines as part of the syllabus rather than as individual handouts at later dates ensures that students can find them when they need them and also that they perceive these writing conventions as an integral part of the course rather than an afterthought. Further, by outlining expectations for style, grammar, mechanics, and other writing concerns in the syllabus rather than in individual assignments, instructors give students the message that those expectations apply to all assignments. When offering writing guidelines, instructors also can refer to pertinent sections of the handbook assigned for the course.

SAMPLE SYLLABUS (EXCERPT)
Guidelines for writing (disciplinary genres)
Organic Chemistry: John Cochran and Patricia Jue

Sample lab notebook entries and formal reports are on reserve in the Cooley Science Library. You will not be performing this experiment; however, the procedure and analysis serve as a model. For a detailed discussion of appropriate writing styles, see *The ACS Style Guide: A Manual for Authors and Editors*, ed. Janet S. Dodd.

PRESENTATION
Laboratory reports should be proofread and typed. Points will be deducted for gross errors in grammar and spelling and for "sloppy" presentation. You will find that clearly (not necessarily "neatly") written laboratory notes serve as a good outline for the laboratory report. Conventionally, reports are not written in the first person ("I did this") or in the imperative ("Do this"). Rather, reports are written in the third person impersonal—as if the experiment did itself!

Formal reports should be concise and well thought out. Consequently, the maximum limit for each report, not including spectra, title page, and reference page, is set to:

Exp I to IV: 2 pages each
Exp V & VI—combined report: 4 pages
Exp VII: 2 pages

All margins should be at least 1", and font size no smaller than 10 or so picas.

In this excerpt from their writing guidelines, Professors Cochran and Jue steer students through one form of academic writing while grounding their work in the larger expectations and constraints of the discipline. In addition to referring students to the appropriate style guide, they explain writing conventions of the discipline and tell students how errors in grammar and spelling will affect their grades.

Notice also how Professors Cochran and Jue provide lengths for papers as well as specifications for manuscript preparation.

Establishing a late-paper policy

Excusing a late paper is always a problem, for the instructor must determine whether the student is telling the truth and whether there is sufficient reason for accepting the paper after the deadline.

A late-paper policy can prevent such quandaries and keep the instructor from being inundated with excuses. One approach is to forbid late papers that have not been arranged in advance; another is to reduce the grade of papers by one level for each day they are late, regardless of reason. Some instructors accept late papers with the proviso that they will not be graded until the end of the semester or that they will receive only a grade and no comments. Both of these stipulations act as strong deterrents to late papers.

Including writing assignments in the syllabus

Some instructors design and distribute assignments as the course goes along. But those who design assignments before the course begins and who have no pedagogical reason for withholding them might want to include them in the syllabus so that students can discover and develop ideas for their papers over the course of the term.

Professor Balonek's inclusion of the first paper assignment in his syllabus not only serves the usual function of a paper assignment but also indicates how the inquiry of the course will be conducted.

By requiring the first paper in the second week of class, the instructor immediately engages the students in active learning. The timing also allows him to provide early feedback without hurting the students' final grade, giving students time to adjust to the demands of the course before they write the next paper.

SAMPLE SYLLABUS (EXCERPT)
Integrating the first assignment into the syllabus
Intelligent Life in the Universe: Thomas Balonek

FIRST PAPER:
Due in class Sept. 13. Write a short two-page essay on the topic "What I *Want* Life in the Universe to Be Like." Discuss any topics you desire, such as what type of life-forms you *want* to exist elsewhere in the universe, where life might exist, how frequently intelligent civilizations occur, how long intelligent civilizations exist, whether any civilizations are attempting to contact us, etc. The essay will be graded, but the grade will *not* be used in determining your course grade.

Scheduling Writing Assignments and Instruction

While this book describes a variety of techniques for teaching writing in the disciplines, it does not suggest that any course should include them all. Nevertheless, as instructors make their choices, they need to consider carefully the question of sequence. What should be taught early in the semester and what saved until later? Such choices depend in part on the level of the course (first-year, graduate), its size, and the relative expertise of its students. A few guidelines may help instructors determine the order of assignments in the syllabus.

Incorporating the handbook into the syllabus

Instructors who assign writing—especially if they teach writing—find it beneficial to adopt a writer's handbook as one of the texts for the course (see pages 26–27). It is seldom sufficient simply to tell students that they should have a good handbook, because owning a handbook and knowing how to use it are two very different things. Instructors who have adopted a specific handbook for the course can make page or section references when assigning and commenting on papers. Further, if all the students in the class own the same handbook, the instructor can use it for in-class writing instruction. The syllabus should therefore list the handbook as one of the texts for the course.

Orientation to and instruction in use of the handbook are especially effective in the early part of the term, before students fall into a minimalist approach to writing. At the beginning of the term (particularly the fall term), they tend to approach their writing from a personal-virtue perspective: *This* time they will "do it right." The handbook, introduced at the beginning of the semester, offers them a means for doing it right. Later in the semester, however (and especially in the spring term) students tend to do only that which is absolutely necessary, by the most expeditious means. If they are not already making productive use of a handbook, it is unlikely that they will begin to do so at this point. If the handbook is introduced late in the term or even once the term is well under way, the instruction may not penetrate the minimalist mode to which students feel their workload has driven them.

Determining when to assign journals, essay exams, and collaborative writing

Including journal-writing early in the syllabus has definite pedagogical benefits. Introduced early in a course, journal-writing counteracts the common notion that academic writing is merely a performance for the teacher. Instead it helps students see academic writing as a way of developing authentic conclusions and interpretations. When journal-writing begins early in the semester, its effects may carry over into students' other writing for the course, especially if one or more formal writing assignments are derived from the journals. (See Chapter 10 for advice on incorporating writers' journals into the course.)

If essay exams are to be given, it is most effective to schedule one early in the course. The instructor's feedback on this first exam gives students guidelines for adopting better study and test-taking strategies for the remainder of the course. Some instructors make the first exam worth only a small percentage of the final grade and then increase the percentage value of exams throughout the semester as students become more proficient test takers. (Chapter 8 offers details on designing essay exams.)

No generic guidelines govern the timing of collaborative assignments, but it may be helpful, especially in lower-level courses, not to introduce graded collaborative work at the beginning of the semester. Students benefit from the opportunity to get to know each other, the instructor, and the material before they embark on graded collaboration, which requires a high degree of mutual trust and respect. (See Chapter 9 for a discussion of assigning and evaluating collaborative writing.)

Determining when to assign and collect research papers

The major research paper that students work on alone and submit at the end of the term has limited pedagogical benefits. Instructors who plan such an assignment might want to consider ways to incorporate the research process into the course so that the paper does not become an end-of-semester, last-minute exercise devoid of any meaning except its completion. Ways to incorporate the major research paper into the course include assigning the work in stages (see pages 110–111); conducting individual consultations on topic choice and development (see pages 35–36); assigning peer response to work in progress (see Chapter 9); and collecting formal outlines a few weeks in advance of the final deadline—a particularly valuable method for large classes where other, more labor-intensive methods are not practical. Among the many alternatives to the research paper are response papers, journals, and collaborative writing (see Chapters 9 and 10). The following staged assignment shows how one instructor gradually introduces students to the research process.

Particularly in introductory courses, instruction and assignments in writing from sources (whether textual sources or laboratory or field data) should precede an integrated research assignment; students need to know how to do the component work before they undertake synthesis. Before tackling a library research paper, for example, they may benefit from an assignment that asks them to

SAMPLE SYLLABUS (EXCERPT)
Assigning the research paper in stages
Art of India: Padma Kaimal

I will also ask you to write a paper for this course, a single paper that I will evaluate at three stages. First you will write 3 or 4 pages describing a work of Indian art exhibited on campus or at a nearby museum. Then you will conduct research on that piece. When that research is completed, you will come to class with a bibliography but without notes and write a draft of your paper in a few bluebooks. Your final draft will then be a polishing and expansion of the in-class text you compose. I will hand out more specific instructions on this paper shortly.

In her syllabus for the course, Professor Kaimal offers an initial description of a staged research paper and explains how the three assignments are connected and will together form the final paper. (Due dates are provided in the weekly schedule.)

Because students are given a clear understanding of what they are to write and why, the project has a higher likelihood of success.

SAMPLE SYLLABUS (EXCERPT)
Assigning two research papers, with opportunity for revision
Reproductive Issues: Victoria E. McMillan

Two scientific review papers (i.e., library research papers) are required for this course:
> Paper #1 (6–7 pages): worth 15% of final grade
> Paper #2 (10–12 pages): worth 30% of final grade

DUE DATES:
> Paper #1: Oct. 15
> Paper #2: Nov. 26

Preliminary topics for both papers—due in class Sept. 10. (One-paragraph written projection required for each.)

Two class sessions will be devoted to critiques of student drafts: Oct. 10 (Paper #1) and Nov. 19 (Paper #2). On these dates you will need to bring in photocopies of part/all of your work-in-progress to distribute to other members of the class; more details to follow.

Individual conferences to discuss rough drafts will replace regular class meetings on Oct. 8 (Paper #1) and Nov. 14 (Paper #2).

If you wish, you may revise Paper #1 and resubmit it, along with your earlier version and my comments, by Dec. 3. The final grade for Paper #1 will then be the average of the grade for the first version and that for the revision.

Professor McMillan's decision to assign two scientific research papers, the second longer than the first and counting for more of the final grade, allows students to apply what they learn from the process of writing the first paper to the second. The second paper is due two weeks before the end of the semester, enabling Professor McMillan to return it before the end of classes. Allowing students to rewrite the first paper permits the instructor to grade those papers at a comfortable pace while still allowing students sufficient time to revise them. An explanation of how revised papers will be figured into the grade helps students decide whether to revise.

summarize a textual source or analyze the author's assumptions or argument. (See pages 236–240.)

Staggering deadlines for various components of research papers (summaries, drafts, and so on) allows instructors to respond to developing papers before the final drafts are due and also gives students a good opportunity to learn and revise. In addition, collecting the final draft of the paper no later than two weeks before the end of the term allows students to read the instructor's responses before the term ends. This provides incentive for students to improve their papers. (See page 70.)

Checklist of potential components of a syllabus for a course in writing in the disciplines

_____ Course name and number

_____ Instructor's name, office number, telephone number, and office hours

_____ Description of the course

_____ List of texts for the course, including a writer's handbook

_____ Description of types of writing instruction to be included in the course

_____ Explanation of the purposes of writing in the course

_____ Description of types of writing assignments to be given

_____ Details of quantity and frequency of writing in the course

_____ Writing guidelines

_____ Criteria for evaluating writing

_____ Policy for late papers

_____ Calendar of writing instruction and assignments

_____ Copies of the writing assignments themselves

_____ Attendance and grading policies

For Further Reading

Connors, Robert, and Cheryl Glenn. *The St. Martin's Guide to Teaching Writing.* New York: St. Martin's, 1989.

Elbow, Peter. "Embracing Contraries in the Teaching Process." *College English* 45 (1983): 327–39.

Gabennesch, Howard. "The Enriched Syllabus: To Convey a Larger Vision." *The National Teaching and Learning Forum* 1.4 (1992): 4–5.

Harris, Mary McDonnell. "Motivating with the Course Syllabus." *National Teaching and Learning Forum* 3.1 (1993): 1–3.

Rubin, Sharon. "Professors, Students, and the Syllabus." *The Chronicle of Higher Education* 7 Aug. 1985: 57.

Russell, David R. "Vygotsky, Dewey, and Externalism: Beyond the Student/Discipline Dichotomy." *Journal of Advanced Composition* 13.1 (1993): 173–98.

CHAPTER 3

Integrating Writers' Resources

In this chapter:

- ☐ Choosing an appropriate handbook
- ☐ Teaching students how to use a handbook
- ☐ Supplementing the handbook with handouts
- ☐ Conferring with students
- ☐ Referring students to tutors
- ☐ A selected bibliography of writers' handbooks and guides
- ☐ Checklist for integrating writers' resources into the course
- ☐ For further reading

Choosing an Appropriate Handbook

Instructors do students a favor when, in addition to requiring a handbook, they help students learn to use it. It helps students to be aware that even the most experienced writers use handbooks to refer to rules of grammar, punctuation, and style. In addition, most handbooks offer suggestions for developing and organizing writing. Of course, use of a handbook does not guarantee perfect writing. But students can begin to see how it can help them with all the writing they will do—in college and beyond.

Textbook publishers are generally willing to provide examination copies of their writers' handbooks, and instructors may want to preview several candidates before choosing one. For example, instructors who want to assign writing exercises to the class (see pages 32–33) should make certain that the handbook they select includes exercises; some do not. Those who intend to concentrate on certain facets of writing, such as style and mechanics or the development of ideas, must be sure to choose a handbook that is strong in those areas. Additional factors in handbook selection are discussed in the following sections.

Handbooks for write-to-learn and disciplinary genres

Because write-to-learn courses are chiefly concerned with improving students' general writing and learning skills, these courses are best accompanied by a comprehensive generic handbook. In addition to serving as a reference for points of grammar, punctuation, and mechanics, comprehensive generic handbooks help students throughout the writing process—from generating ideas and planning to researching, drafting, documenting, and revising. Students will find such handbooks useful for many different courses. (See pages 39–42 for a list of representative handbooks.)

Instructors who want students to learn the conventions of writing in a particular discipline often select a handbook prepared for writers in that discipline. (The bibliography at the end of this chapter offers a sampling.) Such handbooks focus on the various settings for and approaches to writing within a certain discipline. *A Guide to Writing Sociology Papers* by Roseann Giarrusso et al., for example, takes students through the process of writing textual analysis and doing library research, ethnographic research, and quantitative research. A second option for instructors of disciplinary genres is a brief style guide, such as Strunk and White's *The Elements of Style* or Diana Hacker's *A Pocket Style Manual*, which addresses clarity, grammar, punctuation, mechanics, and documentation but not the writing process. Instructors may then provide their students with instruction and handouts on specifics of writing in their discipline. (See pages 33–34.)

Electronic handbooks and ancillaries

Most publishing houses offer an on-line electronic handbook and electronic ancillaries (such as grammar exercises) as supplements for students who purchase their printed handbooks. These are usually compatible with the most commonly used hardware and software and are available to students for free or at a modest price. An electronic handbook enables students to bring onto their computer screens abbreviated versions of key handbook sections for reference as they compose or revise their papers.

Teaching Students How to Use a Handbook

Adopting a constructive spirit

If students are to make good use of a handbook, they must regard it as a helpful reference rather than as an impossible standard of perfection that they can never achieve. Their approach to a handbook is greatly affected by the approach taken by their teachers. It is therefore important that the instructor present the handbook as a tool for researching, drafting, revising, and editing. Students must understand that every writer makes errors and that what separates good writers from poor ones is their ability to revise and edit. They must understand that effective revision involves evaluating and reimagining their work. And students must understand that they cannot correct errors simply by reading through a paper to see if it "sounds right"; effective editing involves a systematic analysis of the paper, a search for errors that the writer knows he or she is prone to commit.

It is seldom helpful for instructors to mark every error in a student's paper, but it is almost always helpful to identify the important errors or to point out those that occur repeatedly. (See pages 211–213 for a fuller discussion of this method of responding and grading.) Specific, focused feedback can guide students' revision especially if it refers students to a handbook for further advice.

Incorporating handbook references into the syllabus and assignments

The instructor can encourage students' familiarity with and use of the handbook by including references to pertinent handbook sections throughout the syllabus. For example, if a biology instructor intends to assign both research and review papers, the syllabus might refer to handbook sections that explain these types of writing.

Instructors can also refer to pertinent handbook sections in assignments so that students consult the handbook *before* writing the paper. In fact, such references can help the instructor structure staged assignments. The first graded stage of a biological review paper in a class using *Writing Papers in the Biological Sciences* might refer students to "Choosing a Topic" in McMillan's chapter "Writing a Review Paper"; the second stage might grade their work on searching the literature (sections 2 and 3 of that chapter); and the third stage might grade their presentation of results (section 4). (For further discussion of staged assignments, see pages 110–111.)

In-class handbook instruction

The handbook can also be used in class, either to give students an overview of its contents or to provide ongoing support for the

SAMPLE ASSIGNMENT (EXCERPT)
Including handbook references in assignments
Racism, Sexism, and Social Darwinism: Mary Lynn Rampolla

Your first writing assignment, due on Sept. 15, is to write a summary of "A shared cultural context" on pp. 31–39 of Stephen Jay Gould's *The Mismeasure of Man.* In writing your summary, you should follow the guidelines set forth in the handout "The Summary." You might also find it useful to look at the summary examples found in sections 48a–b and 49d of *The Bedford Handbook for Writers.*

Before writing your critique, you should read, carefully, the handout "Critical Reading and Critique," which was given to you in class on Sept. 17. You might also find it useful to look at the section on common mistakes in reasoning in section 52f of *The Bedford Handbook for Writers.*

For this course focusing on both disciplinary and write-to-learn genres, Professor Rampolla distributed a sequence of handouts as part of the syllabus at the beginning of the course. These assignments refer students to the handouts and, in addition, direct them to relevant sections of the handbook. For the summary paper, the handbook expands on the handout by offering examples of summary writing. For the critique paper, the handbook supplements the handout by discussing common failures of reasoning.

students' writing at various stages of the process. Giving the students an overview of the handbook chosen for the course is not as superfluous an exercise as it might seem; for many students, a writing handbook is foreign territory, and with some class time devoted to it, they will not enter that territory unaccompanied. On the day when the instructor intends to provide an overview of the handbook, he or she should make sure that the students bring their handbooks to class so that during the instruction they are looking at and working with their own books rather than gazing at a distant volume held up in front of the class.

Using the handbook in class can extend far beyond an overview of its contents, however. Assigning occasional handbook exercises to the entire class and going over important sections in class are also helpful. Before the first paper assignment in a write-to-learn course, for example, the instructor might want to take students through their handbook's discussion of planning the paper. And after the first paper has been returned, it might be useful to spend time on the handbook sections that cover revision or common problems with grammar and usage. Such activities will not produce mastery of those issues, but they will help students become more familiar with the handbook and more inclined to consult it on their own as they revise.

In-class handbook instruction can be made more concrete if it is applied to writing samples from students in the class. Students need to be told in advance that their writing may be used in class and that they can opt not to have their writing made public. Perhaps the best approach is to tell students at the beginning of the semester that from time to time their writing may be distributed in class and that whenever they write something they would not want distributed, they should attach a note to that effect when they hand it in. They should also attach a note if they are willing to have their writing made available to the class but would prefer to remain anonymous.

Sometimes classroom instruction using students' own prose is best conducted with anonymous samples, but at other times it is more beneficial to acknowledge the writers of the samples. Because the choice often depends on subtle interpersonal factors, such as students' previous experience with peer response, many instructors let class members vote on which method they would prefer. In any case, whenever a student's writing is used as a sample, everyone else in the class must be prepared to treat it with respect. Many instructors set down ground rules for peer response, stipulating that no jokes, put-downs, or wry facial expressions will be permissible—during or after class—even between "best friends" who are "teasing" each other.

Although students may observe and discuss errors in the process of peer review, the detection of errors is not the objective; nor does the finding or "correcting" of errors conclude the process. Rather, the writing samples from the class should be used to help students learn to analyze writing and explore options for revision. (See pages 184–185 for advice on conducting in-class response to students' work.)

Professor Howard gave her students a handout containing anonymous writing samples from each class member. The samples became the focus of handbook-based classroom instruction on style and mechanics. Although other errors are present as well, selections 1, 5, and 6 were used in a lesson on the apostrophe; selections 2 and 4 were

SAMPLE HANDOUT
Using students' prose to teach editing
Critical Reading and Writing: Rebecca Moore Howard

---

1. When you are born you are pure due to your inexperience at life. During your lifetime you go through stages of being pure in heart and mind and also being impure. The total choice is up to the person to figure out a way of life that suits them. The soul in my theory is like a lump of clay. It has it's own shape, size and texture and can be molded in certain ways to fit the artists feelings. We are the artists and are given certain characteristics but how we use these characteristics is based on choice and outside stimuli.

2. In *Phaedo*, Socrates portrays women as inferior. Socrates' environment contradicts his attitudes. Socrates' environment basi-

cally illustrates that women were considered powerful. In Homer's *The Odyssey* he explains how Penelope, wife of Odysseus, ruled the kingdom while he was away for twenty years. If it had not been for Helen of Troy, who started the war between Greece and the Trojans for ten years.

3. My evidences that the mind and not the body is what causes this temptation of impurity is based on past experiences. I know that as a young teenager you feel very curious about knowing how it feels to smoke for the first time in your life. This curiosity or knowledge comes from the mind that you want to investigate. Once you're tempted or trapped out of this curiosity there's no way out for you to escape. You start smoking for the first time in your life and feel weird about this novelty. Then after your first reaction you still want to try it again for an improved feeling.

4. Socrates said that "the soul resembles the divine, and the body resembles the mortal" (pg. 119). Socrates believes that the "death" is the physical decomposition of the body once the soul departs. The soul contains many elements, they are: the immortality of knowledge, the passing to one body to another, and the pure and the impure elements when it changes to the existing to the immortal, according to Socrates. For example, when a soul is trying to get into Hades and the soul is pure they can get in and pass through with ease, but if the soul is impure and is polluted, referring to sexual desires, "the soul is dragged back to the visible region in fear of the unseen and of Hades."

5. Not only does the soul see the thing but it sees what the thing truly is. As a philosopher, Socrates would probably find the superior intelligence of the soul quite appealing, and might actually long to die so that he could live on in that particular state. One might wonder why the soul would bother to inhabit a body if it is so highly intelligent on it's own. Socrates also had an explanation for that. When the soul is in the body it lives the life that the body lives.

6. It is clear to see that the body and the soul are two different things which, when separated, go it's own separate ways. The body and the soul cannot possibly "meld together" for after the body dies the soul lives on. The "physical" body disappears for after a certain point the body must decay, but the "spiritual" soul will continue to live on.

7. The disease works like this. The body forces the soul to face many impurities that the soul must reject. The more impurities that the soul lets in, the more impure it becomes. The more impure it becomes determines where you will go when you die and if you are reincarnated, what you will be when you come back.

used to illustrate techniques for correcting sentence fragments and comma splices; selection 3 gave the class practice with placing commas after introductory phrases and clauses; and selections 2 and 7 precipitated a discussion of sentence structure and length.

Including handbook references in responses to student writing

By referring to specific handbook sections in responding to students' work, instructors encourage use of the handbook as a tool in revising and editing. Though generalized instruction is useful, students will better comprehend the handbook's advice on writing and revising if they see how it applies to their own work.

When each paragraph in a paper seems to be a marooned, self-enclosed entity, the instructor might refer the student to the handbook's discussion of transitions. When the verbs don't agree with their subjects, the student might be referred to the section on subject-verb agreement. Instead of simply writing "awkward" or, more enigmatically, "AWK" in the margins of a student's paper, the instructor can try to determine the grammatical cause of the awkwardness. *The Bedford Handbook for Writers*, 4th edition, for example, includes on the inside front cover a brief table of contents with symbols corresponding to many of the topics. For ease of reference, these symbols appear with section numbers in colored tabs at the tops of the pages. For a problem with mixed construction, an instructor using *The Bedford Handbook* could write "mixed" (the symbol) or "11a" (the section number) pointing the student to the appropriate handbook section, where the student would see that the mixed construction *When an employee is promoted without warning can be alarming* could be revised to *Being promoted without warning can be alarming.* If the awkwardness derives from a lack of parallelism, the instructor can write "//" or "9," referring the student to section 9, where the student would find the example *Abused children commonly exhibit one or more of the following symptoms: withdrawal, rebelliousness, restlessness, and they are depressed* revised to *Abused children commonly exhibit one or more of the following symptoms: withdrawal, rebelliousness, and depression.*

Instructors cannot be sure that students will make use of handbook sections referred to in their responses unless they require students to submit a revision. Instructors with heavy workloads may want to assign a grade to the revised version without writing comments. (For advice about grading revisions, see page 69.)

Assigning handbook exercises

Instructors can also tailor the handbook to a class's needs by assigning exercises that address students' specific writing problems. The answer keys provided in instructors' editions of most handbooks make grading exercises easy, and instructors may even want to give students copies of answer keys so that they can check their own work. (Some publishers offer separate answer keys for students.)

When many students in the class are having similar writing problems, the instructor may want to assign the relevant handbook sections and exercises to the whole class. This approach can give class members a sense that they have common needs and concerns about writing, rather than creating the impression that some are "good" writers and others "deficient." However, it has the potential disadvantage of providing writing instruction that may not be equally useful to every member of the class.

Exercises can also be assigned to individual students. After reading a draft of a paper and noticing major or recurring errors, the instructor can assign pertinent handbook exercises for the student to submit at the same time as the revised paper.

Supplementing the Handbook with Handouts

Because few instructors find a handbook that accords precisely with their pedagogical aims and tastes, many write their own handouts on such issues as style, manuscript preparation, idea generation and development, and documentation. Handouts, however, have one disadvantage: Students tend to see them as "what *this* instructor wants" and therefore may not apply the information and advice to their writing in other courses. They tend to believe that published handbooks are of more universal applicability than are instructors' handouts. Thus it is clearly important to choose a handbook carefully so that there is minimal need for supplementary handouts.

This is not to suggest, though, that instructors should not distribute handouts on writing. Handouts can bring specificity and control to the teaching of writing, emphasizing the issues that instructors find most compelling, in terms that they consider effective. Instructors who want more explanation of an issue than they or the handbook can provide might want to check with their colleagues. One of them probably has a good handout on the topic and will be willing to share it.

SAMPLE HANDOUT (EXCERPT)
Using a supplementary handout on discipline-specific writing
Ethnographic Writing: Describing and Interpreting Social Action: David Hess

A GUIDE TO ETHNOGRAPHIC WRITING
II. Writing the Ethnography
    A. Genres: Envisioning a Textual Organization
        1. The Puzzle-Solving Format (e.g., Geertz "Deep Play"). Start with an event (your text) and then examine it from different points of view (your exegesis).
        2. The Time Cycle Format (e.g., Burnett "Ceremony, Rites"). Decide on a time unit (your text—e.g., evening, work shift,

For this course Professor Hess adopted a generic writers' handbook and supplemented it with his original handouts. Part I of the handout describes the research stages, and the passage shown here explains the writing and editing stages. The handout outlines some rhetorical features of an ethnography and illustrates them with references to fieldwork the students might themselves conduct. By citing examples and clarifying points throughout, this handout makes the process more accessible to students.

week, semester, or school year) and then examine it from beginning to end (your exegesis).

B. Framing Devices (Pictures, footnotes, diagrams)
   1. Decide on mode: complementary vs. supplementary relationship to text.
   2. Decide on tone: serious vs. ironic.
C. Point of view
   1. Decide on role of the "I."
      a. To establish authority vs. to establish reflexivity.
      b. How prominent you wish to make the "I."
   2. Decide how much of your dialogue with informants you want to represent (how close you want to be to a fieldwork report versus an analytical study).
   3. Decide how much you want to represent your point of view versus that of your informant(s).
D. Style
   1. Decide on appropriate metaphors.
   2. Decide how the form of the text relates to its content.

Professor Johnson provides students with a three-page handout with directions in English and examples in Spanish. The handout offers tips on sentence structure, sentence length, vocabulary, and verbs. It also urges students to take risks and try new structures rather than use patterns they know well and are sure are correct. This approach encourages students to think of stylistic choices and language acquisition as interrelated enterprises.

SAMPLE HANDOUT (EXCERPT)
Using a supplementary handout with stylistic suggestions
Intermediate Spanish: Anita Johnson

HOW TO SOPHISTICATE YOUR WRITING
II. Avoid the same old sentence pattern of Subject/Verb/Object-Complement (*María escribe la carta* or *María es simpática*). Use more complex and varied sentence patterns.

Simple sentence: *Voy al cine.*
Compound (independent clauses joined by conjunction): *Voy al cine y veo la película.*
Complex (subordinate clause): *Cuando voy al cine, veo películas interesantes.*
Compound-complex (subordinate clause and two independent clauses joined by conjunction): *Cuando voy al cine, veo películas interesantes y como mucho.*

Notice that each of the sample handouts presented here is in outline rather than essay format. The handouts also offer a combination of directions and examples, and they are brief. All of these features make them readily accessible to students.

Conferring with Students

The one-to-one conference

Students are often reluctant to consult an important resource: the instructor. Many are afraid that asking the instructor for help will expose them as inadequate writers. In classes of manageable enrollment, scheduling one-to-one conferences with every student once or twice during the semester may help students overcome this fear, for the conferences establish that students can talk to instructors without having to feel as if there is something "wrong" with their writing (or with themselves as writers).

A great deal can be accomplished in fifteen- or twenty-minute conferences if the instructor (1) avoids reading what the student has written, (2) talks as little as possible, and (3) never picks up a pen except to write down what the student has said. Students come to conferences hoping for answers, but they get the most out of conferences if they are the ones who devise those answers.

Reading the student's work before or during the conference too easily sets up the instructor to give a blueprint for a successful paper; the instructor is expected—and may be tempted—to point out problems and tell the student how to correct them. The instructor may also become entangled in sentence-level issues (such as word choice, grammar, and punctuation) rather than the larger issues of how the student has developed and organized his or her ideas. The latter concerns are more appropriately the focus of writing instruction in the disciplines.

Instead of reading the paper during the conference, the instructor can ask the student to describe its main assertion(s), the reasons he or she believes (or doubts) them, and the problems the student encountered in drafting. This frees the student from the written text, prompting him or her to think about the development of ideas rather than about the words already committed to the page. The instructor should listen and then repeat or synthesize what the student has said: "It sounds to me as if you're saying that. . . ." The instructor can also suggest options: "What would happen if. . . ." And he or she should warn of pitfalls: "I'm concerned that if you say. . . ." Again, the most successful meetings are usually those in which the student does much more talking than the instructor, whose best role is to help the student articulate goals and explore options.

The instructor should also avoid writing on the student's paper. Otherwise he or she becomes proofreader, editor, provider of solutions; and the pencil, once in hand, takes on a life of its own. The instructor becomes carried away with the heady success of solving problems in the paper. But in the bargain, the student loses ownership of his or her writing and does not learn about the writing process. Watching the instructor revise does not teach students how to make their own revisions.

The instructor should pick up the pencil only to act as scribe, writing down what the student says. By taking notes and giving these to the student at the conclusion of the session the instructor saves the student time and helps him or her remember the insights achieved. The instructor might begin a conference by asking the student about his or her plans for the paper or his or her concerns. The conference proceeds with the instructor eliciting from the student the various options that might be pursued and concludes with the two of them weighing the pros and cons of these options. The student does not have to have already begun the writing process for the conference to be successful. If the student is "stuck" or simply hasn't begun work on the paper, the instructor can ask about his or her ideas or problems with getting started and act as secretary, jotting down what the student says. The two of them can then look over these notes, searching for germs of a topic or thesis.

During the conference, instructor and student should sit side by side, at slight angles to each other—not on opposite sides of a desk. This arrangement allows them to go over work together; it also allows them to make eye contact without feeling uncomfortably close to each other. By leaving the door slightly ajar, the instructor provides privacy without making the student feel trapped.

Timing is important for conferences. They are perhaps most effective shortly before a paper is due. If they take place too far in advance of the due date, students will not have begun thinking seriously about the paper and will therefore have little to contribute, nor will they be able to make much concrete use of what the instructor has to say. If the conferences come too close to the due date, students will not have time to make full use of the insights they develop. Depending on the length, difficulty, and importance of the paper and the number of students in the class, the instructor may want to consider holding ten-to-fifteen-minute conferences four to nine days before the paper is due. Ideally, these conferences should be spread over several days; more than three hours of conferences in a day may exhaust the instructor's intellectual energies.

To offset the burden that one-to-one conferences place on the instructor's time, one or more regular class sessions might be canceled to allow for a round of conferences. The pedagogical value of conferences is generally well worth the loss of one or more class periods.

Small-group conferences

For classes that are too large to allow for one-to-one conferences, the small-group conference, in which the instructor meets with two to four students, is a valuable alternative. In the small-group conference the instructor and students discuss strategies for composing an upcoming paper or for revising a recently returned one. Small-group conferences have the advantage of making students feel less on the spot. And as conferences unfold, students often feel less isolated in their writing process, having come to realize that their classmates have similar concerns. The best small-group conferences are ones in which the students develop a problem-solving rapport that extends beyond the conference, and the instructor may want to suggest that groups meet again on their own and continue working together. (For advice on directing peer group work, see pages 184–189.)

Referring Students to Tutors

Many colleges and universities have a writing center (sometimes called a "writing lab" or a "writing clinic") in which tutors are available to consult with students. Most writing centers offer drop-in hours and will also make appointments with students. At most schools the center is staffed in part, if not entirely, by graduate or undergraduate students. Often they are English majors, but sometimes tutors are chosen from all disciplines, with the idea that a multidisciplinary tutoring staff is well positioned to help students with assignments from their various classes. Often the tutors are students who themselves have great facility with writing, but at some institutions tutors are intentionally chosen because they have struggled with their writing and succeeded; thus, they can readily understand the difficulties that their peers may be having. At some institutions the center is staffed partly or entirely by professional tutors and faculty who have volunteered their time or who are given course release for their work.

Benefits of tutoring

Tutoring helps students learn about writing in a concrete rather than abstract context. Figuring out how to formulate a thesis for a political science paper that is due in four days may teach a student much more about principles of theses than will a week of composition class devoted to the subject. Another advantage of tutoring is that it provides students with an alternative to the instructor as a resource for writing. The writing center offers a place where students can get advice on their writing without the volatile influence of the instructor-student power relationship. Because the tutor is not grading the paper, the student may perceive his or her advice to be more "objective." That very feature in turn may constrain tutoring; because the tutor is not the person who grades the paper, the student may perceive the tutor's advice as lacking authority and thus ignore it.

Instructors, too, struggle with delicate dynamics in referring students to the writing center. They are inviting strangers into the intimate teacher-student relationship, and those strangers may intervene in inappropriate ways. Instructors are justly concerned that a tutor might criticize their assignments or grading practices or might actually write students' papers. Yet these types of problems seldom occur in writing centers. At most colleges and universities, the writing center is well managed and its staff well trained. As part of their training, tutors are typically told not to write students' papers or criticize teaching practices, and instructors can generally expect that tutors will respond to students' work in constructive, supportive ways. If evidence accumulates to the contrary, an instructor should consider contacting the writing center director to tell him or her of a situation that may need to be remedied. Instructors may want to contact the writing center in any case. By talking with the director and other staff members, they can learn more about the center's philosophy and strategies and communicate their own hopes and expectations for tutoring.

When and how to make referrals to the writing center

If class size and the instructor's workload permit, the students' first writing resource should be the instructor. In that ideal situation, the instructor can recommend tutoring as a means of expanding the dialogue about students' writing, as a means of providing more extensive advice, or as a second opinion about strategies for improving students' writing. Instructors with large classes or heavy workloads, however, may need to recommend the writing center as the first line of response to students' instructional needs.

In either case, the tenor of the instructor's referral is crucial to the success of the tutoring. Instructors should always strive to make positive rather than negative referrals, depicting the writing center as a resource for all writers rather than as a remedy for papers gone wrong. Instructors teach an important lesson if they dispel the notions that writing is unteachable, that the ability to write is a gift granted to the few, that writing instruction is for the ungifted masses whose prose needs to be made presentable, and that tutoring is for the hopeless cases who do not respond to instruction.

The instructor might, *before* the first paper is due, recommend to all students in the class that they visit the writing center for advice on conceptualizing, developing, and revising their papers. It might be possible to have the writing center director or a tutor come to class and make a brief presentation to acquaint students with the resources available at the center. If, after a set of papers has been returned, students have the option to revise, the instructor might point out to the entire class (not just those who received low grades) that tutors can help in the revising process.

Much less constructive is telling the class that those who are having "problems" with their writing can seek "help" at the writing "lab" or "clinic." Such language puts the students in the position of admitting some sort of deficiency as a prerequisite to tutoring. Seeking tutoring then becomes their punishment or penance for inadequacy. Even less constructive is telling a student, whether in person or in writing, that a paper is so bad that he or she must enlist the help of a tutor. Again, this sort of comment fosters a negative attitude toward tutoring and can reduce its effectiveness.

In addition to recommending tutoring to the entire class, the instructor can encourage individual students by making remarks such as "I don't feel that this paper is expressed in appropriately academic language. I would be glad to go over it with you, and I would also urge you to avail yourself of the resources at the writing center. That way you'll have some ideas for how to write a more effective version."

It should be made clear to students that tutors are not editors or proofreaders. Rather, the tutors' role is to help students improve their own writing. Tutors can go over a paper with students, help them identify strengths and weaknesses, and work with them to develop strategies for drafting, revising, and editing. Finally, follow-up is important to the success of tutoring. If the instructor refers a student to the writing center and later inquires about the success of the consultation, the student is much more likely to regard the referral as a serious one. Talking about what was accomplished by the tutoring also helps students adopt an analytic attitude toward learning writing, which makes it more likely that they will be able to apply what they learned in tutoring to other writing situations.

A Selected Bibliography of Writers' Handbooks and Guides

Each year new textbooks and handbooks are listed in the spring issue of the journal *WPA: Writing Program Administration*. The following samples indicate some of the generic and discipline-specific handbooks and writers' guides available to the instructor of writing in the disciplines.

Comprehensive writers' handbooks

Besser, Pam. *A Basic Handbook of Writing Skills*. Mountain View, CA: Mayfield, 1994.

Carter, Bonnie, and Craig Skates. *The Rinehart Handbook for Writers*. 3rd ed. Fort Worth: Harcourt, 1993.

Crews, Frederick. *The Random House Handbook*. 6th ed. New York: McGraw, 1992.

————, Sandra Schor, and Michael Hennessy. *The Borzoi Handbook for Writers*. 3rd ed. New York: McGraw, 1994.

Fowler, H. Ramsey, and Jane E. Aaron. *The Little, Brown Handbook*. 5th ed. New York: HarperCollins, 1992.

Hacker, Diana. *The Bedford Handbook for Writers*. 4th ed. Boston: Bedford, 1994.

————. *A Writer's Reference*. 2nd ed. Boston: Bedford, 1992.

Hairston, Maxine, and John J. Ruszkiewicz. *The Scott, Foresman Handbook for Writers*. 3rd ed. New York: HarperCollins, 1993.

Hodges, John C., Winifred Bryan Horner, Suzanne Strobeck Webb, and Robert Keith Miller. *Harbrace College Handbook*. 12th ed. Fort Worth: Harcourt, 1994.

Kirkland, James W., and Collett B. Dilworth Jr. *Concise English Handbook*. 3rd ed. Lexington, MA: Heath, 1994.

Kirszner, Laurie G., and Stephen R. Mandell. *The Holt Handbook*. 3rd ed. Fort Worth: Harcourt, 1992.

Lester, James D. *A Writer's Handbook: Style and Grammar*. New York: Harcourt, 1991.

Levin, Gerald. *The Macmillan College Handbook*. 2nd ed. New York: Macmillan, 1991.

Lunsford, Andrea, and Robert Connors. *The St. Martin's Handbook*. 2nd ed. New York: St. Martin's, 1992.

Marius, Richard, and Harvey S. Wiener. *The McGraw-Hill College Handbook*. 4th ed. New York: McGraw, 1994.

O'Hare, Frank, and Edward A. Kline. *The Modern Writer's Handbook*. 3rd ed. New York: Macmillan, 1993.

Perrin, Robert. *The Beacon Handbook*. 3rd ed. Boston: Houghton, 1994.

Troyka, Lynn Quitman. *The Simon and Schuster Handbook for Writers*. 3rd ed. New York: Prentice, 1993.

Comprehensive style guides

Hacker, Diana. *A Pocket Style Manual*. Boston: Bedford, 1993.

Strunk, William, Jr., and E. B. White. *The Elements of Style*. 3rd ed. New York: Macmillan, 1979.

Research guides

Hubbuch, Susan. *Writing Research Papers Across the Curriculum*. 3rd ed. New York: Holt, 1992.

Hughes, Elaine, Jay Silverman, and Diana Weinbroer. *Finding Answers: Conducting and Reporting Research*. New York: Harper, 1994.

Hult, Christine. *Researching and Writing: An Interdisciplinary Approach*. Belmont, CA: Wadsworth, 1986.

Johnson, Jean. *The Bedford Guide to the Research Process*. Boston: Bedford, 1992.

Kennedy, Mary L., and Hadley M. Smith. *Academic Writing: Working with Sources Across the Curriculum*. Englewood Cliffs, NJ: Prentice, 1986.

Lester, James. *Writing Research Papers*. New York: HarperCollins, 1993.

Memering, Dean. *The Prentice Hall Guide to Research Writing*. 2nd ed. Englewood Cliffs, NJ: Prentice, 1989.

Meyer, Michael. *The Little, Brown Guide to Writing Research Papers*. 3rd ed. New York: Harper, 1994.

Weidenborner, Stephen, and Domenick Caruso. *Writing Research Papers: A Guide to the Process*. 3rd ed. New York: St. Martin's, 1990.

Zimmerman, Don, and Dawn Rodrigues. *Research Writing Across the Disciplines.* New York: Harcourt, 1992.

Discipline-specific writers' handbooks and guides

Natural and mathematical sciences

Biddle, Arthur W., and Daniel J. Bean. *Writer's Guide: Life Sciences.* Lexington, MA: Heath, 1987.

Bond, Lynne A., and Anthony S. Magistrale. *Writer's Guide: Psychology.* Lexington, MA: Heath, 1987.

Day, Robert A. *How to Write and Publish a Scientific Paper.* 2nd ed. Philadelphia: ISI Press, 1983.

McMillan, Victoria E. *Writing Papers in the Biological Sciences.* Boston: Bedford, 1988.

Miles, Thomas M. *Critical Thinking and Writing for Science and Technology.* New York: Harcourt, 1990.

Pechenik, Jan A. *A Short Guide to Writing about Biology.* 2nd ed. New York: HarperCollins, 1993.

Wilkinson, Antoinette. *The Scientist's Handbook for Writing Scientific Papers and Dissertations.* New York: Prentice, 1991.

Zeiger, Mimi. *Handbook of Clear Writing in Biomedical Journal Articles.* New York: McGraw, 1991.

Social sciences

Becker, Howard S. *Writing for Social Scientists: How to Start and Finish Your Thesis, Book, or Article.* Chicago: U of Chicago P, 1986.

Biddle, Arthur W., and Kenneth M. Holland. *Writer's Guide: Political Science.* Lexington, MA: Heath, 1989.

Cuba, Lee J. *A Short Guide to Writing about Social Science.* 2nd ed. New York: HarperCollins, 1993. Geared to students of sociology and anthropology.

Friedman, Sharon, and Stephen Steinberg. *Writing and Thinking in the Social Sciences.* Englewood Cliffs, NJ: Prentice, 1989.

Giarrusso, Roseann, et al. *A Guide to Writing Sociology Papers.* Ed. Judith Richlin-Klonsky and Ellen Strenski. 2nd ed. New York: St. Martin's, 1991.

McCloskey, Donald N. *The Writing of Economics.* New York: Macmillan, 1987.

Marius, Richard. *A Short Guide to Writing about History.* New York: HarperCollins, 1989.

Steffens, Henry J., and Mary Jane Dickerson. *Writer's Guide: History.* Lexington, MA: Heath, 1987.

Humanities

Barnet, Sylvan. *A Short Guide to Writing about Art.* 4th ed. New York: HarperCollins, 1993.

———. *A Short Guide to Writing about Literature.* 6th ed. New York: HarperCollins, 1992.

Benjamin, Jules R. *A Student's Guide to History.* 5th ed. New York: St. Martin's, 1991.

Biays, John Sheridan Jr. *Responding to Literature: A Step-by-Step Guide for Student Writers.* New York: McGraw, 1988.

Biddle, Arthur W., and Toby Fulwiler. *Reading, Writing, and the Study of Literature.* New York: Random, 1989.

Cole, SuzAnne C., and Jeff W. Lindemann. *Reading and Responding to Literature.* New York: Harcourt, 1989.

Corrigan, Timothy. *A Short Guide to Writing about Film.* New York: HarperCollins, 1992.

MacAllister, Joyce. *Writing about Literature: Aims and Process.* New York: Macmillan, 1987.

Profitt, Edward. *Reading and Writing about Short Fiction.* New York: Harcourt, 1988.

Roberts, Edgar. *Writing Themes about Literature.* 6th ed. Englewood Cliffs, NJ: Prentice, 1988.

Stanford, Judith A. *Responding to Literature.* Mountain View, CA: Mayfield, 1991.

Business and law

Brand, Norman. *Legal Writing: The Strategy of Persuasion.* 2nd ed. New York: St. Martin's, 1988.

Brusaw, Charles T., Gerald J. Alred, and Walter E. Oliu. *The Business Writer's Handbook.* 4th ed. New York: St. Martin's, 1993.

Griffin, C. W. *Writing: A Guide for Business Professionals.* New York: Harcourt, 1987.

Woolever, Kristin. *Untangling the Law: Strategies for Legal Writers.* Belmont, CA: Wadsworth, 1987.

Multidisciplinary writers' guides and handbooks

Anson, Chris M., and Lance E. Wilcox. *Field Guide to Writing.* New York: HarperCollins, 1993.

Durkin, Diane. *Writing in the Disciplines.* New York: Random House, 1987.

Gere, Anne Ruggles. *Writing and Learning.* 3rd ed. New York: Macmillan, 1992.

Murray, Donald M. *Write to Learn.* 4th ed. New York: Holt, 1993.

Simon, Linda. *Good Writing: A Guide and Sourcebook for Writing Across the Curriculum.* New York: St. Martin's, 1988.

Checklist for integrating writer's resources into the course

CHOOSING A WRITERS' HANDBOOK

_____ Consider a generic handbook for a course focusing on write-to-learn genres or a discipline-specific handbook for a course focusing on disciplinary genres.

_____ Review publishers' examination copies before making a selection.

_____ Ask publishers for examination copies of all ancillaries for the handbook.

_____ Consider whether students will be able to to use the book on their own.

TEACHING STUDENTS TO USE THE HANDBOOK

_____ Treat the handbook as a resource for writers rather than as a standard of perfection.

_____ Refer to the handbook in syllabi and assignments.

_____ Provide an in-class handbook orientation. (Some handbooks provide tutorials on how to use the handbook.)

_____ When grading papers, refer to appropriate handbook sections in your comments.

_____ Assign handbook exercises based on difficulties demonstrated in papers or invite a handbook-based revision of papers.

_____ Use samples of students' own writing for in-class handbook-based instruction.

HOLDING CONFERENCES WITH STUDENTS

_____ Encourage students to regard the instructor as a writer's resource.

_____ Use scheduled conferences as a way of fostering a constructive relationship with all the students in the class.

_____ Schedule conferences four to nine days before a paper is due or immediately after returning one.

_____ Cancel class sessions, if necessary, to compensate for time spent in conferences.

_____ Arrange seats at angles to each other and leave office door partially open.

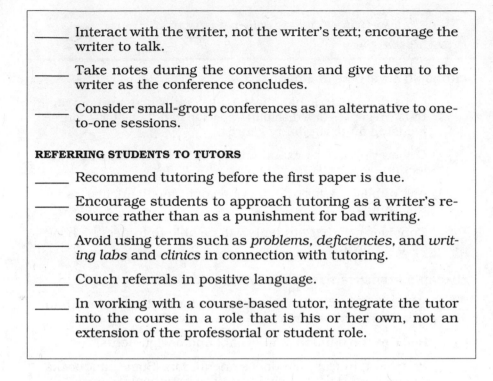

_____ Interact with the writer, not the writer's text; encourage the writer to talk.

_____ Take notes during the conversation and give them to the writer as the conference concludes.

_____ Consider small-group conferences as an alternative to one-to-one sessions.

REFERRING STUDENTS TO TUTORS

_____ Recommend tutoring before the first paper is due.

_____ Encourage students to approach tutoring as a writer's resource rather than as a punishment for bad writing.

_____ Avoid using terms such as *problems, deficiencies,* and *writing labs* and *clinics* in connection with tutoring.

_____ Couch referrals in positive language.

_____ In working with a course-based tutor, integrate the tutor into the course in a role that is his or her own, not an extension of the professorial or student role.

For Further Reading

Freedman, Sarah Warshauer, and A. M. Katz. "Pedagogical Interaction during the Composing Process: The Writing Conference." *Writing in Real Time: Modeling Production Processes.* Ed. Ann Matsuhashi. Norwood, NJ: Ablex, 1987. 58–80.

Harris, Muriel. *Teaching One-to-One: The Writing Conference.* Urbana: NCTE, 1986.

Kuriloff, Pesche C. "Reaffirming the Writing Conference: A Tool for Writing Teachers Across the Curriculum." *Journal of Teaching Writing* 10.1 (1991): 45–58.

Sperling, Melanie. "I Want to Talk to Each of You: Collaboration and the Teacher-Student Writing Conference." *Research in the Teaching of English* 24.3 (Oct. 1990): 279–321.

Stanger, Carol. "The Sexual Politics of the One-to-One Tutorial Approach and Collaborative Learning." *Teaching Writing: Pedagogy, Gender, and Equity.* Ed. Cynthia L. Caywood and Gillian R. Overing. Albany: SUNY UP, 1987. 31–44.

Walker, Caroline. "Teacher Dominance in the Writing Conference." *Journal of Teaching Writing* 11.1 (1992): 65–88.

CHAPTER 4

Teaching the Writing Process

In this chapter:

- ❏ Why teach the writing process?
- ❏ Before students begin the paper—teaching prewriting
- ❏ As students begin the paper—teaching drafting
- ❏ Responding to drafts
- ❏ After students compose the first draft—teaching rewriting
- ❏ Handling multiple drafts
- ❏ Checklist for teaching the writing process
- ❏ For further reading

Why Teach the Writing Process?

The process of writing—how one comes up with ideas, organizes them into written prose, and then reconsiders and revises them—remains mysterious for many students *and* teachers, no matter how frequently or how successfully they engage in that process. Early twentieth-century composition instruction left that mystery unprobed and instead focused on describing the desired features of finished prose. Recently, however, composition researchers—by observing writers at work, interviewing them afterward, and recording "writing protocols" in which students and professionals describe their thoughts and actions as they write—have developed various models of and strategies for the writing process. The very idea of "the" writing process has given way to a recognition of multiple writing process*es* that vary from one writer and one context to another. Moreover, these processes are recognized as recursive rather than linear: Writers do not begin with prewriting and move in an orderly fashion through the

45

various composing stages, finishing with a tidy act of editing. Rather, they may engage in several stages simultaneously, perhaps drafting and editing bits of text even while they are still searching for a thesis. For convenience, though, writing teachers allude to "the" writing process (even though no two processes are the same) and call its components "stages" (even though they are recursive and sometimes simultaneous). Describing the writing process in terms of stages makes writing papers more manageable and less mysterious to students. It also helps them plan their time effectively and allows instructors to schedule sufficient time for assignments.

Instructors may want to offer a systematic introduction to the stages of the writing process. Such an introduction is particularly appropriate in write-to-learn courses because it helps students improve their general writing skills; but students who are expected to produce discipline-specific writing also benefit from advice about the writing process. In learning about the writing process students also learn which patterns and strategies work best for them, and they realize that good writing takes time and is rarely "easy."

Teaching the writing process can be fairly time-consuming, and this discourages some instructors from attempting it. However, much can be achieved in the first five or ten minutes of class at each stage of the writing process. Most instructors who do teach the writing process report that the effort is worthwhile; students learn skills that improve their papers for the class and their writing in general.

Before Students Begin the Paper— Teaching Prewriting

The writing component of an undergraduate course can be called a success if it helps students learn how to generate and develop ideas for writing, for inexperienced writers often believe that good papers come from inspiration or genius that guides the pen across the paper—or the fingers over the keyboard. Good academic writing, they may believe, results from a stream of consciousness much like that attributed to James Joyce. They may not know that there are systematic strategies for making ideas happen, and they may not realize that writers often use these strategies before they begin to compose an essay. In composition theory, the process of preparing to write a paper is variously known as *prewriting, tagmemics, discovery,* and *heuristics.* This book uses the term *prewriting.* The term *prewriting* can be misleading, for often this component of the process involves a considerable quantity of writing. The prefix *pre-,* however, emphasizes the preliminary nature of the activity, the idea that writers may write for themselves *prior to* rather than as a first step in writing for others.

Analyzing the assignment, purpose, and audience

Many disastrous papers are the product of misread assignments. Though instructors should keep writing assignments straightforward and be willing to provide additional explanations, most of the responsibility for understanding must be accepted by the student. Yet college-level assignments tend to be worded and structured very differently from high school writing assignments, and wording and structure vary across the disciplines. Students may therefore benefit from being taught how to analyze writing assignments—both those assigned by the instructor and those they design themselves. They should be able to recognize and understand key words such as *discuss, explore, compare, propose, analyze, explain,* and *research.*

SAMPLE HANDOUT
Analyzing assignments
Prewriting and Essay Design: Sandra Jamieson

ASSIGNMENT ANALYSIS:
As soon as you receive an assignment from any of your professors, ask the following questions:

1. What instruction am I being given? (Circle key words such as *discuss, explore, compare, propose, analyze, explain,* and *research.*)
2. What material/theories does the assignment ask me to include/consider? (Underline words, ideas, and phrases listed in the assignment.)
3. If the assignment begins with a general discussion or quotation followed by an instruction, what is the relationship between the two parts? (Briefly summarize this.)
4. Who is the intended audience for this paper? (If it is not clear from the assignment, assume the audience to be other academics in the discipline who are familiar with the material and might read your work to learn something further about your subject. Assume that your audience knows *at least* as much about the topic as do you and your peers.)
5. What kinds of responses would *not* be appropriate; that is, what are the limits imposed on your paper? For example, plot summary is almost never appropriate in college. (Write out a brief list of what kinds of responses would not be appropriate.)
6. Finally, write a two-to-six-sentence summary of exactly what you are being asked to do. Imagine you are explaining the assignment to a peer who missed class or who simply does not understand the assignment. Don't plan the paper or summarize what you might write; simply *write out in careful detail what you are being asked to do.*

Although this seems to be a lot of work before they start writing, students find such a breakdown invaluable, especially with more complex assignments. The final summary allows Professor Jamieson to check at a glance whether her students understand the terms used in the assignment, the rhetorical mode they should adopt, and the audience whom they should address. It also helps students focus before they begin to generate ideas, thus saving them time.

Careful attention to the wording of an assignment also helps students understand the purpose of their writing. Instructors can help students understand the purpose of an assignment by providing guidelines.

These guidelines help students keep the purpose of lab reports clearly in mind.

SAMPLE GUIDELINES (EXCERPT)
Analyzing purpose for laboratory reports
Organic Chemistry: John Cochran and Patricia Jue

Give enough detail about your materials and methods so that others could repeat your work and obtain comparable results. Report the amounts of reagents and solvents used (mass/volume and moles) since these inform the reader of the limiting reagents and the scale of the reactions.

Because the purpose of high school assignments tends to be evaluative, requiring that students prove that they read the work or did the research, many students are unaware of other purposes in college-level academic writing. Simply explaining why scholars in the discipline write can help students understand the kinds of writing that will be required of them. The idea that the instructor will not simply read papers to evaluate "correct" presentation of received "facts" but will also look for new interpretations, explanations, and connections may be new to many students. Thus it can be helpful to remind them of purpose from time to time as they work on their papers.

Most high school writing assignments are designed with the instructor as audience yet often decree that students "assume an audience totally unfamiliar with the material." This strategy produces

Students often assume that their audience is the instructor who knows everything or the layperson who knows nothing. Both assumptions produce inadequate papers—the former lacking in detail, the latter burdened by minutiae. Imagining an audience of academics in the discipline can help students achieve a balanced relationship with their audience and can encourage them to take their work seriously and perceive themselves as apprentice academics.

SAMPLE GUIDELINES (EXCERPT)
Analyzing audience
Organic Chemistry: John Cochran and Patricia Jue

You should assume that the reader is a fairly competent chemist. It is sufficient to state that you refluxed, distilled, washed with some solution, and evaporated without detailing the apparatus used, unless it was nonstandard and has bearing on your results.

some effective book reports and summaries, and because it may have helped them get good grades in high school, many students are slow to recognize that college writing is often aimed at an informed audience. Instructors can help students by describing the audience in the assignment. The description might include what the audience already knows and what it might expect from a paper.

Students can practice writing for specific audiences by writing paragraphs in different ways for audiences that vary in disciplinary knowledge and academic sophistication. Comparing articles written for a popular market with those written for an academic audience can also help students identify the stylistic and rhetorical features specific to the discipline in which they are writing.

Generating ideas

Most comprehensive handbooks describe a variety of approaches to generating ideas. (See the end of Chapter 3, pages 39–42, for lists of handbooks.) *The Bedford Handbook,* for example, explains *listing,* the process of writing down everything the writer can think of relating to the subject (an especially useful technique for comparison papers because the student can see at a glance the similarities and differences of the items being compared); *clustering and branching* (see the example of a student's clustering and branching on page 52); *asking questions* (see the sample handouts on pages 50 and 55); *journal-keeping* (see Chapter 10 in this book); and *freewriting,* which a student engages in by simply sitting and writing whatever comes into his or her head about the subject, the only rule being that the pen must never leave the paper and must keep moving. In another version of freewriting, *freetyping,* a student turns down the contrast or turns off the screen of the computer and types without stopping for at least fifteen minutes.

Assigning students to read the pertinent section of their handbook, though, does not amount to teaching them how to generate ideas. It is also important to spend class time discussing possible ways to avoid the dread blank page. When assigning a paper, instructors may ask students to consider the different methods described here and select whichever seems most helpful. They then may assign students to hand in their prewriting or share it in peer response groups where they can compare results and discuss the merits of each method. (See pages 184–189.) Or instructors may assign just one method of prewriting to the entire class and then ask students to compare results. If the handbook does not contain a section describing various methods, the instructor can consult colleagues and other handbooks and compose a handout.

There is no "right" writing process; there is only what works for each writer, and even this varies from one occasion to another for the same writer. The instructor who participates in discussions, sharing his or her experiences as a writer, is therefore far more valuable than the instructor who acts as expert, telling students how writing should be done. Some instructors develop handouts that make their own writing process a model for students to adapt to their own purposes. But even while modeling his or her own writing process, the instructor should present it only as a possibility, not a necessity.

Professor Howard assigns this write-to-learn prewriting because she found that students often have a great deal of difficulty with the idea that they should write for themselves before they write for their readers. In response to her directions, many try to write outlines of their paper rather than figuring out what questions they must ask and answer to gather information for an outline. Gradually, though, the students come to realize that their prewriting questions and answers will generate materials that help them form their ideas but that are not included in the actual draft of the paper.

By focusing attention on the assignment itself as a source of prewriting questions, this method ensures that the students will stay focused on the purpose of the assignment. (Another excerpt from this handout appears on page 55.)

SAMPLE HANDOUT (EXCERPT A)
Generating ideas
Prewriting and Essay Design: Rebecca Moore Howard

When you have received a writing assignment, begin with prewriting, a technique that helps you master the materials you are to write about so that you can discover and develop your own logical ideas about them. The "prewriting" you do in this learning stage is for yourself. Once you have completed it, you will be ready to write again, to begin drafting the essay for your professor. These two writing acts, prewriting and drafting, are separate; but the prewriting is essential preparation for successful drafting.

STEP 1. *List the prewriting tasks.* What are the things you must know, before you begin writing, to respond to the assignment? Separate these from each other as much as possible; "similarities and differences," for example, should be two categories, not one. List these things as questions for you to answer as you reread the material (e.g.: Who are the main characters? What role does each one play? What tensions exist between them?). Sometimes some of these questions can be found in the wording of the assignment itself. Usually you will also have to figure out some of the prewriting questions yourself, based on your knowledge of the material.

Do these two things simultaneously but on separate sheets of paper:

STEP 2a. *Write out answers to each prewriting question.* Remember as you do this that you are not organizing your essay; you are just generating material, getting your thinking out on paper. Also, it will save time later if the answers that you write down now include notes referring back to the sources or to the passages in the text—page numbers, chapters, verse and line numbers, etc.

STEP 2b. *Write down all the ideas that occur to you.* Include the brilliant insights, the stupid questions, the complaints, the emotions, the reactions, the things you're reminded of—everything. (Typically these ideas will crowd into your head as you write out your answers to the prewriting tasks. Instead of pushing them aside, forgetting them, or telling yourself that they are irrelevant, *write them down.* Later you may find relevance in things that at first seemed immaterial.)

Defining and developing the topic

Many students don't understand the difference between a topic and a thesis. It is therefore helpful to spend a few minutes teaching them to differentiate between the two (e.g., "This paper will explore the social value of code switching" is a topic, whereas "While code switching is necessary to advancement in mainstream society, it requires its practitioners to surrender ethnic identity" is a thesis). Instructors may want to alert students to topic-statement flag words: *about* ("This paper will talk *about* . . ."); *discuss* ("This paper will *discuss* . . ."); *compare* ("This paper will *compare* . . ."); *ask* ("This paper will *ask* whether . . ."); and so on. Such words almost always signal a topic without any statement of conclusion *about* that topic—a thesis statement.

Students can use a variety of prewriting methods to develop the topic into a thesis. Most methods for generating ideas can also be used to focus the topic; in fact, many students will find that at the end of their idea generation they have identified a topic and perhaps even formulated a provisional thesis. If the general subject is still too broad, students may find clustering and branching (sometimes termed "mind mapping," "thought webs," or "thought balloons") especially helpful. In this method the student writes the general subject at the center of a sheet of paper and then surrounds it by lines pointing toward other general ideas that the subject raises in his or her mind. From each of these ideas the student draws more lines, following the trail of associations as far as it will go. Some students like to draw a circle or a box around each idea to keep the ideas separate. Often as the student looks back over the page and considers the ideas generated from one or more branches, a thesis comes to mind. If it does not, many students find it helpful to make additional connections between ideas with different colors of ink. As a method of generating ideas, clustering and branching tends to attract writers who are uncomfortable with the linear logic of lists and questions.

Student Ezra Lowe produced the following clustering and branching diagram (see page 52) in a class that was learning how to ask and answer questions as a means of prewriting—demonstrating that even though students should be guided through possibilities for prewriting, they should also be given leeway to try other methods.

Stating the thesis

Many essays published in academic journals do not include explicit thesis statements. Of those that do, many do not place the thesis statement at the beginning of the essay. Yet there is value in teaching students to do both these things: placing an explicit thesis statement as a signpost in the introduction to the paper helps the inexperienced or unfocused writer determine what he or she has to say and

Ezra Lowe, a chemistry major, used clustering and branching as a way of generating and organizing his ideas and focusing his topic. His assignment asked him to discuss the ethics demonstrated in the Gospel of Luke, a question he considered too broad. As he drew the branches, he became increasingly aware of his interest in the issue of leadership (explored in the clusters in the top half of the page). Having thus narrowed the topic, he began asking himself prewriting questions on the subject of moral leadership in order to generate a thesis. He color-coded the nodes in this diagram to designate categories like "thesis" and "counterarguments." Of all prewriting methods, clustering makes the least sense to anyone other than the author; however, those who prefer clustering find it invaluable for narrowing the topic and generating a thesis. Some writers will look at Lowe's clusters and branches and immediately see the pattern—those writers should try this method themselves.

SAMPLE OF STUDENT PREWRITING
Defining and developing the topic

how to say it. Even experienced writers find that their writing is often clearer and more focused if they state a thesis at the beginning. Some students argue that their high school teachers told them to place the thesis at the end of the paper so as not to "give it away." Such a strategy often produces convoluted prose as the students struggle not to reveal too much. In disciplines and assignments where it is appropriate, requiring thesis statements in the introduction can disabuse students of this notion of the academic essay as mystery novel.

Although they may know the difference between a thesis and a topic and be able to identify the key words that act as markers of each, many students don't formulate a thesis until after they have written a draft of the paper. In effect, drafting itself serves as a method of prewriting. In such cases the thesis statement may appear in the conclusion, and the instructor may suggest that the student move the thesis to the introduction in the next draft and rewrite the conclusion to expand on the ideas in the paper or summarize main points. Sometimes with very little alteration the whole conclusion can become the introduction. The student then needs to reorganize the draft to make sure that it supports the thesis. (See pages 66–67.) That many writers do not discover their thesis until they have written a draft of the paper further demonstrates that prewriting, drafting, and revising are not linear, mutually exclusive stages; they may very well take place simultaneously or recursively.

SAMPLE THESIS STATEMENTS

"Thesis" that is really a topic: "This paper will explore the social value of code-switching."

Inadequate thesis (because it is merely a statement of fact): "Code-switching is necessary for advancement in mainstream society."

Effective thesis: "While code-switching is necessary for advancement in mainstream society, it requires its practitioners to surrender ethnic identity."

Once students understand that a thesis is not a topic or merely a statement of fact, they can begin to generate sample theses. Real examples of theses can be very useful, and some instructors devote class time to having students revise them collaboratively.

Model thesis statements, though narrow and formulaic, can help students learn how to shape their ideas from topic to thesis. For instance, "This paper will discuss the similarities and differences between X and Y" can be reworded "Although X and Y have very different . . . , they share a similar . . . , and this leads us to conclude . . . ." The first ellipsis mark represents the main differences, the second represents the main similarities, and the third discusses the consequences of these similarities and differences.

This handout effectively summarizes the purpose, location, and function of a thesis in a literary analysis paper. The thesis formula gives students a model to compare with their own theses or to use directly. In addition, Professor Maurer's description of a thesis as "the conclusion of your analysis of the two poems" gives her students a way to think of the difference between a topic (the difference in tone between two sonnets) and the thesis (the causes of those differences).

The general discussion of thesis production and revision reassures students that modifications are a natural—indeed crucial—part of the writing process.

SAMPLE HANDOUT (EXCERPT)
Generating theses
Survey of British Literature: Margaret Maurer

3. Formulate a thesis statement for your essay that will introduce your discussion of the poems. Your statement should come at the end of your introduction, normally at the end of the first one or two paragraphs in an essay of this length [7 pages]. The thesis statement will have this general form:

Both sonnet A and sonnet B are about such-and-such; but whereas the tone of sonnet A is such-and-such, the tone of sonnet B is such-and-such. Formal effects of the two sonnets contribute to this difference in tone.

Note that your thesis, which comes very early in your essay, is actually, in some sense, the conclusion of your analysis of the two poems. In your thinking through, it will probably come out near the end of your preliminary analysis. Do not be surprised, though, if, once you have figured out what you think your thesis is and begun to write the paper that presents to the reader the analysis that led you to your thesis, you then find yourself changing your thesis slightly or even greatly as you work out your argument.

A note of caution: Though it is tempting to use examples of poor theses from students' papers, a student's embarrassment at having his or her work singled out as a negative example can be devastating. If the class discusses everyone's thesis in turn, this embarrassment is somewhat alleviated, although many instructors prefer to make up examples or use anonymous samples from other sections or semesters.

Thorough prewriting should make it easier to generate a specific thesis. A handout describing prewriting strategies might include a section on thesis writing.

Another note of caution: Though handouts can be valuable supplements to writing assignments, many students are overwhelmed by pages and pages describing the writing process or strategies for addressing an assignment. Like good assignments, good handouts should be as succinct as possible. Also, instructors can help students get a handle on material by setting aside class time to discuss assignments and handouts.

SAMPLE HANDOUT (EXCERPT B)
Selecting the thesis
Prewriting and Essay Design: Rebecca Moore Howard

STEP 3. *Write your thesis out in one sentence.* THE THESIS IS NOT SIMPLY AN ANSWER TO THE QUESTION YOUR PROFESSOR POSED; rather, you should think of it as your statement of the results of your prewriting. Going through the prewriting tasks and writing out your answers has kept you focused on your professor's question. Now you are going to report the intellectual results of that exploration. Your prewriting analysis was done in direct response to the question posed; now your essay is done in direct response to the prewriting analysis. In order to write the essay, you are going to have to reflect on the significance of this work you have done. Now state the significance in writing, in one sentence. If you can think of more than one statement that you might make, write each of them down. These are exploratory theses. Select one that you want to write about; or you may find yourself forming a new statement that represents a combination of exploratory theses or goes a step beyond them. Choose or create your thesis statement according to both of the following criteria:

What would you enjoy writing about?

What can you write about that will allow you to use your answers to the prewriting tasks?

This is the thesis statement for your paper. It should be a statement, not a question, and it should declare the main point that you are going to make in the paper, the conclusion that you are going to reach, the explanation of what you saw as you did the work required by the assignment. Your other exploratory theses might now become part of this paper, or you might realize that they are irrelevant to it. (Remember throughout this process that when you write a good essay, you will always find yourself discarding hard-earned, valuable material and ideas because they are just not relevant to the explanation of your thesis, regardless of how generally intelligent they may be.)

In this continuation of the prewriting handout begun on page 50, Professor Howard walks her students through one method of idea generation. Once they have asked and answered a series of prewriting questions, they are ready to focus their topic and generate a preliminary thesis.

The two questions that she asks them to pose are particularly important because students may not realize that topics that they find boring will probably produce boring papers. They may also be frustrated when they produce large quantities of prewriting but do not use much of it (despite the warning that this often happens in successful writing processes).

Generating evidence and counterevidence

"Evidence" is too readily mistaken for "proof." And in endeavoring to produce "proof," students too readily gloss over counterevidence. Their essays begin to sound not like academic explorations of a problem but like a sales pitch for shampoo: all doubts removed, all arguments air-tight. It is always well to spend some class time exploring the tension between wanting to prove one's thesis and knowing that in many disciplines hardly anything is ever proven. Students may nevertheless believe that proof is an essential feature of academic writing, that they must *pretend* to prove their thesis even if they aren't too sure about it. Instructors can explain that the thesis is a statement of *belief* and evidence is the *reasons for* (rather than proof of) that belief. This explanation can go a long way toward helping students write authentic—and more sophisticated—prose.

Such an explanation can encourage students to include counterevidence in their essays—doubts that they may have about the thesis, problems they have not yet resolved, or alternative explanations or interpretations of the topic that they are examining. Inexperienced writers are often afraid that counterevidence will make them look as if they can't make up their minds or don't know the right answer. But when they understand the thesis as a statement of belief and evidence as reasons for that belief, they will feel freer to use counterevidence. It's a good idea to suggest placing counterevidence after the introduction or in the middle of their papers instead of in the conclusion, where it will linger in readers' minds.

Once students have generated an exploratory thesis, it is often helpful for them to make a list of the reasons they have for believing it and another list of doubts or alternative ideas. This latter counterevidence can be organized into a working outline and can help writers evaluate whether they have enough material for the paper.

Planning or outlining

Before the first draft is due, some instructors ask for an outline of the whole paper. Generally this requires that students write the thesis at the top of the page and then list the main point of each paragraph or group of paragraphs. Some instructors require students to use a formal outline, like the following sample outline, while others prefer an informal outline, in which students list key sentences and phrases.

Outlining encourages students to imagine the paper as a whole and helps them evaluate how effectively they are supporting their thesis and organizing ideas. Students who tend to underdevelop their ideas often benefit from composing a formal outline, because the requirement that formal outlines have at least two points under each heading forces students to include more detail. Most handbooks offer a sample outline, like the following. Instructors can urge their students to examine such samples even if they do not require formal outlines.

Many instructors of large classes find that, though it's not possible for them to read a draft from every student, they can review outlines to provide feedback before the final draft is due.

Outlines have the further advantage of countering the notion that papers must consist of five paragraphs: an introduction that states

SAMPLE OUTLINE

From *The Bedford Handbook for Writers*, 4th ed: Diana Hacker (Bedford), 516–17.

Thesis: The great apes resemble humans in language abilities more than researchers once believed, and evidence is mounting that pygmy chimpanzees can understand and perhaps even create sentences.

I. Early ape language studies showed that apes could acquire significant language skills, but researchers failed to prove that apes could create sentences.
   A. Apes acquired impressive vocabularies in sign language and in artificial languages.
   B. Despite charges that they were responding to cues, apes were using language spontaneously.
      1. They performed well in experiments that eliminated the possibility of cuing.
      2. They learned signs and symbols from each other and initiated conversations on their own.
   C. Apes were using language creatively.
      1. They invented creative names.
      2. They may even have lied and joked.
   D. There was once little evidence that apes could order symbols grammatically to form sentences.
      1. The apes' sequences of signs were often confusing and repetitious.
      2. Evidence of meaningful sequences was inconclusive.
II. Recent research with Kanzi demonstrates that pygmy chimpanzees can understand and perhaps even create grammatical patterns.
   A. Kanzi can understand grammatically complex spoken English.
   B. Kanzi has picked up simple grammatical patterns from his caretakers.
   C. Kanzi appears to have developed his own patterns.
III. Evidence suggests that linguistic abilities in humans and apes are part of a continuum.
   A. The skeptics tend to apply a double standard: one for very young human children, another for apes.
   B. In our human ancestors, the ability to communicate in language must have preceded language itself.

Roman numerals indicate broad areas for discussion, and the capital letters and arabic numbers indicate evidence. (Some outlines provide even greater levels of detail.)

The sample thesis included here is a reportorial thesis, and would be appropriate for a paper reporting the findings of scientists studying the language abilities of pygmy chimpanzees. To revise this thesis so that it is more argumentative, (see samples on pages 51 and 53), a student might rewrite it as follows: "The great apes resemble humans in language abilities more than researchers once believed, and the mounting evidence that pygmy chimpanzees can understand and perhaps even create sentences is persuasive." Of course, to accommodate this evision, the outline would have to be modified.

the thesis, three supporting paragraphs, and a conclusion that restates the thesis. The five-paragraph structure may be useful for introducing secondary school students to essay development, but many college students cling to the idea that it describes *all* accomplished academic writing. The job of overcoming this notion may fall to instructors of writing in the disciplines, who may need to repeat the mantra "*thesis + three examples + restatement of thesis does not suffice for developing sophisticated ideas.*" Instructors may also want to assign formal outlines to help students see that the demands of the topic and thesis—not an arbitrary form—should determine the structure of a paper. The class may benefit from going over sample essays (reproduced with permission of former or current students) to examine alternative ways of developing ideas. And certainly students benefit from one-to-one work with the instructor (see pages 35–36) or a tutor (see pages 37–39).

Yet another word of caution: Outlining works best as an organizational technique for material that has already been discovered rather than as a means of generating ideas. Though outlining can help the writer develop and explore ideas, other systems are generally more useful in the earliest stages of the writing process.

As Students Begin the Paper—Teaching Drafting

The process of drafting is very individual, and many students are reluctant to change the method of writing they have always used. Some writers seem unable to compose at the computer, while others find pen and paper too slow and messy. Some like to write in class; others do not. Some write recursively, continually rereading and revising what they have already written as they proceed, while others simply "get down a draft"—rushing to put all of their ideas on paper while the creative juices are flowing. Because of these individual preferences, instructors tend to emphasize prewriting and revision, seeing drafting as part of those stages rather than an entity to be taught separately. Still, instructors may want to consider some aspects of drafting, even if they are not included in the writing pedagogy.

Drafting on a personal computer

Students who have access to personal computers (PCs) should be encouraged to use them—and take the time to learn how to use both Macintosh and IBM/IBM compatibles if the university computer center provides both. Many students find that they can generate more prose more rapidly at the computer, even if their typing skills are limited. Science and math students in particular may feel more confident in front of a computer keyboard than with a pen in their hands. The insert, delete, move, cut, and paste functions of PCs make it easier for students to revise papers. Indeed, students who use PCs spend approximately twice as much time revising as those who use typewriters or typing services. Further, drafts printed out from computers, as opposed to hand-corrected typing, may make it easier for students to spot errors and structural problems—perhaps because we expect printed text to be correct and thus notice when it is not. Instructors often prefer printouts because they do not have to interpret handwriting in addition to following the student's ideas.

Word processing programs also provide on-line services such as spell checking (which should be used by all students) and grammar checking (which is often time-consuming but can prove enlightening and may be more enthusiastically received than traditional grammar instruction isolated from the real-life context of a paper in process). Many also include outlining functions. Some handbook publishers offer on-line handbooks, too, which students can consult while they compose or revise on PCs. Like traditional handbooks, though, on-line handbooks need to be introduced to the students and preferably integrated directly into the course. (See page 27.) By referring to specific computer functions in class, instructors can help students use PCs more efficiently and effectively.

SAMPLE INSTRUCTIONS (EXCERPT)
Drafting on a computer
Cultural Diversity: An Introduction to Cultural Anthropology and Linguistics: Leedom Lefferts

Footnotes: When you use the prescribed notation system described below, most footnote/endnotes are unnecessary. Citations and references are NOT given in the following system. Other information frequently included in notes, such as explanatory data, sidelight information, etc., should be incorporated into the text. If you absolutely need notes, these are numbered sequentially throughout the text and placed on a separate page, titled Endnotes, at the end of the paper, before the References Cited. (WordPerfect users: Endnote placement: Control-F7, 3, then "Generate": ALT-F5, 6, 5.)

When introducing students to a writing technique or textual convention, it is helpful to include instructions for performing that task on a PC. Many students use their PCs only as sophisticated typewriters, so encouraging them to explore computer functions introduces them to new possibilities and gives them more confidence in using computers.

A vast body of literature on computers and writing discusses everything from the relative merits of DOS and Macintosh and teaching in computer laboratories to using computer networks, Hypertext, and interactive media in the classroom. Instructors contemplating computer applications should consult the bibliography at the end of this chapter and discuss their plans well in advance with the computer technician(s) on campus.

A final note about drafting on PCs: "The computer lost my paper" is now a more common excuse for late papers than "My dog ate my paper"—and often it is true. Stressing that students must back up their work on separate disks that they own (rather than disks that they share with others) and that computer error will not be accepted as a reason for late papers reduces the frequency of computer problems. Raising this issue at the beginning of the semester saves considerable frustration later.

Reducing anxiety

Because the writing process is individual, it is highly unlikely that students will work at the same pace or in the same way as those around them, yet these differences cause considerable anxiety. Students may well appear at their instructor's office asserting that they "can't write"—meaning that they would like to stop writing now, please. Often all they need is reassurance that their topic is sound and their thesis acceptable and that everyone has trouble getting started or keeping going. Sometimes students can't get started on the paper because they haven't finished (or started) prewriting. If they have no idea what they are going to say, they need to work more on generating ideas, starting to write only when they feel that they have something to say. This problem isn't the much-feared "writer's block" so much as it is the writer's equivalent of getting a muscle cramp from trying to run without first warming up the muscles (a metaphor most students readily understand).

Other students will announce that they have decided to change their topic, not because they were inspired to go in new directions but because they gave up the old direction in despair. Unless they agree that the original topic has little potential, most instructors try to steer such students back to it because of the amount of work already invested in it. Starting on a new topic, the student is likely to get behind. By asking the writer to explain the attraction of the original topic, the instructor can sometimes revive interest in the topic and help the student discover solutions to impasses. At such points, it can be helpful to remind students that the writing process is recursive and that writers are always generating (and reviving) ideas, researching background, writing, and revising; this should not be something to fear.

It is also helpful to assure students that many people—even professors—reach a point of despair during the writing process; the difference is that most experienced writers have come to accept despair as part of the process. This reassurance may not reduce students' frustration or anxiety, but it does let them know that they are "normal." In addition, by speaking to students as fellow writers, instructors encourage students to speak and think about themselves as writers rather than bumblers. As students learn to discuss writing frustrations and satisfactions with others, they feel more comfortable seeking help. (See pages 35–39.)

Responding to Drafts

Teaching writing is most effective when instructors not only tell students the desirable features of their completed manuscripts but also respond to works in progress and depict these processes as conversations between writers and readers. Readers usually notice surface features, such as spelling and punctuation, first, but writers—and thus writing instruction—must begin at the other end of the process, with the development of ideas.

R. Baird Shuman's research reveals that students can tolerate only a limited number of negative comments in the margins or body of a paper—approximately five—after which they either cease to read comments or become overwhelmed (Hairston) and are unable to learn from them (Harris). Indeed, L. V. Arnold has shown that there is no significant difference in writing improvement between students whose teachers marked every error and made extensive comments and those whose teachers made only a few comments and error corrections. Thus limited, more thorough comments may be most useful. Obviously, the types of comments and method of commenting will be determined by the needs of the students and the pedagogy of the instructor, and as with other areas of writing pedagogy, there is no "correct" method. Comprehensive marking of students' errors, though, is an inefficient use of time.

Instructors' written comments can assist students' revisions, but only if students read them. Some instructors return papers with comments but no grades as a means of forcing students to read the comments carefully. Others require students to write a summary of the comments, list common errors, or write a response to each comment. If the paper is to be rewritten, these responses are then handed in with the final paper, along with the earlier draft(s) and comments. If the paper is not being revised, error summaries and lists can be applied to later papers and handed in along with them.

Students also need to learn to see an instructor's comments as the response of a *reader* of the paper. Too easily they will see the instructor's comments as the voice of authority to which they must defer when revising, an attitude that stifles their own analysis and reimagining of the paper. The tone of the instructor's comments on drafts and papers is crucial. Most useful to student writers is an understanding of the effect of their prose on readers rather than a catalog of supposedly text-bound "strengths" and "weaknesses." Comments like "I didn't understand this" are more meaningful than the cryptic "Clarity needed"; and "Now I've lost sight of your thesis" is more helpful than "Relevance?" Responses from other students can also help students imagine their papers from the perspective of readers and help them learn to become better readers themselves. (See pages 184–189 for information about setting up peer groups.)

Instructors' comments on drafts can take the form of editing and other marks within the body of the text, comments and explanations in the margins, and comments on the paper as a whole made at the end. Some instructors adopt only one of these methods, while others adopt a combination, sometimes as determined by the specific needs of an individual. Students whose native language is not English, for example, may need more explanation of surface errors such as punctuation than native speakers who have not yet learned to proofread.

Writing comments at the end of the paper

Many instructors argue that the most effective form of response to drafts is the comment at the end of the paper because it helps students to see the paper as a whole. The instructor first reads the paper through without comment and then reads it again more slowly, noting issues of particular concern but still not writing comments. Finally the instructor writes a fairly extensive comment about the paper as a whole. Rather than looking for the thesis in the first paragraph and commenting on its efficacy in the margin, the instructor making holistic comments discusses the role of the thesis in the overall paper, perhaps explaining how effectively it drives the organization or how well the evidence supports it.

This comment, written in response to a paper on Ntozake Shange's novel *Sassafrass, Cypress, and Indigo* is probably much longer than most instructors imagine writing on a draft; however, it was the *only* comment, and as such took considerably less time than marking points of confusion, lack of evidence, and citation errors in the margins. The paper contained some very good ideas but lacked an organizing principle or clearly articulated thesis— promising only to discuss Mitch's and

SAMPLE INSTRUCTOR RESPONSE
Writing holistic comments
African American Women Writers: Sandra Jamieson

Carlos,

I enjoyed reading this draft; you make some really astute observations. I especially like your point about the more subtle influences of place on the inhabitants—I hadn't thought about it in that way before, but I think you are absolutely right. You support all of your assertions with effective textual references and quotations (although I expected to see a reference to the fact that Sassafrass had started to write a play about Alvin Ayler once; wouldn't that seem to support your argument that she would like to write?). Check the handbook for rules about quotations of more than four lines, though; there is a specific way to format and introduce such quotes.

As a reader, I found myself frustrated at several points. You make some great observations, but I was often unsure *why* you made those observations. You also organize them in a rather confusing manner— for example, you discuss Sassafrass's attitude to her environment, then you discuss Mitch's music and painting, and then you return to

Sassafrass's efforts to improve their home. I can see how you might think of these things in that order, but does that make it the most effective way to include them in your paper? My answer is "no." There's a reason for this lack of consistent organizational strategy, though; there is no clear thesis asserted in this paper! As I read it again it seemed to me that you were arguing that Mitch inhibits Sassafrass's creativity by failing to perceive art as broadly as she does. His concept of art is the narrow Western notion which values "art for art's sake," so Sassafrass's appliquéd banners, patchwork cushions, and macramé wall hangings don't count because they have a purpose above and beyond being beautiful. Because he denigrates them, Sassafrass too comes to see her art as "merely" craft and herself as a failed artist (practicing a "charade of homebodiness"). Is this pretty much your thesis? If it is, don't make your readers play a guessing game; state it up front in the introduction, and then organize your paragraphs to support it—beginning, perhaps, with a discussion of what S. considers to be art, then contrasting it with M.'s perception (and discussing his own artistic production perhaps), following this with a discussion of the psychological consequences of their conflicting interpretation, and then, finally, with a discussion of S.'s work as art. Your introduction might discuss the historical tension between definitions of "art" and "craft," perhaps even suggesting that an understanding of M. and S.'s disagreement will shed light on the problems with such narrow and fixed definitions.

Reread the paper and your prewriting notes and see if this strategy would work. If I got your thesis wrong, write out the correct thesis and try to organize your material to support it. Remember, your paper should help me more fully understand the novel and perhaps human beings in general. If you get stuck, come and talk to me!

Don't forget to spell-check and proofread your final draft. (Pay particular attention to sentence structure and transitions—once you have reorganized this it will be considerably easier to make effective transitions.)

Sandra Jamieson 11/11/90

Sassafrass's attitudes about art.

It also had fairly significant problems in sentence structure and transitions, but it is a waste of time to point these out when such a radical revision of organization is required. A paper that is straining for meaning frequently contains more surface-level errors than a more finished version, so attention should be paid to global revision first.

Writing comments in the margins

Some instructors responding to drafts write in the margins during a first reading, commenting at points where confusion occurs or where prose, argument, evidence, structure, or style is particularly pleasing. It is important that comments in the margins be as specific as possible. A check mark, for instance, does not explain *why* the prose next to it is effective, so it rarely provides practical help despite its value as encouragement. Also, the infamous "AWK" is open to many interpretations (see Rankin), and instructors are more helpful if they explain *why* an instance of awkward prose interrupts the reading.

In responding to papers as they read, instructors should keep in mind that students will probably be overwhelmed by too many comments. Thus, only substantiated interruptions should be noted in the margins. Other problems can be summarized at the end of the paper.

Some instructors prefer to write a series of numbers next to areas of text and then write or type their comments on a separate sheet keyed to those numbers. This method is also very effective for instructors receiving papers as electronic mail or through a computer network. Again, the key is not just to make marks and comments but also to explain them. (Some instructors annotate directly in students' electronic texts. See pages 65–66 for an example.)

Perhaps because they have observed what Shuman's, Hairston's, and Harris's findings corroborate, many instructors try to limit their comments to the most important points or the most repeated errors. Some require students to respond to each suggestion and observation with a check, question mark, or comment. This at least ensures that the students read and consider the comments at the time of

For some of his homework questions, Professor Valente asked his introductory mathematics students to explain the results of mathematical equations *in words* rather than in equations. Valente observes that because the calculations were often made by computer (using a program called Mathematica) a vast chunk of time was freed up for his students to begin to ask *Why?* rather than simply *What?*

By commenting on their actual writing and articulation as well as their calculations, he affirms the importance of writing and teaches writing skills his students can take with them to other courses.

SAMPLE INITIAL RESPONSE DURING READING (WRITE-TO-LEARN COURSE)

Critical and Qualitative Thinking: Kenneth G. Valente

1. Firstly, the graph $y = x^2$ will be C times greater or lesser than $y =$

    very nice

    x^2 but not equal to 0. For example, look at graphs A and AI.

    A is $y = x^3$ and AI is $y = 2x^3$; therefore, AI is 2 *times* greater than A. Also,

    if there is a negative or positive, the direction of the graph is

    drawn another way. *Can you be more precise here?*

revision. Also, responding to teachers' comments forces students back into an active relationship with their papers, encouraging them to take responsibility for revision instead of simply typing changes suggested by the instructor.

Making marks in the text

Students can generally explain and correct at least half of the mechanical errors in their papers if those errors are simply marked without further comment. Therefore, extensive explanations of errors in grammar, punctuation, usage, and mechanics are usually unnecessary. In fact, some instructors just mark the margins next to errors and return the paper to the student for correction. In *Writing with Power* Peter Elbow suggests underlining effective passages with a straight line and ineffective ones with a "wiggly" line. Some instructors use different-colored pens to achieve the same effect. Shuman suggests marking and explaining in detail the first three major errors and then drawing a line across the page to indicate that the rest of the paper was read simply for content.

Still other instructors read over papers with special attention to certain aspects of writing. These might be points that have been discussed recently in class—perhaps the use of active rather than passive verbs—or problems that occur repeatedly in a particular student's work. After marking strengths and weaknesses in particular areas, the instructor writes comments at the end of the paper that summarize those strengths and weaknesses and offers suggestions for improving the writing. In their final comments, instructors using this method, known as *trait analysis,* emphasize that they didn't mark all errors or places where the writing was effective.

However errors are indicated, the marked-up draft is revised and resubmitted, and the instructor explains the remaining errors, helping students learn to proofread and revise more effectively. Requiring students to hand in final drafts for grading ensures that they will try to revise and edit their work and allows instructors to assess how helpful their comments have been.

SAMPLE REMARKS
Commenting within the paper
Essay Organization and Development: Rebekah Lautersack (student) and Rebecca Moore Howard (instructor)

[**Rebekah, I have annotated the first 2 ¶s to give you some ideas for sentence-level revisions. The two that seem most compelling are pronoun-antecedent agreement (you really need to consult §22a of the handbook) and verb tense (you're switching back and forth between present and past). §13b of the handbook tells you**

The first two paragraphs are remarks made by Professor Howard. The next two paragraphs are the beginning of Rebekah Lautersack's draft, with in-text comments by the instructor in bold.

Because Professor Howard's composition

students use a computer network, they submit their work in electronic rather than hard-copy form. This system enables the instructor to make annotations directly within students' texts, as Professor Howard did for this student's work-in-progress. Because the paper excerpted here was a late-stage draft, the instructor concentrated on sentence-level concerns. She marked only the first two paragraphs, identifying recurrent errors that the student could then check in the remainder of the paper. Identifying a particularly compelling idea, though, Professor Howard did encourage the student to develop it.

Instructors using a network of Macintosh computers generally insert their comments in a darker, heavier font. Macintosh or IBM compatible networks can also install one of several software packages designed to allow internal response by instructors or other students.

to be consistent and gives you some pointers about recognizing verb tense shifts. But if you're stumped about which tense you should be in, follow the general guideline that when writing about literary works and their creators (everything assigned in English— as well as a lot of philosophy and foreign languages), it is customary to use the present tense, since the work of art is "alive," even though its creator isn't. When writing in *your* major, however, it is customary to use the past tense for things that happened in the past.

Since you're at the end of your writing process, things like pronoun agreement and consistent verb tense are your primary concerns. But I have noted one place in the text that I think might benefit from development, since it seems to contain germs of important ideas.]

In the books *The Souls of Black Folk* by W. E. B. DU Bois and *The Education of Henry Adams* by Henry Adams, both twentieth century thinkers communicate their personal struggles with forces characteristic of their times. Adams grapples primarily with the short comings **[Make this one word, shortcomings.]** of formal education and its relevancy to the slew **[Where I come from, *slew* is very informal. You might want to try something like *myriad* or just plain *many*.]** of changes which erupt at the turn of the twentieth century while DU Bois **[Make sure you spell (and capitalize) your authors' names very precisely throughout the paper.]** is faced with the severity and persistency of America's color line. Each thinker is also faced with the notion of personal failure despite their **[You have a problem of pronoun-antecedent agreement here. See §22a of the handbook.]** accumulated insights and revolutionary spirit, yet they both remain optimistic that through a spirit of probing, consciousness-expanding education, the problems they each faced **[Careful—keep your verb tenses consistent.]** can be remedied. Because each thinker perceives this transition into the twentieth century with such poignancy and prescience, their **[Pronoun-antecedent agreement again . . .]** perspectives, struggles, and solutions have become immortalized.

Henry Adams, the apparent product of State Street, Capitalism, and the scion of the powerful Adams' **[Nope. No apostrophe here, because it's not a possessive.]** family, in actuality "in a half-hearted way, struggled all his life against State Street, Banks, Capitalism altogether." (Adams, 335) His ideals were noble, high and virtually unobtainable; thus, it is not a surprise that in his own eyes, Adams views himself primarily as a failure. **[The preceding two sentences are dynamite. You should consider developing the ideas in them, because they're really interesting.]** The stringency of his aims and his quest for education propel him into a series of experiences which work to stress the chaotic nature of life in general. Rather than becoming a unifying factor in Adams's life, his education only compounded his instinctual feeling that chaos is the dominant reality in life.

After Students Compose the First Draft— Teaching Rewriting

Outlining after the first draft

Students may find that outlining is useful not only before writing but also *after* the first draft. At this stage of the writing process, outlining helps them see how well they have developed and explained their arguments and ideas. Students are particularly delighted to discover that outlining after a first draft can help them figure out where to flesh out (or cut) the essay to meet a minimum (or maximum) page requirement. (Outlining after a draft is a fine alternative to resetting margins and fonts, cramming in more quotations, or transforming concise sentences into long, windy ones; it suggests ways to expand papers *conceptually*, rather than *cosmetically*.)

As with pre-draft outlines, post-draft outlines can be formal or informal. Although making a formal outline for longer research papers (see pages 56–58) can sometimes seem cumbersome, fitting the material from a first draft into outline form helps students to study the skeleton of their papers and thus recognize structural and organizational problems often difficult to discern by reading the paper itself. By reviewing such a skeleton, students can tell at a glance when they have provided sufficient detail and support and when such information is lacking, and they can assess whether they have arranged their argument and evidence effectively. In short, successful post-draft outlines help students find and improve the weakest areas of their papers.

Instructors whose class size prevents them from reading a draft from every student can review a post-draft outline and provide feedback before the final draft. Also, formal outlines help instructors, teaching assistants, and tutors determine where to focus their attention as they discuss papers with students.

Reconsidering audience and purpose

Though a first draft is sometimes composed primarily for the writer, the second should address the writer's audience. Revising for a specific audience often requires global revisions in which the student, after imagining the whole paper from the perspective of readers, makes major changes in content and focus so that the paper more effectively addresses the concerns and expectations of readers. Instructors can help by reminding students of the intended audience if it was mentioned in the original assignment or by writing out a brief description of the intended audience, including what that audience might already know and expect from a paper. (See pages 47–48.)

Revising for purpose requires students to imagine the desired effect of the whole paper; then they must consider how well each part serves the purpose. Many students find outlines a valuable aid in considering how well they stick to their purpose. For each section or paragraph they should ask questions such as "How well does this explain the overall argument of the paper?" "How well does this support my thesis?" "Will this help convince my readers that my interpretation is logical?" "Would the experiment be replicable on the basis of this discussion?" and so on. They can then make revisions on the basis of their answers. Peer reviewers can use the same strategy. (See Chapter 9.)

Attending to tone and disciplinary conventions

Students should regard a paper's tone as an issue for the final revision of the paper. (Tone conveys an attitude toward a subject and may be distanced or personal, depending on the purpose and audience of a paper.) Disciplinary conventions of writing—for example, a discipline's preference for the active or passive voice or its practices for documenting sources—should also be latter-stage concerns of revision. Though students may be aware of and working on these issues throughout the writing process, an excessive concern with them before the final revision can focus too much attention on sentence-level rather than global issues, which can lead to inadequately developed ideas and even writer's block.

At the revision stage, students might find it useful to look at the paper as a whole to help them gauge whether its tone and structure are appropriate for its purpose and discipline. They might read it as if it were a lecture to be given in a class in that discipline, considering revisions wherever tone seems inappropriate or content inadequate for the audience. Revisions for tone and disciplinary conventions, however, will generally be at the sentence level, most often occurring in specific places such as the conclusion, the discussion of findings, or the integration of quotations. In *disciplinary courses,* instructors might devote class time before the paper is due to peer revision groups or whole-class discussion of tone and conventions. (See pages 184–189 for suggestions on how to organize peer revision groups and pages 166–168 for suggestions on how to engage the entire class in discussion.) To focus such sessions, some instructors hand out anonymous samples of student papers from other sections or semesters (with the permission of those students) and discuss their tone and the ways in which the writers apply disciplinary conventions. Others assign a journal article that demonstrates a desired style and tone and then discuss its rhetorical features in class. This can be very enlightening for students who are unused to thinking of professional writing as *writing* rather than simply as a transparent source of information. Realizing that all writing is the product of choices and strategies can help students revise their own. Revision in this context comes to be seen as a natural and inevitable part of the writing process rather than as punishment for "bad" writers.

Revising on a personal computer

Personal computers have radically changed the way many students work, helping them produce effective revisions with much less effort. Because students working on computers can easily rearrange words and paragraphs and insert and delete text, it's much easier for them to reorganize and refocus papers and make sentence-level revisions. Instructors have also benefited from students' use of personal computers. For one thing, they can feel free to require multiple drafts when they know students don't have to retype papers at each stage of revision. Also, clean printouts are much easier to read than papers that have been handwritten or hand-corrected. Of course, computers do not change students' tendency to procrastinate, but instructors can help students meet final deadlines by requiring advance drafts, by assigning peer response groups (see Chapter 9), or by sending students to the writing center.

Instructors can help students revise on the computer by taking some time to tell them how to use basic computer functions or having a member of the computer lab staff do so. Spell checkers and grammar checkers are useful tools to be aware of, but students should still be encouraged to refer to their handbooks when revising their papers on the computer. Grammar checkers, in particular, recognize only symptoms typical of certain errors, and they can make mistakes. Therefore, writers should not make changes suggested by a grammar checker without referring to specific rules first.

Revising through interactions with readers

Students revise most effectively when they see an instructor's comments as reactions from a *reader*, not as orders from an authority figure. If students see the instructor merely as an authority, they may be stifled in reimagining and revising their papers. (See pages 60–61 for advice on responding to papers.) Students may start moving away from instructor-bound revisions if they are given the opportunity to take part in peer groups, or "writers' workshops," in which they will hear a variety of readers' suggestions for revision. Such groups help students understand that there may be several valid suggestions or opinions about any given paper, and the writer's role in revision is to decide which suggestions are best suited to his or her goals and purposes. In addition, by contributing suggestions to peers, students get further insights about revision—insights they can apply to their own writing.

When taking part in peer groups, students need to be trained as readers and guided through the process of peer response. (See Chapter 9.)

Handling Multiple Drafts

Although most students cite time limitations as their reason for not redrafting, the real reason is often procrastination produced by a fear of revising. That fear, in turn, is born of a lack of revision skills and confidence. The prospect of revising papers produces anxiety in students for a number of reasons. Perhaps the most common can be called "fear of commitment." If students expend considerable effort on a paper and still receive a poor grade, they perceive that they lack writing ability—just as they feared. If, on the other hand, they receive a poor grade for a paper that they know was not their best work—a paper they never committed to—they do not risk finding out exactly what they can or cannot do. What many students do not know is that failed papers often result from lack of *revision* skills rather than lack of *writing* skills per se. As they practice revision strategies, students will find themselves more successful at reworking their papers and thus be more willing to revise in the future.

A good way for students to learn revision is to rework multiple drafts of one paper, rather than trying to transfer an instructor's comments and insights on one paper to the writing in another. By thoroughly revising one paper students learn general principles through applying them in a specific context. If students are given the option to revise papers as many times as they like, though, some will hand in a draft every week. For many instructors, it will be practical to read only one preliminary draft of each paper. Jeffrey Sommers suggests giving deadlines for revision, observing that such a practice mirrors that of academic writers who "may revise and revise, but ultimately . . . must conclude" because of the demands of real deadlines (239).

Checklist for teaching the writing process

GENERAL TIPS ON TEACHING THE WRITING PROCESS

_____ Consider assigning a handbook, writer's guide, or discipline-specific guide.

_____ Consider using supplemental handouts.

_____ When giving the first writing assignment, summarize components of the writing process and refer students to supplemental resources (e.g., handbook sections, handouts, office hours, tutoring services).

_____ Allow class time to discuss the relationship between prewriting, drafting, and revising.

_____ Allow class time to discuss discipline-specific conventions.

_____ Consider grading various components of the writing process (such as notes, drafts, and outlines) in addition to, or as part of, grading the finished product.

_____ Make sure that students have sufficient time for all stages of working on a paper (two weeks for all papers, three or more for papers involving extensive research).

EXPLAINING THE WRITING PROCESS TO STUDENTS

_____ Emphasize that there is no "correct" writing process.

_____ Emphasize that students need to experiment and determine for themselves which writing strategies work best for them.

_____ Explain that different types of writing may call for different strategies.

_____ Stress the importance of allowing sufficient time for revision (no fewer than three days before the final draft is due).

WRITING RESPONSES TO DRAFTS

_____ Read the entire paper before writing any comments.

_____ Determine the most important areas to comment on and try not to go beyond them.

_____ Keep marginal comments within manageable proportions (three per page).

_____ Make comments as specific as possible. (Avoid simply writing "AWK.")

_____ Tell writers what they're doing well along with what they could improve.

_____ In a final comment, summarize your reactions as a reader, then provide an overall analysis of the paper's effectiveness.

For Further Reading

Prewriting

Beaugrande, Robert. "The Processes of Invention: Association and Recombination." *College Composition and Communication* 30 (1979): 260-67.

Beck, James P. "Predrafting: On Having Students Write before We Teach Them How." *Journal of Teaching Writing* 5 (1986): 71-76.

Caernarvon-Smith, Patricia. *Audience Analysis and Response.* Pembroke, MA: Firman Technical Publications, 1983.

Faigley, Lester, et al. *Assessing Writers' Knowledge and Processes of Composing.* Norwood, NJ: Ablex, 1985.

Flower, Linda S. *Problem-Solving Strategies for Writing.* 4th ed. New York: Harcourt, 1993. Flower argues that to transform writer-based prose into reader-based prose, students need to integrate rhetorical concerns into the early stages of the composing process.

Hayes, J., et al. "Writing Research and the Writer." *American Psychologist* 41 (1986): 1106–13. The authors contend that process-oriented instruction gives students substantial guidance for generating text.

Johannessen, Larry R., Elizabeth A. Kahn, and Carolyn Calhoun Walter. *Designing and Sequencing Prewriting Activities.* Urbana: NCTE, 1982.

Kiniry, Malcolm, and Ellen Strenski. "Sequencing Expository Writing: A Recursive Approach." *College Composition and Communication* 36 (1985): 191-202.

Murray, Donald. "Write before Writing." *College Composition and Communication* 29 (1978): 375–81.

Nelson, Jennie. "This Was an Easy Assignment: Examining How Students Interpret Academic Writing Tasks." *Research in the Teaching of English* 24 (1990): 362–96.

Schwartz, Mimi. *Writer's Craft, Teacher's Art: Teaching What We Know.* Portsmouth, NH: Boynton/Cook, 1990.

Smagorinsky, Peter. "The Writer's Knowledge and the Writing Process: A Protocol Analysis." *Research in the Teaching of English* 25 (1991): 339–64.

Smith, E. *Conducting a Follow-up Study of Students in Writing Courses.* ERIC 1984. ED 247 596. The author found that students continued to use freewriting, brainstorming, and outlining as invention techniques two years after taking a writing course.

Stewart, Donald. *The Authentic Voice: A Pre-Writing Approach to Student Writing.* Dubuque: Brown, 1972.

Witte, Stephen P. "Pre-Text and Composing." *College Composition and Communication* 38 (1987): 397–425.

Writer's block

Clark, Beverly Lyon. "On Blocking and Unblocking Sonja: A Case Study in Two Voices." *College Composition and Communication* 43 (1992): 55–74.

Daly, John A., Anita Vangelisti, and Stephen P. Witte. "Writing Apprehension in the Classroom Context." *The Social Construction of Written Communication.* Ed. Bennett A. Rafoth and Donald L. Rubin. Norwood, NJ: Ablex, 1988. 147–71.

Leader, Zachary. *Writer's Block.* Baltimore: Johns Hopkins UP, 1991.

Rose, Mike. "Rigid Rules, Inflexible Plans, and the Stifling of Language: A Cognitivist Analysis of Writer's Block." *College Composition and Communication* 31 (1980): 389–401.

———. *When a Writer Can't Write: Studies in Writer's Block and Other Composing-Process Problems.* New York: Guilford, 1985.

————. *Writer's Block: The Cognitive Dimension.* Carbondale: Southern Illinois UP, 1984.

Responding to drafts

Anson, Chris M., ed. *Writing and Response: Theory, Practice, and Research.* Urbana: NCTE, 1989. This book provides essays on many aspects of responding to writing and offers thorough reviews of the literature on the subject.

Arnold, L. V. "Writer's Cramp and Eyestrain: Are They Paying Off?" *English Journal* 53 (1964): 10–15. The author points to studies that reveal no significant difference in writing improvement between students whose teachers mark every error and make extensive comments and those whose teachers make only a few comments and error corrections.

Butler, J. F. "Remedial Writers: The Teacher's Job as Corrector of Papers." *College Composition and Communication* 31 (1980): 270–77. According to Butler, instructors who limit their comments and corrections to grammar encourage students simply to "fix" grammar but not to work on any other aspect of papers during revision.

Connors, Robert J., and Andrea A. Lunsford. "Teachers' Rhetorical Comments on Student Papers." *College Composition and Communication* 44 (1993): 200–23. Referring to statistics on the types and purposes of comments on student writing, the authors argue for concrete responses and a more personal voice in comments.

Cooper, Charles, and Lee Odell, eds. *Evaluating Writing: Describing, Measuring, Judging.* Urbana: NCTE, 1977.

Edwards, Renee. "Sensitivity to Feedback and the Development of Self." *Communication Quarterly* 38 (1990): 101–11.

Elbow, Peter. *Writing with Power: Techniques for Mastering the Writing Process.* New York: Oxford UP, 1981. Elbow suggests replacing marginal comments with underlining in the text: a straight line under passages that work and a "wiggly" line under passages that do not work.

————. "Ranking, Evaluating, and Liking: Sorting Out Three Forms of Judgment." *College English* 55 (1993): 187–206. Elbow contends that evaluating papers without giving grades is at times beneficial for students, as it teaches them to like their writing (which, in turn, allows them to evaluate it more effectively).

Hairston, Maxine. "On Not Being a Composition Slave." *Training the New Teacher of College Composition.* Ed. Charles W. Bridges. Urbana: NCTE, 1986. 117–24. Hairston summarizes the scholarship on why students do not learn from extensive marginal comments and suggests nine ways to provide students with "quality feedback rather than overwhelming them with more advice than they can absorb and more criticism than they can tolerate."

Harris, Muriel. "Evaluation: The Process for Revision." *Journal of Basic Writing* 1:4 (1978): 82–90. The author contends that above a certain "minimal level," students learn from marginal comments "in inverse proportion to the amount of instructor notation on the page."

MacAllister, Joyce. "Responding to Student Writing." *Teaching Writing in All Disciplines.* Ed. C. Williams Griffin. San Francisco: Jossey-Bass, 1982. 59–66. MacAllister contends that instructors do not need to write many marginal comments or use correct grammatical terminology to respond effectively to student papers. Instead, she argues for holistic grading, clearly established evaluative criteria, and peer response at the drafting stage.

Mallonee, Barbara, and John R. Breihan. "Responding to Students' Drafts: Interdisciplinary Consensus." *College Composition and Communication* 36 (1985): 213-31.

Miller, Hildy. "Kaleidoscope of Values: Composition Instructors, Noncomposition Faculty, and Students Respond to Academic Writing." *Journal of Teaching Writing* 9 (1990): 31–43.

Rankin, Libby. "An Anatomy of Awkwardness." *Journal of Teaching Writing* 9 (1990): 45–57. Rankin discusses the many uses, interpretations, and perceptions of the marginal notation "AWK."

Schwartz, Mimi. "Response to Writing: A College-Wide Perspective." *College English* 46 (1984): 55–62.

Schwegler, Robert. "The Politics of Reading Student Papers." *The Politics of Writing Instruction: Postsecondary.* Ed. Richard Bullock and John Trimbur. Portsmouth, NH: Boynton/Cook, 1991. 203–26. According to Schwegler, teachers tend to suppress value-laden responses to student writing, replacing them with "formalist and implicitly authoritarian" comments.

Sommers, Nancy. "Responding to Student Writing." *College Composition and Communication* 33 (1982): 148–56. Sommers's study of the written responses to student papers concludes that many teacher comments fail to help students engage the issues or purposes of their writing.

White, Edward M. *Assigning, Responding, Evaluating: A Writing Teacher's Guide.* New York: St. Martin's, 1991. This guide contains a chapter on responding to student writing.

Willingham, Daniel B. "Effective Feedback on Written Assignments." *Teaching Psychology* 17 (Feb. 1990): 10–12.

Zak, Frances. "Exclusively Positive Responses to Student Writing." *Journal of Basic Writing* 9 (1990): 40–53. Zak contends that students may benefit more from "exclusively positive comments."

Revising

Beach, Richard, et al. "Factors Influencing Self-Assessing and Revising by College Freshmen." *New Directions in Composition Research.* Ed. Richard Beach and Lillian S. Bridwell. New York: Guilford, 1984. 149–70.

Flower, Linda, et al. "Detection, Diagnosis, and the Strategies of Revision." *College Composition and Communication* 37 (1986): 16–55.

Harris, Muriel. "Composing Behaviors of One- and Multi-Draft Writers." *College English* 51 (1989): 174–91.

Herrington, Anne J., and Deborah Cadman. "Peer Review and Revising in an Anthropology Course: Lessons for Learning." *College Composition and Communication* 42 (1991): 184–99.

Hillocks, George. "The Interaction of Instruction, Teacher Comment, and Revision in Teaching the Composing Process." *Research in the Teaching of English* 16 (1982): 261–78.

Kearns, Michael. "Topical Knowledge and Revising." *Journal of Teaching Writing* 9 (Fall/Winter 1990): 195–208.

Lovejoy, Kim B. "The Gricean Model: A Revising Rhetoric." *Journal of Teaching Writing* 6 (1987): 9–18.

Murray, Donald. "Internal Revision: A Process of Discovery." *Research on Composing: Points of Departure.* Ed. Charles R. Cooper et al. Urbana: NCTE, 1978. 85–103.

Wallace, David L., and John R. Hayes. "Redefining Revision for Freshmen." *Research in the Teaching of English* 25 (1991): 54–66.

Personal computers

Bacig, Thomas D., Robert A. Evans, and Donald W. Larmouth. "Computer-Assisted Instruction in Critical Thinking and Writing: A Process/Model Approach." *Research in the Teaching of English* 25 (1991): 364–83.

Boiarsky, Carolyn. "Fluency, Fluidity, and Word Processing." *Journal of Advanced Composition* 11 (1991): 123–34.

Burns, Hugh. "Computers and Composition." *Teaching Composition: 12 Bibliographical Essays.* Ed. Gary Tate. Fort Worth: Texas Christian U, 1987. 378–400. Some of the literature reviewed in this essay is a little dated, but Burns includes a wealth of valuable introductory and advanced information.

Curtis, Marcia S. "Windows on Composing: Teaching Revision on Word Processors." *College Composition and Communication* 39 (1988): 337–43.

Elder, John, Betsey Bowen, Jeffrey Schwartz, and Dixie Goswami. *Word Processing in a Community of Writers.* New York: Garland, 1989.

Fulwiler, Toby. "Programs for Change: Computers and Writing Across the Curriculum." *Composition Chronicle* 2 (Dec. 1989): 8–10.

Gebhardt, Richard C. "Computer Writing and the Dynamics of Drafting." *Journal of Teaching Writing* 5 (1986): 193–202.

Gillis, Philip D. "Using Computer Technology to Teach and Evaluate Prewriting." *Computers and the Humanities* 21 (1987): 3–19.

Handa, Carolyn, ed. *Computers and Community: Teaching Composition in the Twenty-First Century.* Portsmouth, NH: Boynton/Cook, 1990. This book includes essays on computer networking, pedagogical uses of computers in writing instruction, collaborative learning and computers, using personal computers to teach idea generation, and designing an effective computer classroom. Includes a fairly comprehensive ten-page bibliography.

Holdstein, Deborah H., and Cynthia Selfe, eds. *Computers and Writing: Theory, Research, Practice.* New York: MLA, 1990.

Joram, Elana, et al. "The Effects of Revising with a Word Processor on Written Composition." *Research in the Teaching of English* 26 (1992): 167–93.

Montague, Marjorie. *Computers, Cognition, and Writing Instruction.* Albany: SUNY UP, 1992.

Myers, Linda, ed. *Approaches to Computer Writing Classrooms: Learning from Practical Experience.* Albany: SUNY UP, 1993.

Sirc, Geoffrey. "Response in the Electronic Medium." *Writing and Response: Theory, Practice, and Research.* Ed. Chris M. Anson. Urbana: NCTE, 1989. 187–208.

Stenzel, John, Linda Morris, and Wes Ingram. "The Effects of Minicomputer Text-Editing on Student Writing in Upper Division Cross-Disciplinary Courses: Results of a Study by the Writing Center, University of California, Davis." *Computers and Composition* 6.2 (1989): 61–79.

Tuman, Myron C., ed. *Literacy Online: The Promise (and Peril) of Reading and Writing with Computers.* Pittsburgh: U of Pittsburgh P, 1992.

CHAPTER 5

Teaching and Responding to Style, Grammar, and Punctuation

In this chapter:

❏ The place of style, grammar, and punctuation in the pedagogy of writing in the disciplines

❏ Teaching and responding to style

❏ Teaching and responding to grammar and punctuation

❏ Checklist for teaching and responding to style, grammar, and punctuation

❏ For further reading

The Place of Style, Grammar, and Punctuation in the Pedagogy of Writing in the Disciplines

Teaching style, grammar, and punctuation from the writer's perspective

Instructors, like all other readers, immediately notice surface features of writing, and errors in usage, grammar, sentence structure, spelling, and punctuation seem to leap off the page. Gradually, readers also register the text's assertions and notice how they are organized and presented. Writers undergo the reverse process. Their first concern is what to say; then they begin to consider how to say it; then they write the essay. Finally, they attend to surface form. Obviously, the processes of reading and writing are not so neatly linear; nevertheless, the preceding illustration shows how the perspective of writers and readers differs.

It is not at all unusual for instructors to approach the teaching of writing from the perspective of the reader. Indeed, many novice writing instructors believe that teaching style, grammar, and punctuation *is* teaching writing—that there is nothing more. Gradually, though, they come to realize that sentence-level features are a product of the development and presentation of ideas in their social context, the academic discipline. As they become more experienced, they tend to realize that it's more important to deal with content and development first, then address sentence-level concerns. Further, grammar and usage are best addressed in context rather than in drills. As Richard Braddock, Richard Lloyd-Jones, and Lowell Schoer reported in 1963, decontextualized grammar instruction does little to improve one's ability to write in correct, standard English.

Though style, grammar, and punctuation are best presented as editing concerns and latter-stage concerns of the writer, instructors can significantly demystify the writing process if they point out to inexperienced writers that style, in particular, is intricately tied to the development and presentation of ideas; changes in one affect the other. Style—how one structures sentences and chooses words—is not simply an arbitrary feature "added on" at the latter stages of composing; it is part of the conceptual choices that a writer makes. Style, in other words, is the product not just of editing choices but of rhetorical choices.

Approaches to teaching style, grammar, and punctuation

"Perhaps the most subtle conflict that arises when we try to improve students' writing . . . stems from the fact that few of us write with complete confidence and ease ourselves" (Dubrow 89). Heather Dubrow's observation is particularly applicable to the issues of style, grammar, and punctuation. Few of us consider ourselves experts in these subjects; therefore, we may be reluctant to teach them. In a course in writing in the disciplines, moreover, it is seldom appropriate to dedicate much time to sentence-level concerns, except insofar as they are specific to the discipline.

Yet instructors cannot ignore difficulties that their students have in writing Standard English. One effective way to help students is to pair or group them for peer response to papers and to stipulate style, grammar, and punctuation as specific (but preferably not exclusive) concerns. (For details about orchestrating peer response to writing, see Chapter 9.) Students know a great deal more about style, grammar, and punctuation than they may realize, and every student, no matter how uncertain or inexperienced as a writer, has expertise to share with his or her classmates. Many instructors hand out lists of questions for students to ask of each paper they read ("Do all of the subjects and verbs agree?" "Is the verb tense consistent throughout the paper?" "Is the language appropriate to the subject and audience?"); others suggest that students refer to the handbook and perhaps use the handbook's editing symbols to make corrections; still others suggest that students note just obvious errors. Of course, instructors can also help students with style, grammar, and punctuation. (See pages 81–90.)

Teaching students who use nonstandard dialects of English

Academic culture often regards Standard Written English—defined by the "rules" in dictionaries and writers' handbooks—as the "correct" or "pure" form of English. All other forms of English, therefore, seem acceptable only as they come close to that "correct" form. However, the sociolinguistic perspective on dialects, embodied in the work of Dennis Baron and William Labov, casts the matter in quite a different light: Standard Written English, they argue, is simply one of many dialects of English. It is the form appreciated by the most intellectually powerful members of the culture and is "correct" only insofar as it is their code of choice. Were a different group to gain social ascendancy, a different dialect might become the standard. Thus, every dialect is "correct" in that it embodies the ideals of its culture and facilitates ready communication among members of that culture.

This sociolinguistic perspective can help instructors respond more effectively to student writing. Students who are told that the way they and their families speak (and write) English is "wrong" or "bad" generally react defensively, for they may see the way they use language as part of their identity. This defensiveness does not produce the most effective environment for learning. Instructors adopting a sociolinguistic perspective, however, do not characterize one grammatical structure as "right" and another as "wrong," but rather one as conformity to Standard Written English and the other to a different dialect. An example of nonconformity evidenced by speakers of other dialects and speakers of other languages are dropped *-ed* and *-en* verb endings, which are absent in some American English dialects and which have no grammatical cognate in many languages. The absence of such verb endings does not mean that the writer lacks a concept of past tense but that the past in his or her language or dialect is marked in a way other than a terminal *-ed* or *-en* (or its translated equivalent). Such a difference, Mina Shaughnessy points out, can lead to yet other problems with Standard Written English. Because in some American English dialects the pronunciation of *giving* and *given* is nearly identical—*given'* and *given*—the student striving to manipulate Standard Written English may produce a sentence such as "This is one responsibility *giving* to you in college" (Shaughnessy 100).

Again, the teacher of writing in the disciplines may not be equipped to do the dialect analysis necessary to help speakers of nonstandard dialects master Standard Written English. But the instructor can avoid identifying nonstandard usage as "not English" or "not good English." Such usage *is* good English—a good example of a dialect other than Standard Written English or of a multidialectal student's effort to master the standard. Nevertheless, students have a better chance of succeeding in the writing they do academically and professionally if they learn the standard. A remark to this effect, along with handbook references, tutor referrals, and instructor-student conferences can be helpful to speakers of other dialects. The instructor can initiate important conversation, in class or in conferences with individual students, about how every dialect is as "right" and as effective as every other one in its own context, but that in academic contexts Standard Written English is the preferred code.

Standard Written English is best taught as a language form whose mastery widens one's range of social and professional possibilities, just as would the acquisition of a foreign language. Because Standard Written English is the accepted form in most academic and professional writing, people who want to advance in those settings must learn it. Although Shirley Brice Heath describes traditions of linguistic plurality in the United States, she stipulates, "Access to the wider society outside one's own primary group has, however, consistently been dependent on knowledge of English, and upward mobility in that society has called for facility in using a standard variety of English" (19).

Teaching students for whom English is a second language

Students who speak English as a second or third language (ESL students) often reveal traces of other language patterns in their writing, even if they speak without an accent. As a transition to mastering English, some students think in another language and translate to English as they write. Muriel Harris observes that the absence of certain vowels in written Arabic can cause students whose first written language is Arabic to omit vowels in English. She notes, too, that Spanish sentences are typically longer than those in American English, which may cause students whose first written language is Spanish to write sentences many Americans would consider "overly long" (99). Some features appear in both the written and spoken English of ESL students, such as the absence of articles (*a, an, the*) in many Asian dialects or the lack of relative pronouns in Arabic (Harris 99). Features of second language interference are easier to identify in a student's writing when the instructor has already heard them in the student's speech.

Instructors who speak more than one language often recognize grammatical constructions from other languages and can identify them as such to the student. Even monolingual instructors, though, can ask students whether their native language is something other than English and might be intervening in their English prose. Instructors might also ask students questions like "How would you organize this sentence in your native language?" to try to understand why an ESL student might have written a sentence in a particular way.

Mark LeTourneau identifies "inflection of nouns, verbs, and adverbs; count and non-count nouns (those which can be counted and have plurals and those which cannot); prepositions; tenses; definite articles; and word order" as causing particular problems for those learning written English (qtd. in Harris 100). Instructors who are aware of such problem areas can be more sensitive and helpful to ESL students, perhaps referring them to appropriate ESL sections in their handbook or writing guide.

Students experiencing significant second language interference can benefit from the one-to-one instruction provided by peer tutors, even if those tutors are not trained in ESL methods. Alternatives to tutoring are peer review groups or informal pairings with students known to the instructor to be suitable informal advisers. (See pages 37–39 for a discussion of peer tutoring.) Once they are satisfied that the students are working on their English writing skills, many instructors focus their comments on content or praise advances in style. They offer encouragement without emphasizing how slow the acquisition process is.

Identifying and teaching students with learning disabilities

Students whose in-class writing (e.g., for essay exams) is knowledgeable but riddled with errors in style, grammar, and spelling without any discernible patterns of error and whose out-of-class writing (e.g., for research papers) is significantly better could be suffering from a learning disability. Carolyn O'Hearn identifies confused homonyms and near-homonyms, frequent spelling errors, transposed letters, punctuation errors, and capitalizing letters in the middle of words as common traits in the handwritten prose of learning-disabled students (often referred to as LD students). She offers examples such as *which/witch, use/you,* and *as/has, becuase* (for *because*), *dose* (for *does*), *sonething* (for *something*), and *proBaBly* (for *probably*). These "flag[s] that signal Learning Disability," as O'Hearn puts it (299), rarely occur in the prose of students who don't have learning disabilities.

Under Public Law 94-142 (passed in 1975), all learning-disabled students are entitled to educational assistance reimbursable by the federal government, so diagnosis is important. Though it is obviously unwise for instructors unskilled in special education to attempt to diagnose learning disabilities, it is more harmful to ignore the possibility in some students. Rather than telling students that they probably have a learning disability, instructors may suggest that students consult a special education expert on campus if there is one or send samples of students' writing to such experts for evaluation. In any case, it is important that students get the message that learning disabilities are treatable and they are not a sign of inferior intelligence. It is often helpful to explain that "learning disability" means that the brain is not able to process one aspect of language learning effectively, not that one is a poor learner in general. Indeed, reaching college with a learning disability generally requires more intelligence and diligence to compensate for the areas of difficulty.

A number of articles suggest strategies for helping students with learning disabilities. (See page 94.) For example, some instructors schedule weekly or biweekly meetings with learning-disabled students to help them with specific elements of their writing. (See *Teaching One-to-One* by Muriel Harris for effective strategies.) Instructors might also consider making referrals to the writing center, especially if tutors have been trained to work with learning-disabled students.

Teaching and Responding to Style

Responding to awkward prose

Students are often aware that their writing "doesn't sound right" but can't figure out how to improve it. Regardless of what they may or may not realize about their prose, though, it is unlikely that students will learn anything useful from the comment "awkward," or the more cryptic "AWK," in the margins of their papers. However, instructors can help students understand the causes of awkward sentences by referring them to pertinent sections of the handbook for specific direction in revision and advice about sentence structure and grammar.

The teacher of writing in the disciplines is unlikely to have had formal training in sentence structure and grammar and therefore may be reluctant to identify the source of students' writing problems. The following guide can be helpful in diagnosing some of the problems that cause awkward sentences.

> *Look for stilted prose.* Assuming that academic writing should sound "formal," some students avoid using first- or second-person pronouns (*I, you*), or they rely too much on passive constructions. Stilted sentences like this one can result: "One has to examine one's feelings when one encounters the type of situation that was encountered by the writer of this paper." In many situations, the active voice is preferable to the passive (see the following paragraph), but instructors should make students aware of the conventions of the discipline they are

writing in. Also, instructors who see that students are struggling to avoid using *I* or *you* in contexts where these pronouns would be appropriate should note this in their papers. It may also be helpful to refer students to the handbook's discussion of point of view and active versus passive voice.

Look for indirect, wordy structures. Though scientific writing commonly uses the passive voice, many disciplines prefer the directness of the active voice, regarding "The Normans invaded England in 1066" as more direct than "England was invaded by the Normans in 1066." Some writers bury central ideas in prepositional phrases—for example, "One can understand the values of a nation by looking at its advertising" instead of the more direct and succinct "A study of advertising reveals the values of a nation." Instructors should also make students aware of wordiness or repetition, which can slow down and frustrate readers. It may be helpful to tell students that any words that can be deleted from a sentence without changing its meaning are probably unnecessary. Students might also be referred to the handbook's advice on eliminating wordiness.

Look at the way ideas are ordered and connected. Sometimes prose is awkward because the writer hasn't paid enough attention to the presentation of ideas, making sure that one idea flows smoothly and logically to the next. In addition, the writer may not have provided transitional words or phrases to help readers make connections between ideas. Consider the following sentences: "It may not be realistic to expect a battered woman to leave an abusive situation immediately. She may be emotionally or economically dependent on the batterer. Social service workers should try to help her understand that abusive patterns will probably continue and that leaving is, ultimately, the best solution." The ideas in these sentences stand apart from each other instead of working together to make the point the writer intended. By reordering sentences and providing transition, the writer communicates thoughts more clearly: "Because a battered woman may be emotionally or economically dependent on the batterer, it may not be realistic to expect her to leave an abusive situation immediately. Nevertheless, social service workers should try to help her understand that abusive patterns will probably continue and that leaving is, ultimately, the best solution." By connecting ideas and providing transitions, the writer also gets rid of choppiness, another common writing problem. Students who need help with ordering and connecting ideas can be referred to the handbook's discussion of paragraph development and transitions.

Look for errors in parallel structure. A sentence may sound awkward because its components are not parallel, that is, they are in different grammatical forms. Consider this example:

"Every day the participants in the study spent time talking with other participants, writing in their journals, and they listed their expectations for the next day's work." To make the sentence elements parallel, the writer must revise the clause "they listed their expectations" to a phrase introduced by an *-ing* verbal like *talking* and *writing.* Revised, the sentence reads: "Every day the participants in the study spent time talking with other participants, writing in their journals, and listing their expectations for the next day's work." Most handbooks offer advice and examples for students having problems with parallel structures.

Look for shifts in point of view, verb tense, mood, and voice. Shifts in person ("Every student wants to know what your instructor expects") or number ("Every student wants to know what their instructor expects,") are common, and in such cases, it's often easier to make both elements plural ("Students want to know what their instructors expect"). Shifts in tense ("I saw what looks like three frogs"), mood ("Step 1 is to choose a topic. Step 2, narrow your topic"), and voice ("The electorate answered Marvin's question, and he was told to stay with the party") may also show up in students' papers. Again, it may be helpful to refer them to appropriate sections in the handbook.

Awkward sentences may also result from mixed constructions, misplaced and dangling modifiers, or imprecise language. Most handbooks offer advice in all these areas.

Helping students write varied sentences

The general length and complexity of sentences can vary from discipline to discipline. For example, writing in economics tends to have far fewer dependent clauses and phrases than might appear in an English paper.

Yet certain principles of sentence structure do cross disciplines, for example, the principle that sentences should be varied in both length and structure. If too many sentences are of the same length or structure, the prose takes on a singsong or a turgid quality. Most handbooks discuss how to write varied sentences, and instructors may refer students to these discussions in class or in comments on papers. When sentence length and structure are a problem for many students, some instructors bring examples of turgid or choppy prose to class and discuss how they could be improved, perhaps showing how short, simple sentences might be combined or long, complex sentences broken in two. The examples can come from student prose or from publications in the discipline. Some instructors use examples of their own unrevised and revised prose to demonstrate how to construct varied sentences. Such a strategy reinforces the notion that all writers—even instructors—need to revise.

Responding to excessively formal or informal prose

Besides noting that a certain degree of formality is usually appropriate in academic writing, instructors can help students find the right words by encouraging them to focus on their subject and audience: What are they writing about, and for whom? A history major writing about the impact of the Great Depression for an audience of fellow historians probably should not use language like the following: "The Great Depression was a real bummer for U.S. workers; one-fourth of them were out of work by 1932." Slang words like *bummer* might, however, be appropriate for an imaginative account of coming of age written for an English class.

Of course, instructors need to be sensitive to possible sources of students' word choices. For example, students who seem to be using excessively informal language may really be experiencing dialect interference. The transitive verb *dis,* for example, means "to show public disrespect to" in several dialects of American English. If the students do not recognize this verb as dialect, they may use it in their academic writing and be confused or insulted when their instructors tell them that *dis* is "not a word" or "not a verb." They know from their day-to-day speech that it is both. If students are told that the word is "slang" or "informal" usage, they may feel that their language—and thus their culture—has been *dissed* and therefore may begin resisting instructors' comments and advice. In responding to papers that use such words, instructors should explain how the language affects them as readers. (For example, in the case of the word *dis:* "This word stopped me. Though I realize it is a word in everyday speech, it is not used in academic prose. Because it will not be familiar to all of your readers, it might interrupt them as they try to follow your argument.")

Some students, believing that academic prose features high-flown words, write sentences in which the language is unnecessarily complex. In their responses, instructors can point out places where simpler words or phrases might be substituted for complex language or jargon. Instructors might also assure students that clear, simple writing does not signal a lack of expertise or authority. (See pages 81–82 for advice on responding to stilted prose.)

The one-to-one conference is especially helpful to writers who are having problems using language appropriately. The personal approach of the conference can help students feel more comfortable exploring alternatives to their writing styles. Conferences also allow students to discuss why they make certain word choices. (See pages 35–37 for advice on conducting conferences.)

Helping students use words correctly

Popular and academic journals alike lament the "fact" that literacy is on the decline, conquered by electronic media. Specifically, they are referring to print literacy—facility with words in reading and writing—as opposed to facility with words in speech. Words that college students of yore could recognize in reading and use in writing may be unfamiliar to today's students. Yet the fact that today's students may not have great facility with print vocabulary does not mean they have no respect for or awareness of it. However much they want to improve their print literacy, though, inexperience may cause them to use words inaccurately. They may confuse *inhibit* and *inhabit* or use *disinterested* when they mean *uninterested.*

Instructors may be uncertain about how to respond to papers in which a lot of words are misused. Though marking every error will certainly give students the message that they have a problem, it may also overwhelm and discourage them. A more effective approach might be to write a comment at the end of the paper that summarizes the errors. In addition, it might be helpful to do trait scoring (see pages 211–213), in which the instructor marks only major or prevalent errors in word usage. For example, a student who tends to confuse words that sound alike (*cite/sight/site, accept/except*) will probably find it more useful to be told that than just to see individual errors marked with no general comments. Being aware of the problem might make the student more willing to consult a dictionary or a handbook's glossary of usage while writing. It is also important to tell students what they are doing well. Making a note of well-chosen words can be helpful encouragement.

If homonym and near-homonym mixing is common in a paper, the student may be learning-disabled. Instructors can encourage such students to make an appointment with a specialist in learning disabilities. The specialist can help students devise learning strategies and adapt the learning environment to their special needs. (See pages 80–81 for a more extensive discussion of working with learning-disabled students.)

Helping students avoid sexist language

Mankind sounds so much more lofty than *people* and so much more straightforward than *humanity* or *humankind* that students reach for the word without thinking that they might be reproducing a masculine orientation in their culture. Many students, however, are aware that a sentence like "If the student wants to improve his writing, he should read his handbook" sounds exclusionary. They may try to get around the problem by using a plural pronoun with a singular antecedent: "If a *student* wants to improve *their* writing, *they* should read *their* handbook." Politically correct, grammatically incorrect.

Though sexist language does not necessarily betoken sexist thought, it can constrict both writers' and readers' visions of the possibilities open to one gender or another. Thus, as much as possible, instructors should try to help students use language that is not only grammatically correct but gender-neutral. When students are apparently unaware that they are using sexist language, instructors should let them know. If they seem to be struggling to avoid sexist language, instructors can help them with alternatives.

Students might be referred to their handbook's suggestions for avoiding sexist language. Alice F. Freed offers a list of such suggestions in her book *Teaching Writing: Pedagogy, Gender, and Equity.* Though oriented toward instructors' classroom talk, her advice is also applicable to students' writing:

1. Deliberately alternate between *he* and *she* for indefinite pronominal reference. Another alternative is to say *he or she* as in the sentence "When a linguist is analyzing data, he or she should consider all available interpretations of the material."
2. When speaking of a hypothetical student, subject, informant, patient, client, writer, researcher, or other randomly chosen human, do not assume the sex of the individual.
3. Avoid the generic use of *man;* instead use *humans.*
4. Avoid stereotyped and fixed phrases that express bias such as *man and wife, fathers and sons, forefathers,* etc.
5. When speaking, do not assume the sex of individuals based on their occupation. That is, do not assume when speaking that all doctors are men, that all nurses are women.
6. Use parallel constructions and word choices when referring to women and men. Avoid phrases such as *men and girls, men and ladies.*
7. Purposely choose nonconventional, nontraditional examples of your own when speaking, in order to break expected stereotypes. For example, speak of a boss who asks her secretary if he can work overtime.
8. Avoid making jokes that are at the expense of any portion of your audience—however innocent you may think the comments are.
9. Do not assume that only the men or boys or only the women or girls in a group are capable of answering particular types of questions. That is, do not assume that the sex of the members of the group determines their behavior, their knowledge, or their interests.
10. When discussing the contents of articles, stories, novels, and various kinds of studies, look for any possible sex-related bias in the material and bring these to the attention of the group or try to elicit comments about these biases. (86–87)

Teaching the style of the discipline

In addition to the general concerns of style that this chapter has already addressed, writing instructors who are focusing on disciplinary genres—helping students become members of a discipline—must consider teaching stylistic features of that discipline. The most obvious of these are documentation and citation systems. (See pages 131–132.) But many other stylistic features distinguish the discourse of each discipline, and even students in introductory courses can be brought to understand some general distinctions. The sciences commonly use the passive voice, while the humanities tend to avoid it. Engineers generally have a more sparse prose style than philosophers. And though the pronoun *I* is usually inappropriate in a chemistry laboratory report, it is often acceptable in personal response papers in cultural studies.

It is helpful if instructors can tell students not only what the stylistic conventions are but also why they are used. For example, scientists usually use the past tense to describe steps and results of an experiment because each experiment is seen as a discrete entity—something that has occurred and can be replicated by others who follow the steps properly. In an English course, however, descriptions of action in a nineteenth-century novel are written in the present tense, for qualities of novels—and other art forms—are seen to exist in a kind of timeless present.

To help students become familiar with the conventions of their discipline, some instructors distribute lists of stylistic features or key words that students might be unfamiliar with. Students may learn even more from assignments that ask them to read professional prose in the discipline and identify and discuss points of style. Such assignments might ask students the following questions about a piece of writing: "How would you describe the style of the writing?" "Does the author seem distanced from the subject or does he or she seem to have a personal stake in it? (Note whether the author uses first person or third person.)"

To some extent students are always engaging in a kind of imitation when they write academic prose, often with disastrous results if that imitation is unguided, as David Bartholomae points out in "Inventing the University." A guided imitation of academic writing, however, can be an effective way of teaching students stylistic conventions of the discipline. Further, assignments that call for imitation encourage students to slow down, pay attention to the words they are reading, and realize that every word has a rhetorical purpose and impact. (See sample assignment on page 88.)

Of course, academic writing isn't merely an imitation of established styles; it is also a product of writers' experiences and perspectives. And instructors, even as they teach the style of a discipline, must be open to the many different ways students express ideas. For a long time, the impersonal, forceful prose associated with males has been privileged in the academy and, according to Janice Moulton, the positivist mode of argumentation used in the sciences has been extended to argumentation in all disciplines. Increasingly, however, scholars are asserting that other styles of arguing and expressing ideas must be acknowledged and fostered.

By asking students in her upper-level Latin class to imitate and change styles, Professor Pinault also encourages stylistic flexibility in the students' own writing. Guided imitation teaches students what elements of style are appropriate to imitate and thus may help prevent inadvertent plagiarism.

SAMPLE ASSIGNMENT
Teaching style through imitation
Latin Prose Authors: Jody Rubin Pinault

FIRST PAPER ASSIGNMENT

Compose a letter in English in the style of Seneca's epistles. Remember to analyze first Seneca's sentence structure, diction, prose rhythm, and prose ornaments. Also, after rereading his letters, consider carefully which late-twentieth-century topics would be most successful if presented in the Senecan manner.

SECOND PAPER ASSIGNMENT

Take the Seneca letter that you wrote for the first paper assignment and rewrite it in Cicero's style. Before you start, carefully analyze how Cicero's style differs from Seneca's. Take into consideration sentence structure and length, diction, repetition, rhetorical devices, and prose rhythm. Study the English interpreters of Ciceronian style that we have discussed in class.

Feminist scholars have noted that, in many cases, women speak in prose voices that are different from those of men, and those scholars propose alternatives to privileged methods of academic inquiry and writing—alternatives that include women's voices. In their article "Feminist Theory and Practice in the Writing Classroom," Anuradha Dingwaney and Lawrence Needham recommend coalition writing, in which members of a group set and pursue their own agendas. Moulton explores alternative methods of argumentation in which an argument is evaluated based on the strength of its assertions instead of its being invalidated through counter examples, as in the positivist mode.

While providing examples of discipline-specific prose, instructors should consider offering samples of work from writers with a variety of styles and backgrounds. By seeing the diversity of writers who have contributed to a discipline, students of various cultural backgrounds may understand that they, too, have something to contribute.

Teaching and Responding to Grammar and Punctuation

Grammar

Instructors outside the English Department who pay attention to grammar in students' papers reinforce the notion that all writers should try to use correct grammar regardless of their discipline. Few instructors, however, can afford to spend time marking and explaining every grammatical problem in students' papers. Instead, they may mark major or prevalent errors, referring students to appropriate sections in the handbook. The following list, though by no means complete, covers some common problems to look out for. (See pages 211–213 for an explanation of trait analysis.)

> *Sentence fragments:* "Dr. Hewitt argued for passage of the legislation. *Even though she had opposed it in the past.*" (Joining the fragment to the sentence eliminates the problem: "Dr. Hewitt argued for passage of the legislation, even though she had opposed it in the past.")
>
> *Fused sentences (also known as "run-on sentences"):* "Thirty people began the study only twenty-five completed it." Joining the two independent clauses with a comma and a coordinating conjunction eliminates the problem: "Thirty people began the study, **but** only twenty-five completed it." Using a semicolon and a conjunctive adverb is also effective: "Thirty people began the study; **however**, only twenty-five completed it."
>
> *Comma splices:* "Settlers didn't have enough draft animals to plow the land, they had poor access to water supplies." Adding a coordinating conjunction after the comma eliminates the problem: "Settlers didn't have enough draft animals to plow the land, **and** they had poor access to water supplies." A semicolon and a conjunctive adverb also fixes the problem: "Settlers didn't have enough draft animals to plow the land; **moreover**, they had poor access to water supplies."
>
> *Errors in subject-verb agreement:* "Each of the subjects were given a placebo." Reminding students to check that verbs agree with their subjects in number and person can help them catch more obvious errors, but making verbs agree with indefinite pronouns requires more careful attention. A handbook's discussion of indefinite pronouns could help them make the correction: "Each of the subjects **was** given a placebo."
>
> *Errors in pronoun-antecedent agreement:* "Everyone works on their own project." Reminding students that the indefinite pronoun *everyone* is singular allows them to fix the antecedent as they revise the sentence: "Everyone works on **his or her** own project." Often this error occurs because students are trying to avoid gender-specific language. Learning to fix the error in this specific circumstance may help students remember the rule in other instances.

Handbooks offer much more thorough discussions of these issues and other similar ones (such as case of personal pronouns, *who/ whom,* and use of adjectives, adverbs, and irregular verbs). Some writers' handbooks also offer advice for students who speak English as a second language, and some even include special sections on common ESL problems. (See pages 79–80 for advice on teaching ESL students.) In addition to referring students to the handbook, instructors may want to spend some conference time helping students with grammar. Where class size prohibits one-to-one conferences, some instructors circle the first few instances of major or prevalent errors in students' papers and note the sections of the handbook that students should consult. They then require students to correct all of the errors of the type that have been circled and resubmit the paper.

Punctuation

As in the case of grammatical errors, it's not desirable for instructors to mark every punctuation error in students' papers. Again, noting major or prevalent errors and describing them to students may be the most effective approach. By writing a summary like the following at the end of a paper rather than just marking individual errors, an instructor offers more helpful and specific guidance: "Sometimes you use commas where they aren't necessary, such as between compound elements that aren't independent clauses or between cumulative adjectives. I've pointed you to the appropriate sections of the handbook so that you can see some examples." Most handbooks offer thorough advice and examples for punctuation usage, and instructors should refer students to this advice in class, in their comments on papers, and possibly in conferences. Writing centers can also help students improve their punctuation skills.

Checklist for teaching and responding to style, grammar, and punctuation

TEACHING STYLE, GRAMMAR, AND PUNCTUATION

_____ Treat style, grammar, and punctuation as late stages of the composing process.

_____ Use peer response pairs or groups so that students can share expertise, but don't allow these groups to make style, grammar, and punctuation their sole concern.

_____ Offer one-to-one conferences in which you mark and explain errors in a section of a student's paper; then have the student return for a follow-up conference after attempting to correct the same errors in the remainder of the paper.

_____ Engage in one-to-one mentoring of students who use excessively formal or informal language.

_____ Guide students toward gender-neutral language.

TEACHING THE STYLE OF THE DISCIPLINE

_____ Explain discipline-specific conventions in style and provide handouts.

_____ Assign analyses of the style of professional writing in the discipline.

_____ Provide diverse examples of writing in the discipline to show that "style" is actually made up of many voices.

RESPONDING TO STYLE, GRAMMAR, AND PUNCTUATION

_____ Don't ignore style, grammar, and punctuation, or students may believe that such matters are unimportant.

_____ Decide whether to respond to and grade style, grammar, and punctuation in students' papers, or whether to respond to such errors without grading them.

_____ Mark only the more important or pervasive errors.

_____ Provide handbook references when you mark errors and make comments.

_____ Identify causes of awkward prose rather than simply labeling the writing "awkward."

_____ Treat error as a transgression not against "good" or "correct" English but against the conventions of Standard Written English, the dialect of the academy.

_____ Consider the possible influences of other cultures or languages as the source of writing problems.

For Further Reading

Teaching style, grammar, and punctuation

Baron, Dennis. "Why Do Academics Continue to Insist on 'Proper' English?" *Chronicle of Higher Education* 1 July 1992: B1–2.

Bartholomae, David. "Released into Language: Errors, Expectations, and the Legacy of Mina Shaughnessy." *The Territory of Language: Linguistics, Stylistics, and the Teaching of Composition.* Carbondale: Southern Illinois UP, 1986. 65–88.

———. "Inventing the University." *When a Writer Can't Write.* Ed. Mike Rose. New York: Guilford, 1985. 134–65.

Braddock, Richard, Richard Lloyd-Jones, and Lowell Schoer. *Research in Written Composition.* Urbana: NCTE, 1963.

Brooks, Charlotte K., ed. *Tapping Potential: English and Language Arts for the Black Learner.* Urbana: NCTE, 1981.

Cazden, Courtney B., and David K. Dickinson. "Language in Education: Standardization versus Cultural Pluralism." *Language in the USA.* Ed. Charles Ferguson and Shirley Brice Heath. New York: Cambridge UP, 1981. 446–68.

Connors, Robert. "Mechanical Correctness as a Focus in Composition Instruction." *College Composition and Communication* 36 (1985): 61–72.

———. "The Rhetoric of Mechanical Correctness." *Only Connect: Uniting Reading and Writing.* Ed. Thomas Newkirk. Upper Montclair, NJ: Boynton/Cook, 1986. 27–58.

Dingwaney, Anuradha, and Lawrence Needham. "Feminist Theory and Practice in the Writing Classroom: A Critique and a Prospectus." *Constructing Rhetorical Education.* Ed. Marie Secor and Davida Charney. Carbondale: Southern Illinois UP, 1992. 6–25.

Dubrow, Heather. "Teaching Essay-Writing in a Liberal Arts Curriculum." *The Art and Craft of Teaching.* Ed. Margaret Morganroth Gullette. Cambridge: Harvard UP, 1984. 88–102.

Freed, Alice F. "Hearing Is Believing: The Effect of Sexist Language on Language Skills." *Teaching Writing: Pedagogy, Gender, and Equity.* Ed. Cynthia L. Caywood and Gillian R. Overing. Albany: SUNY UP, 1987. 81–92.

Gage, John T. "Philosophies of Style and Their Implications for Composition." *College English* 42 (1980): 615–22.

Giannasi, Jenefer M. "Language Varieties and Composition." *Teaching Composition: Twelve Bibliographical Essays.* Ed. Gary Tate. Fort Worth: Texas Christian UP, 1987. 227–64.

Hairston, Maxine. "Not All Errors Are Created Equal: Nonacademic Readers in the Professions Respond to Lapses in Usage." *College English* 43 (1981): 794–806.

Hartwell, Patrick. "Grammar, Grammars, and the Teaching of Grammar." *Rhetoric and Composition: A Sourcebook for Teachers and Writers.* 3rd ed. Ed. Richard L. Graves. Portsmouth, NH: Boynton/Cook, 1990. 163-85.

Haswell, Richard H. "Error and Change in College Student Writing." *Written Communication* 5 (1988): 479–99.

———. "Minimal Marking." *College English* 45 (1983): 600–04.

Haugen, Diane. "Coming to Terms with Editing." *Research in the Teaching of English* 24 (Oct. 1990): 322–33.

Heath, Shirley Brice. "English in Our Language Heritage." *Language in the USA.* Ed. Charles Ferguson and Shirley Brice Heath. New York: Cambridge UP, 1981. 6–20.

Labov, William. *Language in the Inner City: Studies in the Black English Vernacular.* Philadelphia: U of Pennsylvania P, 1973.

———. "The Logic of Nonstandard English." *Georgetown Monographs on Language and Linguistics* 22 (1969): 1–31.

Lloyd-Jones, Richard. "Primary Trait Scoring." *Evaluating Writing: Describing, Measuring, Judging.* Ed. C. R. Cooper and L. Odell. Urbana: NCTE, 1977. 33–66.

Moulton, Janice. "A Paradigm of Philosophy: The Adversary Method." *Discovering Reality: Feminist Perspectives on Epistemology, Metaphysics, Methodology, and Philosophy of Science.* Ed. Sandra Harding and Merrill B. Hintikka. Boston: Reidel, 1983. 149–64.

Ohmann, Richard. "Use Definite, Specific, Concrete Language." *College English* 41 (1979): 390–97.

Pringle, Ian. "Why Teach Style? A Review-Essay." *College Composition and Communication* 34 (1983): 91–98.

Rankin, Libby. "An Anatomy of Awkwardness." *Journal of Teaching Writing* 9 (Spring/Summer 1990): 45–58.

Roy, Alice M. "Alliance for Literacy: Teaching Non-native Speakers and Speakers of Nonstandard English Together." *College Composition and Communication* 35 (1984): 439–47.

Rubin, Donald L. "The Influence of Communicative Context on Style in Writing." *The Development of Oral and Written Language in Social Contexts.* Ed. A. D. Pellegrini and T. Yawkey. Norwood, NJ: Ablex, 1984. 213-32.

Scannell, Dale P., and Jon C. Marshall. "The Effect of Selected Composition Errors on Grades Assigned to Essay Examinations." *American Educational Research Journal* 3 (Mar. 1966): 125–30.

Smitherman, Geneva. *Talkin and Testifyin: The Language of Black America.* Detroit: Wayne State UP, 1986.

Sosnoski, James J. "The Psycho-Politics of Error." *Pre/Text* 10 (Spring/Summer 1989): 33–54.

Stanley, Julia. "'Correctness,' 'Appropriateness,' and the Uses of English." *College English* 41 (1979): 330–35.

Walvoord, Barbara E. Fassler. *Helping Students Write Well: A Guide for Teachers in All Disciplines.* 2nd ed. New York: MLA, 1986.

Cultural and second language interference

Harris, Muriel. "Cultural Differences." *Teaching One-to-One: The Writing Conference.* Urbana: NCTE, 1986. 87–94. Harris includes a discussion of Kaplan's models of "cultural thought patterns" and their effect on the structure of student papers.

Janopoulos, Michael. "Reader Comprehension and Holistic Assessment of Second Language Writing Proficiency." *Written Communication* 6 (1989): 218–37. According to research, classes containing nonnative speakers of English and native-speaking instructors should not use holistic grading, in which readers "read through" surface errors to focus on content. In these classes, native speakers are less able to read through errors of nonnative speakers and are thus less able to evaluate content fairly.

Kaplan, Robert B. "Cultural Thought Patterns in Inter-Cultural Education." *Language Learning* 16 (1966).

LeTourneau, Mark. "Typical ESL Errors and Tutoring Strategies." *Writing Lab Newsletter* 9.7 (1985).

Shaughnessy, Mina. *Errors and Expectations: A Guide for the Teacher of Basic Writing.* New York: Oxford UP, 1977.

Xu, George Q. *ESL/EFL Composition: A Selected Annotated Bibliography.* Bloomington, Ind.: ERIC/RCS, 1989.

Responding to learning-disabled students

Martin, Judy L. "Removing the Stumbling Blocks: 25 Ways to Help Our Learning Disabled College Writers." *Teaching English in the Two-Year College* 18 (1991): 283–89. This article includes a definition of "learning disabled," some classic features for nonspecialists to be aware of, and suggestions for "removing the stumbling blocks"—including reducing the importance of spelling in the overall grade, rethinking the relationship between surface errors and content, and paying particular attention to the kinds of responses written on papers.

O'Hearn, Carolyn. "Recognizing the Learning Disabled College Writer." *College English* 51 (1989): 294–304. O'Hearn includes a useful bibliography of more specialized sources, including essays on teaching students with specific learning disorders ranging from dyslexia to strephosymbolia.

Vogel, Susan A. "Learning Disabled College Students: Identification, Assessment and Outcome." *Understanding Learning Disabilities: Interdisciplinary and Multidisciplinary Views.* Ed. Drake D. Duane and Che Kan Leong. New York: Plenum, 1985. 179–98.

Vogel, Susan A., and Mary Ross Moran. "Written Language Disorders in Learning Disabled College Students: A Preliminary Report." *Coming of Age: Selected Papers from the 18th International Conference of the Association for Children and Adults with Learning Disabilities. The Best of ACLD 3.* Ed. William M. Cruikshank and Janet W. Lerner. Syracuse: Syracuse UP, 1982. 211–25.

CHAPTER 6

Designing Writing Assignments

In this chapter:

- ❏ Features of the writing assignment
- ❏ Pedagogical uses of writing assignments
- ❏ Multistaged assignments
- ❏ Sequenced assignments
- ❏ Checklist for designing writing assignments
- ❏ For further reading

Features of the Writing Assignment

Although assignments vary according to discipline, instructor, and course, some general principles about wording, presentation, and scheduling can help instructors design effective assignments that stimulate interesting papers.

Presenting the writing assignment as part of the course

Students will get the most out of writing assignments that draw directly on course materials or skills learned in the course rather than those that are presented as isolated tasks divorced from the rest of the learning process. An economics professor who gives writing assignments out of a composition textbook, for instance, may have the best intentions of improving students' writing skills, but if the assignments have no relation to the material of the economics course, students are likely to view the work as an irrelevant chore to be gotten out of the way. Assignments integrated into the subject of the course are more likely to engage students and thus produce better writing.

Wording the assignment

Printing and distributing copies of the assignment will make expectations clear and give all students a common understanding of the assignment. The wording of the assignment should clearly state its purpose, and instructors should go over the wording with the class, perhaps suggesting that students circle key terms (*explain, evaluate, describe, compare, argue for or against*). Instructors can help

This thorough assignment statement ensures that students know exactly what they are being asked to do—and why. The first two sentences contain the key words *interpretation* and *more than a description*, which indicate the purpose of the assignment and the kind of writing required. The third sentence gives examples of appropriate topics; the fourth explains the heart of the assignment ("how opposing sets of social categories . . . are articulated in one or more symbolic domains"); and the fifth and sixth suggest ways to approach the assignment.

This assignment is part of an ongoing project at Rensselaer Polytechnic Institute called *Reading Rensselaer*, a cumulative collection of students' ethnographic descriptions of the college. By including students' papers in the collection, Professor Hess invites students to participate in the world of anthropological data collection.

SAMPLE WRITING ASSIGNMENT
Making the purpose clear
Introduction to Cultural Anthropology: David Hess

Write a cultural interpretation of one aspect of campus life. This should be more than a description; it should be your interpretation of the meaning of local culture. In the past, students have selected topics such as social categories articulated in a field hockey practice session, the way fraternities and sororities carve up space and time in the library, the first date as a ritual, etc. In any case, look at how opposing sets of social categories (m/f, rich/poor, black/white, native/foreign, fresh./soph./jr./sr./grad . . . , etc.) are articulated in one or more symbolic domains (space, time, food, ritual event, laboratory research, a job, etc.). Try to work in terms of opposing sets of symbols, mediating terms, and correlation between opposing symbols, as we have seen in the Kypseli movie, my presentation of Brazilian magic rituals, or the essays and discussions on structuralism. A diagram may be helpful, but it is not necessary.

students recognize that those key words specify the rhetorical purpose of the assignment. Instructors can also help students by providing additional explanations of purpose when necessary. For instance, students should know whether they are supposed to prove one point or to explore several alternatives, and they should also know whether they are expected to repeat what they have learned or to demonstrate applications of that knowledge. If the assignment is designed to develop knowledge that students have gained in the course, to expand on the course content, or to help the instructor gauge the students' comprehension, instructors can also state this in the assignment.

Some instructors ask students to summarize in their own words what the assignment is asking them to do, writing their interpretation of it (perhaps explaining it to someone who doesn't understand), and briefly describing how they might go about completing it. Skimming through these descriptions can enable the instructor to identify problems in his or her wording of the assignment and then clarify any confusing issues in class or in individual conferences.

Clarifying assignments

An instructor who knows that an assignment is complicated or who has already received disappointing results from it may be tempted to compensate with an overdetailed explanation. Lucid explanation of the purpose of the assignment and the instructor's expectations is, of course, essential, as is anticipating and answering students' questions. Yet lengthy assignments containing several pages of extensive advice and explanation will probably overwhelm students. Instructors might more profitably clarify and simplify the wording of the assignment than explain it. Sometimes the need for extensive explanation signals an unnecessarily complex assignment that should be revised or discarded.

Instructors can anticipate students' questions by listing and answering some typical questions on the assignment handout. Or they can ask students to write one or more questions about the assignment on a notecard and hand it in the day after the assignment is given. Instructors can then answer the questions in the next class orally or in writing (or perhaps using E-mail).

To further clarify an assignment, some instructors suggest strategies for approaching it, including a brief outline of a process students might follow for gathering data or organizing material. Even if students should be able to figure out a strategy for themselves, the anxiety surrounding a writing assignment can prevent some from doing so. Using a numbered list of steps can prevent their missing steps or following only those that appear easiest. Again, moderation is advised: Instructors using such an approach should be aware that excessive advice can intimidate students or can lead to uninspired, formulaic papers such as students may have become accustomed to producing in high school.

The following example shows how an assignment could be revised to offer clearer guidelines for students.

Although this assignment, on Lorraine Hansberry's *A Raisin in the Sun,* is succinct and clear in its demand, Professor Jamieson says that it was not successful. To satisfy this assignment, students had to define both terms and explain why they concluded that Mama is either a realist or an idealist. Though explaining that conclusion is the purpose of the essay, many students became bogged down in definitions, and some even read the second clause to mean that they should "explain what evidence" they used to determine their definitions.

SAMPLE WRITING ASSIGNMENT
An assignment that didn't work
African American Literature: Sandra Jamieson

Is Mama a realist or an idealist? Define both terms, and explain what evidence you used to make your judgment.

The assignment could be rewritten:

TOPIC: Is Mama a realist or an idealist?

—The answer to this question will be the thesis of your paper.
—Before you can decide on your answer to the question, you must develop a written definition of each term. You should explain these definitions in your paper, perhaps in the introduction.
—As you prepare to write, make a list of all the evidence that explains why you believe your thesis, and use that list to help structure the paper.
—Don't forget to list counterevidence that might contradict your thesis, and include a passage showing why the counterevidence is not as persuasive as your evidence.

Another way to ensure the clarity of an assignment and anticipate students' problems and questions is for instructors to test the assignment by imagining themselves writing the paper according to the instructions provided. Some instructors list for themselves a number of sample theses or research questions and sketch out sample outlines. Others list the information they expect to find in the finished paper. Both approaches allow instructors to evaluate and revise assignments before distributing them to students. Such evaluations can also make grading easier. A third strategy for evaluating the effectiveness of assignments is for instructors to put themselves in the shoes of that one student who always manages to misunderstand assignments and bungle experiments. What can he or she do wrong with this assignment? The answers can help instructors formulate clear advice and explanations.

Offering choices

The best assignments do not leave students too free to interpret yet allow several possible approaches that can lead to effective papers. The revised assignment achieves this, whereas the initial statement of the assignment might make students feel too confined by the need to define. Simply asking "What is Mama's attitude toward life?" would give students too much freedom. Another possible revision that would not produce satisfactory results is "Explain the consequences of Mama's idealism," which gives students too narrow a focus by preventing them from arguing that she was not an idealist.

The most effective assignments offer two or three choices of topic or of rhetorical mode (comparison, description, argumentation, or more creative options), depending on the topic and the discipline. Only a few students would take up the option of writing a Socratic dialogue between Luke's Jesus and Plato's Socrates, but those who succeed at it demonstrate impressive knowledge of the dialogue form and style, as well as mastery of the beliefs and values of the two subjects. More important than their simply knowing these things is that they learn them in order to be able to write the paper rather than learning them so that they may regurgitate them in a more traditional form. A creative option such as this works well for some students and not at all for others. Gerard Cox asserts that no more than 70 percent of any class responds well to any particular method of teaching writing, and he urges instructors to vary teaching methods so that the 30 percent who were unmoved by one method have an opportunity with a second or third (112). The efficacy of offering choices can be applied to types of writing assignments as well.

SAMPLE WRITING ASSIGNMENT (EXCERPT)
Offering choices
Introduction to Political Science I: Michael Johnston

Here are a few suggested topics; you may use or modify any of them, or use them to help you formulate your own. A one-page prospectus spelling out a proposed topic will be due on Monday.

Professor Johnston gives his students a wide variety of writing topics, allowing them to select different rhetorical methods in addition to different theorists and topics.

The first option allows them to use course material to analyze a public issue they might be interested in. By specifying Bagehot's and Edelman's methods, he ensures that the students have adequate tools for analysis, but he gives them freedom to select an issue for analysis.

The second option calls for a different style of writing but on a much more focused topic. Although analysis is involved in comparison-and-contrast papers, many students find them more accessible, and some students would prefer not to select their own topic.

In the third option Professor Johnston allows students to imitate the choices facing political scientists analyzing an issue while still offering only three options as the basis for their analyses.

The fourth option allows for greater creativity. Developing their own model will engage students in theories rather than simply using them as tools for analysis.

The final option calls for a more creative but no less rigorous paper. While few students will be likely to attempt it, those who choose this option will probably do a very good job and appreciate the challenge and the freedom.

—Use Bagehot and Edelman to analyze an important aspect of American politics, such as the role of the mass media, or our particular style of election campaigns.

—Compare and contrast Dahl's and Marx's views of the structure of political power in capitalist society.

—Analyze a recent conflict or government decision in terms of the concepts offered by two of the following: Dahl, Bachrach and Baratz, or Schattschneider.

—Develop an alternative model of politics to Easton's or an alternative model of political change to Huntington's.

—Write a speech responding to Solzhenitsyn's Harvard speech.

Scheduling the assignment

The time frame of an assignment depends on many factors—the complexity of the assignment, the number of writing assignments given in the term, the expected length of the paper, the amount of research required, and so on—but a schedule should be clearly spelled out in the initial assignment handout. A research paper that spans the whole term will require interim deadlines for drafts, peer review, instructor's response, and revision. A weekly three-page paper assignment may require nothing more than turning it in. In a two- or three-week time frame from initial assignment to final draft, an instructor might schedule a rough draft or outline at the end of the first week, giving students time to respond to the instructor's comments and consult with tutors, peer reviewers, and other mentors. Many instructors plan to give students enough time to mull over the assignment before they begin writing. Even students who don't begin writing until the night before a deadline will benefit from an "incubation" period during which their minds can actively or subconsciously engage with the topic. A final note: Some instructors give students insufficient time—perhaps two weeks—to write a paper based on extensive reading or research. The time frame may only give them enough time to complete the reading or research. Instructors must be sure, too, that if the writing assignment is based on material covered in class, the students will have ample time for writing the paper after the class has completed those materials. Make sure to give students a realistic deadline for getting *all* the necessary work done.

Pedagogical Uses of Writing Assignments

In addition to testing a student's reading, writing, thinking, and research skills, a good writing assignment can help students understand how these skills relate to the course and the discipline. Many instructors have been influenced by William Perry's study of Harvard undergraduates, which found that students' cognitive development occurs in stages, proceeding from dualistic thinking, in which they believe that information is simply "right" or "wrong," to an ability to deal with contradiction and ambiguity. Perry's conclusion that assignments should be directed to a student's current cognitive level while at the same time challenging him or her to develop more sophisticated thinking and writing skills has led to a variety of models for writing pedagogy. Among them are multistaged and sequenced writing assignments, which move students through the stages over the course of a semester. (See Cox 91; Flower and Hayes; and pages 110–114 of this book.)

Other writing instructors trace their pedagogy to Brazilian literacy educator Paulo Freire, who argues that far from being empty vessels waiting to be filled with information or skills, students possess a great deal of relevant knowledge. They just don't know how to use it to generate writing topics or explore academic issues. Students who "know the material," for example, can fail tests because they do not know how to apply their knowledge.

Formal papers as well as informal writing assignments are an opportunity to teach students how to apply what they know. Keeping journals (Chapter 10), writing annotated bibliographies (pages 121–122), and summarizing their reading (pages 237–240) can all assist students in this endeavor. Any of this informal writing can help students assess their understanding of a piece of writing, forcing them to determine its main argument, its most convincing evidence, and its underlying assumptions. Such interaction is a more effective study tool than underlining or highlighting what seem to be important passages.

Introducing students to discipline-specific writing

If the purpose of the course is to help students become members of the discipline, formal writing assignments might introduce the writing style and structures characteristic of writing in the discipline. (See pages 86–88.) By learning to write like an insider, students become more fully immersed in the discipline.

These five options allow students to try out different forms of scientific writing. Professor McMillan, a biologist, emphasizes that all five require "conventional scientific style and format," which exposes students to the standards for scientific writing and the various approaches a scientist can take to the material.

SAMPLE WRITING ASSIGNMENT (EXCERPT)
Writing in the discipline
Reproductive Issues: Victoria E. McMillan

Both papers 1 and 2 should be review papers in conventional scientific style and format. Each paper may take one of the following general forms:

1. State-of-the-art review
2. Historical review
3. Comparison-of-perspectives review
4. Synthesis-of-two-fields review
5. Theory or model-building review

An effective way to start teaching discipline-specific writing is to point out its features in readings for the course. Some instructors select one or two journal articles and explain the features that conform to the discipline's standards. Another effective approach to assignments is to specify as audience other members of the discipline and to require writing in imitation of a journal's style. Such assignments involve students in the work of the discipline and move them beyond mere performance for a grade. A related assignment asks students to write out a brief audience analysis and then to write for that audience; this helps them learn conventions of writing for other members of the discipline.

Assignments that call for comparison can also help students grasp important features of disciplinary discourse. In history, for example, an assignment asking for transcription of a handwritten document in the library holdings or for comparison of two synchronous reports of the same event will significantly increase students' understanding of the issues confronted by historians. Students in comparative literature can compare two translations of the same text. Like journals, such assignments need not be graded qualitatively and need not use up class time. Assigning them in the first few weeks of the term will set the tenor of the class as active rather than passive and will encourage students to see themselves as participants in the discipline rather than as empty vessels waiting to be filled with knowledge. Such assignments give students increased access to course material and a greater sense of engagement with the readings and lectures and thus help achieve an unstated purpose of most courses: inspiring enthusiasm for the field.

SAMPLE WRITING ASSIGNMENT
Engaging in the discourse of the discipline
Roots of Western Civilization: Tom Howard

Your first writing assignment is to compare the version of Book IV of *The Odyssey* in your textbook for this class with the two other translations of Book IV that are on reserve for this section of GNED 101 in the library. You may focus on any aspect of the various translations that you wish. Similarities as well as differences may be included in your discussion. There is no minimum or maximum length for this assignment, but it is difficult to envision a successful completion of the assigned task in less than three pages. The average length of responses to this assignment in past semesters has been five to seven pages. The record length is seventeen pages—long may that record stand!

For your information, the translation by William Cullen Bryant was published around 1870, while that of T. E. Shaw (Lawrence) first came out in 1932.

Professor Howard reports that he is always astounded at the range of responses to this assignment. Book IV of *The Odyssey* consists of just over 800 lines, yet students have identified hundreds of differences in the translations. Even more important than the language differences they identify are the rhetorical differences they often discover.

Effective assignments in some disciplines require students to broaden their perspective beyond the course material by applying what they've learned to events, works, or theories outside the course itself or to an element of the course that has not been studied in depth—a poem, a historical moment, the behavior of a metal or a chemical.

Classics Professor Pinault's creative assignment helps her students use their knowledge of Hippocrates by applying his theories to the elements of the campus ecosystem. Pinault reports that her students enjoy this assignment and generally produce very thoughtful and creative work.

SAMPLE WRITING ASSIGNMENT
Writing beyond the course itself
The Art of Persuasion: Jody Rubin Pinault

For our next class, write one typed page on the following:

Determine from a map which direction Colgate's main campus faces (north, south, east, west), where our water comes from (spring, lake, river), and what kind of weather has prevailed this year. According to the author of the Hippocratic writing *Airs, Waters, Places,* what diseases would affect communities with such an orientation, this type of water supply, and this pattern of weather? Then, using deductive reasoning, predict what diseases one would expect the inhabitants of Colgate to experience this year.

Stimulating critical thinking and fostering student growth

Using writing assignments to stimulate critical thinking and foster student growth brings to the foreground the goals of write-to-learn genres, in which instructors teach students *how* to think rather than simply *what* to think. Teaching students to think critically as they read texts and listen to lectures helps them interact with the course material and invites them into the world of academic inquiry. Write-to-learn courses that teach critical thinking skills along with writing skills produce students who are better writers in general *and* in the discipline. Critical thinking includes the ability to keep an open mind when presented with new material; to value the opinions and arguments of others even when they differ from one's own; to take ideas seriously, even while evaluating them and judging their logic and supporting evidence; to see the broader implications of ideas and fit them into larger frameworks; and to integrate new knowledge into one's world picture and make the necessary adjustments to other ideas—no matter how painful.

Traditional models of education in which the instructor has the "truth" and hands it to students as nuggets to be preserved do not promote the acquisition of critical thinking skills. This does not mean that the instructor should relinquish control, cease to lecture, or pretend that he or she does not know more than the students do. Rather, teaching critical thinking requires that instructors share all

SAMPLE WRITING ASSIGNMENT
Fostering critical thinking
Language and Gender: Sandra Jamieson

CRITICAL THINKING QUESTIONS

Ask these questions of each reading you do for this class and write out your answers to prepare for class discussion.

Using these notes, you will be required to write three brief papers in which you compare methodologies, biases, or treatment of evidence in several of the readings (due dates on syllabus).

1. What credentials qualify the author to write on this subject?
2. Does the author state his or her position on or relationship to this topic?
3. What critical or methodological tools does the author use to explore the issue/subject?
4. What other critical or methodological tools might he or she have used?
5. What difference would that have made to the argument/theory/conclusion?
6. What biases does the author reveal and how do they limit the text?
7. What counterevidence/conflicting theories/research does the author ignore?

These questions help students read and respond to critical and literary theory. While every student may not be able to answer every question, the attempt changes students from passive learners to critical thinkers. For the first few reading assignments, Professor Jamieson collects the answers at the end of every class. Once she knows that the students can answer the questions, she collects them, only occasionally (requiring students to have them prepared "just in case"). The students present their answers orally in class as a way to begin discussion of the reading or to provoke questions at the end of a lecture.

Brief writing assignments build on the questions by asking students to use them as the basis for comparisons among readings. (For the first paper, Professor Jamieson places two very different readings back to back and briefly discusses the differences to help students understand the method.) Simply asking questions like these (adapted to the discipline) can change the way students relate to texts and encourage them to see authors as scholars in a larger field rather than as holders of unqualified truths.

they know about their subject—including how practitioners in the discipline think, write, and evaluate—not just the facts. Critical thinking skills can be fostered by asking students to write evaluations of their readings and lectures, to compare and contrast, and to question. Some instructors encourage students to be active readers by handing out on the first day a list of ten to twenty of the most important questions they might ask about a text in their discipline.

In write-to-learn courses, teaching students to think critically will give them tools to evaluate and edit their own writing. Teaching them to ask content-specific questions of their reading will help them learn to ask similar questions of their writing.

If the course is focused on disciplinary genres, intending to introduce students to the material and discourse of a specific discipline,

---

Professor Pinet, a geologist, suggests collecting the answers to the first question and discussing the validity of each one with the class. "Then choose one, mentally perform the test for the class, and generate a hypothetical outcome. Examine the 'test data' and pose the second question." As a third step, the class considers the question "What if the outcome of the test had been as follows . . . ?" Students, Pinet says, "should specify the arguments for their assertions."

Professor Pinet observes that "this type of exercise develops critical thinking, while also promoting an attitude of skeptical inquiry. Besides, it's fun!" This pedagogical technique can be used in both introductory and advanced courses of any size.

SAMPLE WRITING ASSIGNMENT
Teaching critical thinking in the discipline
From "Ramblings and Notions about the Teaching of Critical Thinking: Suggestions for Colleagues": Paul R. Pinet

---

Once an interpretation, hypothesis, or speculation is proposed, a useful way of evaluating it critically is to devise a means of testing its validity. For each interpretation, hypothesis, or speculation you propose, ask the following question:

> "What kind of test, experiment, or observation might we make in order to falsify this hypothesis?"

Write out your answer, which we will discuss in class.

Once we have established that your test is valid, ask the second question:

> "Assuming that these are accurate results, what is their significance for the hypothesis?"

critical thinking skills are even more central. While teaching students scholarly approaches to research and writing can help them *act* like academics, and teaching them the writing style of the discipline can make their prose *sound* like that of academics, only through learning critical thinking skills can they actually come to *think* like academics and develop the habits of study that instructors in the discipline expect (often unconsciously).

Expanding the range of the course

Students may, without realizing it, select a particular course because they have some questions or concerns they hope it will address. By the middle of the term, however, they are often able to identify questions and specific areas of interest. Writing assignments can provide them with opportunities for exploring those interests. Some instructors design writing assignments based entirely on the issues students have raised in class discussion, journals, or informal writing. Others give students the option of designing their own writing assignments or even require that they do. Such assignments can expand the range of the course. Students welcome the opportunity to explore areas of personal interest, and they often retain more information from the active learning of self-sponsored research than from data passively received from lectures.

SAMPLE WRITING ASSIGNMENT
Expanding the range of the course
Reproductive Issues: Victoria E. McMillan

PAPER TOPICS
Feel free to choose any topic that relates to the course, including material not specifically covered in the syllabus. Following is a list of suggested topics; these are all very broad, and will need to be narrowed down considerably. You may also think of other topics not on this list.

— Conception/fertilization—some biological aspect (e.g., sex determination; aspects of ovulation; twins, etc.)
— Menstruation—some biological aspect (e.g., synchrony of menstruation among college women; amenorrhea related to athletics or anorexia; dysfunctional menstrual bleeding; toxic shock syndrome, etc.)
— Menopause (e.g., risks of osteoporosis; estrogen replacement therapy; social or psychological aspects)

This assignment allows students to write on almost any topic related to the course, a writing-intensive seminar for first-year students. It would not be possible to cover all of these issues in depth in one semester; but, by offering students the choice of exploring one topic as a research project, Professor McMillan broadens the scope of the course and encourages students to pursue interests that they bring to or develop from the course.

The inclusion of social, cultural, legal,

The inclusion of social, cultural, legal, and historical aspects of some of these topics also encourages the students to perceive the larger social context of biological issues and to get beyond their personal beliefs in their writing.

—Pregnancy (e.g., birth defects related to specific substances, such as thalidomide, nicotine, alcohol; nutritional needs during pregnancy; risks or problems, such as toxemia)

—Childbirth (e.g., causes of the onset of labor; Lamaze or other birthing methods; midwives—legal or historical aspect; cesarean section—surgical methods, advantages and risks, increasing incidence in some hospitals)

—Cancer of the reproductive tract (e.g., risk factors/treatment options for testicular, breast, cervical, ovarian, or uterine cancer)

—Other diseases or disorders of the reproductive tract (e.g., ovarian cysts, fibroid tumors of the uterus, endometriosis, etc.)

—Sexually transmitted diseases (aspects of specific diseases, such as herpes, gonorrhea, syphilis, chlamydia; AIDS — epidemiology, treatment options, ethical or legal aspects, etc.)

—Birth control (e.g., effectiveness/risks of particular contraceptive methods; legal, social, or historical aspects)

—Abortion (e.g., current legal issues; risks of different methods; psychological effects; cross-cultural topics, etc.)

—Infertility in men or women—specific causes/treatments

—New reproductive technologies (e.g., *in vitro* fertilization; sperm banks; surrogate motherhood; prenatal surgery, etc.—some aspect not fully covered in class)

—Maternal or infant mortality issues (e.g., cross-cultural comparisons; options for various health care plans, etc.)

Other assignments might encourage students to apply the knowledge and skills gained in the course to issues of more immediate relevance in their everyday lives. They might, for example, explore the politics of a local issue, analyze the educational policies of their high school, or apply a principle from physics to a design problem. In doing so they will make the material of the course their own and produce more thoughtful papers.

Using writing assignments to monitor the course

Instructors can use writing assignments throughout the course to assess how prepared students are for the material, how they are assimilating the material, and what thought processes they use to complete assignments. One has only to teach a course twice to realize that no two groups of students are alike, and this is perhaps most clearly evidenced in their writing. An assignment that works one year might not work the next, causing frustration for the instructor and unsatisfactory experiences—and grades—for the students. Some instructors use brief writing assignments in the first week of class to help them judge how well students are prepared for the material of

SAMPLE WRITING ASSIGNMENT
Applying course material
Introduction to Quantitative Social Research: Robert Elgie

Surveys represent a data collection procedure particularly well suited to eliciting attitudes, feelings, beliefs, opinions, etc. It is your task to identify a particular domain of attitude, belief, opinion, or feeling whose configuration among Colgate students you believe it would be interesting and important to examine this semester using a survey research design.

This domain should be one:

—for which you expect to find considerable variation among Colgate students.

—for which you might expect such variation to be patterned. By "patterned" I mean that there is the potential to find substantial differences in expressed attitude among identifiable groupings (subpopulations) of Colgate students.

Professor Elgie allows his students to explore some social or cultural aspect of student life on their campus while using the techniques of social research. Leaving the choice of topic entirely open gives students the freedom to apply the techniques of their discipline to something of particular relevance to their everyday lives.

the course and for writing. This information helps them design and adapt subsequent assignments. Instructors need not lower their expectations in response to an unevenly prepared group, but they can be aware of the need to offer more explanation and instruction to some groups than to others or to plan individual meetings with some students and refer others to tutors (see pages 37–39).

Throughout the course, instructors can give brief writing assignments—in class or as homework—to gauge the comprehension of the students and the speed with which they assimilate ideas and adopt new strategies. If a course is still in development, these assignments can alert the instructor to the need to scale down the workload, to spend more time on the readings, or to provide more sophisticated material. Such assignments can vary from reviews of, responses to, or summaries of the course material to more complex comparisons or applications. In a political science or economics course, students might be asked to apply a theory they have learned to a current event; for a math class they might try explaining in writing how to solve an equation; and chemistry students might explain the contents of a household product.

Instructors can also use writing assignments to learn how students think, and this information can help them gauge how to present the course material more effectively and to anticipate challenges and resistances they might meet. Some instructors require that students explain, usually at the end of a paper or report, how they arrived at their conclusions or what the implications of their findings might be. In disciplines where it is inappropriate for students to trace their thought processes, instructors may want to require occasional written responses or discussions in conferences. Some instructors have found E-mail an ideal way to talk with students about writing.

Instructors who modify their courses as a result of what they learn from these assignments demonstrate that they care about the students' learning experiences. However students and instructors communicate about writing, such conversation helps students feel more engaged with and enthusiastic about learning course material.

This brief assignment given to a small class encourages students to apply their classroom knowledge of economics to current events and allows Professor Grapard to gauge how well the students understand the material. The in-class reports help students practice succinct analysis, and the questions and comments help them refine their ideas before they write the paper. This strategy is especially valuable for identifying students who may need help with a writing assignment scheduled to follow the in-class analysis.

SAMPLE WRITING ASSIGNMENT
Monitoring the course through writing assignments
Introduction to Economics: Ulla Grapard

Find an article in Sunday's *New York Times* that interests you and that you can relate to the study of economics. Each of you will choose a different story, and you will be expected to talk about it briefly (five minutes maximum) to the rest of the class. We will also have general class discussion. Consult each other to avoid duplicating stories.

The following questions may help you think about the content of your story and how to write it up and present it to the class.

—What is the main question that this feature story or news story deals with?
—Why is this topic important now?
—What economic aspects are involved?
—Whom is this question important to?
—Why are you interested in this issue?
—Identify at least one question that you feel should be addressed— but was not—in the article.

Multistaged Assignments

Multistaged assignments are especially valuable for students who are writing a research paper for a particular discipline for the first time or are writing an academic essay for the first time. They can be equally valuable for students who have somehow made it through four years of college without learning how to structure an academic paper. Such assignments are literally given in stages, broken up into a series of smaller assignments, each focusing on one aspect of the paper. The first stage might ask students to identify an area or a topic and describe why it interests them. They might be asked to write one or two paragraphs on the topic and then one sentence summing up why they care about it. Next they generate a question or series of questions and integrate these into a general discussion of the topic. The instructor collects that assignment and comments on the choice of topic and suggests where the topic needs more development or focus. Students might then revise their questions and discussion into a working introduction to a research paper. The second stage might require an annotated bibliography on the topic. In the third stage students refine their topic question and the instructor reviews it. In the fourth stage students conduct the research or reading required and organize an outline of the paper. The fifth stage is to write a draft.

Multistaged assignments can help students who are overwhelmed by the process of conducting academic research or doing focused reading on a topic and who might otherwise leave themselves insufficient time to produce acceptable work. (Such assignments also benefit students who use bad papers produced at the last minute as "proof" that they can't write.) Breaking assignments down into manageable stages paces students and helps them develop confidence and skill with all the tasks that go into producing good writing. (Chapter 4 offers suggestions for teaching students to address the component stages of the writing process.) Multistaged writing assignments also allow instructors to spend time in class or in conferences explaining features like thesis, evidence, citation, and counterevidence and to teach students how to use their handbook (see Chapter 3). These discussions may occur in class or in scheduled meetings during office hours. As Muriel Harris explains, one-to-one meetings between instructor and student may be as short as ten minutes yet still be effective if the students know beforehand exactly what they are required to do.

Sequenced Assignments

Sequenced assignments are carefully designed to give students experience in different writing situations with different techniques. Sequenced assignments are of two types, generally called *cognitive* and *situational* (Gene Krupa uses the term "situational writing" while Charles Schuster calls it "situational sequencing").

A situational sequence of assignments asks students to write about a given topic for different audiences, making necessary adjustments in style. They might be asked to imagine themselves as a member of the local community writing to the university president or a student writing to a neighbor; they might write a letter to a politician protesting a local policy, then play the role of the politician's research assistant researching the issue and writing a report, and finally adopt the stance of the politician responding to the letter. Each of these assignments helps students focus on audience and position themselves in various discourse communities.

Situational sequencing is more germane to some disciplines than others and is particularly appropriate in the social sciences. However, a chemistry instructor could ask students to describe a process for a group of visiting middle school students, then describe it again for their instructor, and finally discuss it with a visiting chemistry instructor.

Cognitive sequencing works on the same principle as situational sequencing, but assignments are designed to help students learn various writing skills rather than to focus on audience and task. Cognitively sequenced assignments are given in stages, each focusing on one writing skill and building on the skills used in previous assignments. (Scholars such as William Perry claim that at any moment one can place students on a scale of cognitive development by testing their writing, thinking, and study skills. Cognitive sequencing is designed to help students move up that scale by using previously acquired skills to tackle increasingly complex tasks.)

In a literature course, the first cognitively sequenced assignment might ask students to explicate a text, the second to use their explication as a basis for evaluating another writer's use of metaphors, and the third to discuss the use of metaphors in the work of a group of writers. Such sequencing gives students the opportunity to practice and develop a succession of writing skills.

In composition courses, sequencing often follows a pattern of rhetorical modes developed by Janice Lauer, Janet Emig, Andrea Lunsford, and Gene Montague, who argue that writing skills develop from "private" (expressive) writing, through "public" (descriptive, persuasive, and evaluative) writing, to "college" (research and critique) and "business" (report) writing, and that college composition courses should mirror that pattern. Students might first write a narrative, perhaps the story of how they solved a problem. The second assignment might call for description, perhaps of some aspect of the narrative or of the problem itself. Students then evaluate that description and finally conduct research on the problem or topic—research that provides background information or potential solutions.

Students need to be able to summarize an author's purpose, thesis, evidence, logic, and assumptions before they can analyze the text. By assigning summary writing in the first two weeks of the semester and following it with critique, Professor Rampolla helps her students develop the

SAMPLE WRITING ASSIGNMENT
Sequenced assignments
Racism, Sexism, and Social Darwinism: Mary Lynn Rampolla

FIRST-YEAR SEMINAR 005: FIRST WRITING ASSIGNMENT
Your first writing assignment, due Sept. 15, is to write a summary of "A Shared Cultural Context," on pp. 31–39 of Stephen Jay Gould's *The Mismeasure of Man.* In writing your summary, you should follow the guidelines set forth in the handout "The Summary." You might also find it useful to look at the summary examples found in *The Bedford Handbook for Writers,* sections 48b and 49d.

Along with your finished summary, you should hand in all of your notes and rough drafts.

FSEM 005: SECOND WRITING ASSIGNMENT

Your second writing assignment, due Sept. 29, is to write a critique of Chapter XV (pp. 439–460) of Gobineau's *The Moral and Intellectual Diversity of Races*. Before writing your critique, you should read, carefully, the handout entitled "Critical Reading and Critique," which was given to you in class on Sept. 17. You might also find it useful to look at the section on common mistakes in reasoning in *The Bedford Handbook for Writers*, section 52f.

In writing your critique, make sure that you do the following things:

1. Analyze the author's purpose for writing.
2. Identify the author's thesis and the evidence he adduces to support that thesis.
3. Evaluate (a) the author's use of his evidence and (b) the logic of his argument.
4. Describe how the author deals with opposing viewpoints, or, alternatively, note what issues he overlooks.
5. Identify the assumptions that underlie the argument.

FSEM 005: FINAL WRITING ASSIGNMENTS

Two of the chief purposes of a First-Year Seminar are to increase your competence in writing research papers and improve your ability to use effectively the library for scholarly research. In your first two assignments, you practiced two fundamental skills for academic writing: the summary and the critique. Your remaining writing assignments for this class will all lead toward the production of a 12- to 15-page research paper.

The Topic

The assigned readings for this class focus on the influence that widely held social views about race and gender had on the development and application of scientific thought in the nineteenth century. Most of the texts we will be reading are the products of scholars: naturalists, anthropologists, educators, etc. For your research paper, you will look at the problem from another angle by exploring how, and to what extent, these "scholarly" ideas were popularized. In other words, you will be looking at popular notions of the nineteenth and early twentieth century about race and gender and asking to what extent these popular ideas reflect the "scholarly" views we are studying in class.

There are many ways you can begin to explore this topic, and your first job will be to narrow your focus. Some suggestions for areas to explore include: (1) encyclopedias (look at articles on race; evolution; African, Asian, and Native American people; various ethnic groups; etc. Within this field, you might compare American and

techniques they need for all of the assignments that follow. Her list of essential elements of critique writing ensures that students incorporate their summary skills into the second-stage assignment.

Instructors using in-class workshops (see pages 182–187) could also ask students to summarize and critique one another's drafts using the same criteria that they applied to published texts.

Professor Rampolla's assignments encourage students to seek help and advice in the handbook selected for the course.

English encyclopedias; look at the different editions of the same encyclopedia and see if the ideas change over time; etc.); (2) popular entertainments (look at novels; the operettas of Gilbert and Sullivan, etc.); (3) popular magazines (like *Punch,* in England); or (4) catalogs from exhibitions (like World's Fairs or special Smithsonian exhibits). At this stage, ask the library staff for help: They'll be happy to offer suggestions. You should plan on spending at least a week exploring our library and holdings, narrowing the paper topic to a focus.

After this, you'll be ready to start.

The Writing Assignments

1. Your first assignment will be an annotated bibliography. I'll be giving you a handout explaining bibliographies next week. This assignment will be worth 15% of your final grade. Due Oct. 15.
2. A summary of one of the articles in your bibliography or of a section of one of the books in your bibliography. The text you choose to summarize should be no longer than 10 pages, and you should give a photocopy of it to me, along with your summary. This assignment will be worth 15% of your grade. Due Oct. 20.
3. A critique of an article or book in your bibliography. Once again, you should either photocopy the article you are critiquing or loan me the book. Due Nov. 3, worth 15%.
4. Your prewriting for your paper, worth 5% (we'll be talking about prewriting in class). Due Nov. 12.
5. Your thesis, worth 5%, due Nov. 19 (we'll also be talking about theses in class).
6. Your masterpiece: 12–15 pages, typed, double-spaced, worth 25%, and due on Dec. 3.

Any part of this assignment may be rewritten, and I would be delighted to look at rough drafts, or talk about your project, at any stage of its development. Please feel free to drop in or make an appointment.

Checklist for designing writing assignments

INTEGRATING THE ASSIGNMENT INTO THE COURSE

_____ Connect the assignment to the course content.

_____ Determine the pedagogical purpose of the assignment.

_____ Use the assignment to monitor students' progress in and understanding of the course.

WORDING THE ASSIGNMENT

_____ State the purpose of the assignment.

_____ Suggest strategies for responding.

_____ Design the assignment to allow for more than one "right" answer.

USING THE ASSIGNMENT FOR A VARIETY OF PURPOSES

_____ Design the assignment to help students comprehend and synthesize course materials.

_____ Use the assignment to stimulate critical thinking.

_____ Use the assignment to introduce discipline-specific writing conventions.

_____ Use the assignment to facilitate communication between student and instructor.

_____ Use the assignment to expand the range of the course.

_____ Offer students choices of topic and approaches.

ATTENDING TO THE MECHANICS

_____ Hand out printed copies of the assignment.

_____ Offer sufficient but succinct explanation.

_____ Give students sufficient time to consider the assignment, write, and revise.

_____ Communicate your expectations for students' responses and your grading criteria.

For Further Reading

Bartholomae, David. "Inventing the University." *When a Writer Can't Write.* Ed. Mike Rose. New York: Guilford, 1985. 134–65.

Bazerman, Charles. *Shaping Written Knowledge: Genre and Activity of the Experimental Article in Science.* Madison: U of Wisconsin P, 1988.

Bean, John C., Dean Drenk, and F. D. Lee. "Microtheme Strategies for Developing Cognitive Skills." *Teaching Writing in All Disciplines.* Ed. C. Williams Griffin. New Directions for Teaching and Learning 12. San Francisco: Jossey-Bass, 1982. 59–66.

Becker, Howard. *Writing for Social Scientists.* Chicago: U of Chicago P, 1986.

Bogel, Frederic V., and Katherine K. Gottschalk. *Teaching Prose: A Guide for Writing Instructors.* New York: Norton, 1984. Especially useful are "Classroom Activities" (46–85) and "Designing Essay Assignments" (87–113).

Carter, Michael. "Problem Solving Reconsidered: A Pluralistic Theory of Problems." *College English* 50 (1988): 551–65.

Cox, Gerald H. "Designing Essay Assignments." *Teaching Prose: A Guide for Writing Instructors.* Ed. Frederic V. Bogel and Katherine K. Gottschalk. New York: Norton, 1984. 87–113.

Drenk, Dean. "Teaching Finance through Writing." *Teaching Writing in All Disciplines.* Ed. C. Williams Griffin. New Directions for Teaching and Learning 12. San Francisco: Jossey-Bass, 1982. 53–58.

Elbow, Peter. "Reflections on Academic Discourse: How It Relates to Freshmen and Colleagues." *College English* 54 (1991): 135-55.

Flower, Linda. "The Construction of Purpose in Writing and Reading." *College English* 50 (1988): 528–50.

Flower, Linda, and John R. Hayes. "The Cognition of Discovery: Defining a Rhetorical Problem." *College Composition and Communication* 31 (1980): 21–32. The authors compare the processes adopted by students engaged in problem solving, drawing conclusions about the cognitive process.

Freire, Paulo. *Pedagogy of the Oppressed.* Trans. Myra Ramos. New York: Seabury, 1968. Freire explains how literacy empowers students, making them free. Based on his adult literacy work in Brazil, Freire's approach is a learner-focused pedagogy in which students begin by "naming [their] world" and addressing their own concerns in writing.

Fulwiler, Toby. "Writing: An Act of Cognition." *Teaching Writing in All Disciplines.* Ed. C. Williams Griffin. New Directions for Teaching and Learning 12. San Francisco: Jossey-Bass, 1982. 15–26. Fulwiler explains how students learn through writing.

Geertz, Clifford. *Works and Lives: The Anthropologist as Author.* Palo Alto: Stanford UP, 1988.

Gottschalk, Katherine K. "Classroom Activities." *Teaching Prose: A Guide for Writing Instructors.* Ed. Frederic V. Bogel and Katherine K. Gottschalk. New York: Norton, 1984. 46–85.

Griffin, C. Williams, ed. *Teaching Writing in All Disciplines.* New Directions for Teaching and Learning 12. San Francisco: Jossey-Bass, 1982.

Harris, Muriel. *Teaching One-to-One: The Writing Conference.* Urbana: NCTE, 1986. This book contains thorough discussion of the use of individual conferencing in the teaching of writing, including a helpful section on considering the influence of cultural differences in the writing process, second language interference in writing, and learning disorders (87–101).

Harris, R. Allen. "Rhetoric of Science." *College English* 53 (1991): 282–307.

Heath, Shirley Brice. "An Annotated Bibliography on Multicultural Writing and Literacy Issues." *Quarterly of the National Writing Project and the Center for the Study of Writing and Literacy* 12.1 (1990): 22–24. Heath annotates sixteen books and articles on multicultural and bilingual literacy and includes a discussion of writing instruction and assignment design.

Herrington, Anne. "Basic Writing: Moving the Voices from Margin to Center." *Harvard Education Review* 60.4 (1990): 489–96. Herrington describes redesigning a class to include the voices of marginalized students and discusses writing assignments and written responses to readings. Although Herrington's discussion focuses on a composition course, the strategies she suggests and reasons she gives for them are relevant across the disciplines.

Herndl, Carl G. "Writing Ethnography: Representation, Rhetoric, and Institutional Practices." *College English* 53 (1991): 320–32.

King, Barbara. "Using Writing in the Mathematics Class: Theory and Practice." *Teaching Writing in All Disciplines.* Ed. C. Williams Griffin. New Directions for Teaching and Learning 12. San Francisco: Jossey-Bass, 1982. 39–44.

Kiniry, Malcolm, and Ellen Strenski. "Sequencing Expository Writing: A Recursive Approach." *College Composition and Communication* 36 (1985): 191–202.

Krupa, Gene H. *Situational Writing.* Belmont, CA: Wadsworth, 1982.

Lindemann, Erika. "Making and Evaluating Writing Assignments." *A Rhetoric for Writing Teachers.* 2nd ed. New York: Oxford UP, 1987.

Lunsford, Andrea. "Cognitive Development and the Basic Writer." *College English* 41 (1979): 39–46. Lunsford proposes writing assignments to help students develop and practice more complex cognitive skills. Her discussion focuses on students she identifies as operating below the concept-forming level and thus unable to "decenter." She provides a good summary of theories of cognitive development.

Lynn, Steven. "A Passage into Critical Theory." *Background Readings for Instructors Using* The Bedford Handbook for Writers. 2d ed. Ed. Glenn Blalock. Boston: Bedford, 1994.

MacDonald, Susan Peck. "Problem Definition in Academic Writing." *College English* 49 (1987): 315–30.

McKeachie, Wilbert J. *Teaching Tips: A Guidebook for the Beginning College Teacher.* 8th ed. Lexington, MA: Heath, 1986.

Maimon, Elaine P., Barbara F. Nodine, and Finbarr W. O'Connor, eds. *Thinking, Reasoning, Writing.* New York: Longman, 1989.

Myers, Greg. *Writing Biology.* Madison: U of Wisconsin P, 1990.

Perry, William. "Cognitive and Ethical Growth: The Making of Meaning." *The Modern American College: Responding to the New Realities of Diverse Students.* Ed. Arthur Chickering. San Francisco: Jossey-Bass, 1981. 76–116. Analyzing a study of Harvard students, Perry argues that students begin the college process as "dualists" who believe in and search for objectively determined right and wrong answers.

Pinet, Paul Raymond. "Understanding the Language of Argument and the Methods of Science." *Journal of Geological Education* 37 (1989): 197–201. Pinet includes sample "probing questions" to develop critical reading skills and suggestions for teachers: developing exercises, problem sets, exam questions, and essay assignments. He also discusses journal-keeping and organizing class debates.

Schneiderman, Beth Kline. "Designing a New Writing Assignment for a Literature Course." *Teaching English in the Two Year College* 19 (Oct. 1992): 210–14.

Schuster, Charles. "Situational Sequencing." *The Writing Instructor* 3 (Summer 1984): 177–84.

Spellmeyer, Kurt. "A Common Ground: The Essay in the Academy." *College English* 51 (1989): 262–67.

Spivey, Nancy Nelson. "The Shaping of Meaning: Options in Writing the Comparison." *Research in the Teaching of English* 25 (Dec. 1991): 390–418.

Stotsky, Sandra. "On Learning to Write about Ideas." *College Composition and Communication* 37 (1986): 276–93.

———. "Types of Lexical Cohesion in Expository Writing: Implications for Developing the Vocabulary of Academic Discourse." *College Composition and Communication* 34 (1983): 430–40.

Walvoord, Barbara E. *Helping Students Write Well: A Guide for Teachers in All Disciplines.* 2d ed. New York: MLA, 1986.

White, Edward M. *Assigning, Responding, Evaluating: A Writing Teacher's Guide.* New York: St. Martin's, 1991.

Williams, James. "Preparing to Teach Writing." *Background Readings for Instructors Using* The Bedford Handbook for Writers. 2d ed. Ed. Glenn Blalock. Boston: Bedford, 1991. 191-96.

Young, R. E., Alton Becker, and K. Pike. *Rhetoric: Discovery and Change.* New York: Harcourt, 1970.

CHAPTER 7

Assigning Research Papers Using Laboratory, Field, and Library Data

---

In this chapter:

- ❏ Helping students make the transition to college-level research,
- ❏ Assigning annotated bibliographies
- ❏ Assigning reviews of the literature
- ❏ Assigning research proposals
- ❏ Assigning library research papers
- ❏ Assigning laboratory and field notebooks
- ❏ Assigning laboratory and field reports
- ❏ Assigning policy analysis
- ❏ Checklist for assigning research papers
- ❏ For further reading

Helping Students Make the Transition to College-Level Research

Most students arrive in their college classes believing that they know exactly what is required in a research assignment and confident that they can carry one out to the satisfaction of their instructors. Most are wrong. The differences between what is termed the "research paper" in high school and what college instructors mean by the term can lead to frustration and confusion for both students and instructors. Therefore, before assigning any type of college research, many teachers of writing in the disciplines assess their students' assumptions and expectations. Many find even juniors and seniors mystified at having received inexplicably low grades for college research papers that they believed they wrote well.

Keith Hjortshoj, who teaches writing at Cornell University, describes the typical high school research project:

> Choose a topic; go to the library and get lots of information from sources; write all that down on notecards; sort that information into topical paragraphs; add a perfunctory introduction to the beginning and a perfunctory conclusion to the end. It's a sort of research-facilitated memory dump. (Personal communication, 3 Nov. 1993.)

Such research projects serve a function in high school: They introduce students to a range of resources; they teach elementary library research; and they raise the possibility that there is more than one answer to any given question. But college instructors, especially of first-year students, will find that they have to disabuse their students of their high school–based preconceptions about research assignments.

College assignments require students to make a transition from regurgitation of accepted "truth" to active exploration and refutation of ideas, a transition that can be quite overwhelming. The notion that research requires students to assume authority over their material and assert a position about it is new to most of them. Also new to most students is the notion that they are writing for other members of the discipline—not primarily for the instructor.

Many instructors of writing in the disciplines find it helpful to explain the purpose of academic work in that discipline as a means of helping students see themselves as fledgling members of the discipline. College research writing must of necessity take a disciplinary genres focus because it has a different form in each discipline and is at the heart of most disciplines. Instructors can help students understand the role of research by explaining that in college their task is to write for other academics about topics that can be interpreted or explored in a variety of ways. Explaining that forms such as laboratory research, fieldwork, and library research follow different conventions and are addressed to different audiences can help students comprehend disciplinary differences as well as the intricacies of research and research writing.

Even if students understand how college research papers differ in purpose and audience from high school research papers, they still may be reluctant to abandon old methods of collecting and reporting information. Therefore, it is important that instructors design research assignments that require students to develop the habits of research, interpretation, and reportage expected in a particular discipline or the academy in general. For example, assigning and providing thorough guidance for laboratory notebooks will help students prepare for the final report by making them attend to detail as well as sift through and interpret information. The field notebook can serve a similar role in some social science research. Neither type of notebook, however, overcomes all misconceptions about research; thus, it can be helpful to uncover such misconceptions by asking students what they think they are required to do while researching. In the humanities, this question could be addressed in students' research journals or dialectical notebooks (see pages 196–197) as they record their reactions, thinking processes, and any connections they make while conducting research.

Instructors can also help students make the transition to college-level research by giving them a new way to think of library sources. In high school, many students rely on encyclopedias and articles from popular magazines while doing research. College students, however, must understand that, though encyclopedias and popular magazines can help them begin to understand less accessible research in the field, such sources often merely summarize and oversimplify original research. Further, instead of looking up to such sources, students should see themselves in dialogue with the sources to interpret and explain original research. And as students become even more skilled and confident with research, they should see themselves as more sophisticated than the encyclopedias and magazines they once relied on. Eventually, they will be capable of entering into dialogue with the research itself. Writing annotated bibliographies, reviews of the literature, and research proposals can help students develop more sophisticated attitudes and approaches to sources.

Assigning Annotated Bibliographies

The annotated bibliography is a widely applicable academic writing assignment. In a write-to-learn course, instructors use annotated bibliographies to encourage students to practice and perfect their reading and library research skills. Such an assignment can be followed by a research paper in which the students select five to ten of the sources in support of a thesis. As a discrete assignment unconnected to a larger paper, compiling a bibliography leads students to focus only on the research element and teaches them how to conduct exhaustive searches and engage texts. Following the citation rules of the discipline while compiling the entries, students learn discipline-specific conventions. Equally important is their need to write comprehensibly yet succinctly.

This assignment requires students to find ten sources on a person of their choice and write an annotated bibliography. Answering the questions posed in the assignment forces students to pay attention to relevant issues as they conduct their research. Requiring that the annotations serve a larger purpose than simply summarizing thesis and content helps students perceive the purpose of academic research.

SAMPLE ASSIGNMENT (EXCERPT)
Writing an annotated bibliography
Ethnicity and Identity in the U.S.: Sandra Jamieson

When reviewing a source, consider the following questions about the person you are researching:

1. When was he/she alive?
2. What role did he/she play in American history?
3. What role did he/she play in world history?
4. What connections did he/she have to other people/events?
5. How did contemporaries view him/her?
6. How do scholars evaluate his/her role?
7. How does the author of this text view your subject?
8. What contradictions do you notice between your sources? How do you explain them?
9. What biases do you see in the texts you read?

Your annotations as a whole should provide the answers to 1, 2, and 3. A good biographical bibliography also answers 4–9. You will have to be selective in the material you choose to annotate.

You should consult texts from as many disciplines as possible, and consider the author's discipline as you write entries. For example:

> This historian traces the role of X in the history of the emancipation movement, describing his appearance at anti-slavery meetings and his correspondence with other activists. She also discusses the various reactions to his speeches and articles and compares public reaction to X and Y. She seems to consider X more important than Y because he was a better speaker and more sociable at large gatherings. (She suggests that Y was shy, but X enjoyed the attention.)

State the author's thesis (in articles it is generally in the abstract and/or the introduction; in books it is often in the preface or at the beginning of the introduction).

When you find a book with only one or two pages on your topic, cite it, list those pages at the end of the citation (see your handbook for instructions), and then discuss those pages in the annotation.

Annotated bibliographies assigned in intermediate and upper-level courses can be used as a form of or prelude to a review of the literature. Highly focused annotations (emphasizing one aspect of the text, like the assignment by Moran in the next section) can also help students determine the scope of a potential research topic and plan their research prior to writing a research paper.

Assigning Reviews of the Literature

A review of the literature can take the form of a complete paper or of one stage of a longer paper. Although format and style vary from one discipline to another, the purpose and method remain the same, making literature reviews an excellent means for teaching both discipline-specific conventions and general academic writing skills and strategies.

In introductory courses in which students are still learning how to write literature reviews, some instructors assign a list of texts for review, choosing books or articles that they themselves have already read. They can then evaluate the content of the review in addition to the form. Peer review groups allow students to compare responses

SAMPLE GUIDELINES
Writing a review of the literature (anthropology)
Women, Work, and Family: Mary Moran

GUIDELINES FOR CRITICAL BOOK REVIEWS
A critical book *review* is NOT a book *report.* That is, it does not simply summarize the contents of a book to "prove" that you have read it. Rather, a successful book review should contain the following:

1. A *brief* summary of the *argument.* This should be accomplished in *no more than a page,* preferably a few paragraphs. Note that you are not asked to summarize the *book* here but the *argument.* What does the author want you to *believe* when you finish reading her/his book?
2. Locate this particular work in the context of our course reading. Does the book belong to a particular school of thought or movement within the ongoing debates we have been covering? How is it similar to/different from what we have been reading in class?
3. *Evaluate* both the *argument* and the *contribution* of the book to the field of research on gender, work, and the family.
   a. Does the argument convince you that the author's perspective is valid? *Why* or *why not?* Are there serious and obvious flaws in the way the data was collected, organized, interpreted, and presented? What biases, subtle or otherwise, are evident in the author's analysis? This is where you can really "take the book apart."
   b. Does this book advance our understanding of the relationship between gender, households, and the economy? Is it a contribution to the knowledge, or does it "do more harm than good"? *Why?*

This assignment leaves no doubt about what is expected. Professor Moran establishes a step-by-step procedure for the students to follow as they review literature within the context of the course. This teaches students how to approach texts from within a specific framework for a specific audience rather than trying to discuss them from all possible positions for all readers.

and explore alternatives (see pages 184–189). Providing a handout explaining exactly what is expected from a review can give students a firm basis for this assignment and future research assignments.

By listing several different formats and then emphasizing that each must contain the same sections and satisfy the same requirements, Professor McMillan helps her students understand that content is the most important feature of the literature review, regardless of discipline.

She uses organizational terms (introduction, body, etc.) that students will recognize from other types of writing. The acknowledgments section reminds students that their peers are also fledgling members of the academic community whose opinions, ideas, and advice are significant.

SAMPLE GUIDELINES
Writing a review of the literature (biology)
Reproductive Issues: Victoria E. McMillan

FORMAT FOR PAPERS

Both papers #1 and #2 should be review papers in conventional scientific style and format. Each paper may take one of the following general formats:

1. State-of-the-art review
2. Historical review
3. Comparison-of-perspectives review
4. Synthesis-of-two-fields review
5. Theory or model-building review

Whatever your aims and approach, your review should include the following:

ABSTRACT (briefly summarizes major points covered in paper).
INTRODUCTION (gives brief background material to orient reader; frames the issue/topic to be discussed; states clear thesis/ aims and scope of paper).
BODY (provides concise, critical review of pertinent literature, with extensive documentation of sources; not labeled as a section, but may use subheadings for easier organization. May also contain figures and/or tables).
CONCLUSIONS (gives brief summary, as needed, but mainly provides insights, discusses significance of selected studies or issues; suggests new perspectives or directions for research; assesses impact of current knowledge on society, etc.).
ACKNOWLEDGMENTS (gives credit to others—for example, your classmates—for help with preparation of paper).
LITERATURE CITED (lists complete bibliographic information for all references cited in paper, presented in conventional scientific format).

Assigning Research Proposals

Establishing criteria

The phrase *research proposal* means something slightly different in different disciplines, demanding different frameworks, analyses, writing styles, language, and methodology. Students who have written research proposals for a biology class may have no idea how to write them for a sociology class, so criteria must be established at the outset of such an assignment. Instructors whose goal is to teach some elements of discipline-specific discourse generally explain the purpose of the research proposal in the context of the discipline while teaching students how to write one.

SAMPLE ASSIGNMENT (EXCERPT A)
Establishing criteria for a research proposal
Introduction to Quantitative Social Research: Robert Elgie

ASSIGNMENT 5: SURVEY RESEARCH PROBLEM STATEMENT
Surveys represent a data collection procedure particularly well suited to eliciting attitudes, feelings, beliefs, opinions, etc. It is your task to identify a particular domain of attitude, belief, opinion, or feeling whose configuration among Colgate students you believe it would be interesting and important to examine this semester using a survey research design.

This domain should be one:

—for which you expect to find considerable *variation* among Colgate students.

—for which you might expect such variation to be *patterned*. By "patterned" I mean that there is the potential to find substantial differences in expressed attitude among identifiable groupings (subpopulations) of Colgate students.

Please do not feel that the attitudes to be examined need to be about Colgate-specific phenomena or issues. In fact, in some ways I would prefer that the topic have a broader scope.

Students work hardest and most enthusiastically on projects they are interested in and feel to be personally relevant; therefore, when teaching a new skill, many instructors assign a general topic and allow students to select their own area of interest, as this assignment does.

By limiting the scope of the project, Professor Elgie gives his students easy access to a large pool of data (students on their campus) without the additional effort involved in approaching subjects in an external community.

Explaining methodology

Once the criteria are established, students need to know how to design their proposal. Since structure, format, and procedure vary among disciplines, students are well served by careful explanations. Handouts explaining the procedure are more helpful than lectures or notes written on the board. They are even more beneficial when accompanied by or referring to samples. In addition, discipline-specific handbooks contain helpful suggestions for students and include sample proposals and papers. (See pages 41–43.)

Many teachers of writing in the disciplines find that producing a research proposal for library research helps students focus their topic and anticipate problems they might encounter in finding sources. Asking very basic questions like "What do you propose to explore?"

In this continuation of his assignment, Professor Elgie carefully establishes the step-by-step procedure that students must follow. By then summarizing the goal of a research proposal, he provides a means for evaluating the whole process and the final draft of the resulting research paper.

Providing examples of "comprehensive, well organized and clearly written" proposals from previous semesters gives the students models to imitate and a clear idea of what is required.

SAMPLE ASSIGNMENT (EXCERPT B)
Explaining methodology for a research proposal
Introduction to Quantitative Social Research: Robert Elgie

ASSIGNMENT 5: SURVEY RESEARCH PROBLEM STATEMENT

Having settled on an appropriate attitude domain, prepare a 4–6-page *proposal* for analysis of it. In this proposal:

—Carefully describe the attitude domain to be explored. What facets of it are you particularly interested in?
—Provide a rationale for selecting this topic and focus. What makes it especially interesting and worthwhile?
—Develop some hypothesis that you believe would help us to predict the position of individual students with respect to the attitudes to be investigated.
—Embed this hypothesis in a simplified model that you believe could help explain the patterning of the domain of attitudes being examined.
—Include a flow chart representation of that model.

If you are at all uncertain as to how to write up this proposal, remember this: to the degree that you do this well, you will have written a good problem statement and theory section for a research paper on this topic and made it reasonably easy to identify what data needs to be gathered in a survey instrument to study the attitudes you are interested in and test the hypothesis you have proposed. You should aim to make your proposal at least as comprehensive, well organized, and clearly written as the examples you have seen from previous semesters.

"Why do you propose to explore this?" "How will you conduct this research?" and "What will be the value of your findings?" encourages students to consider their topic, methodology, and purpose in depth.

The background section of this research proposal assignment can help students focus their research by considering why the topic interests them and what they already know about it. Professor Jamieson says that she returns to this section when students seem to

SAMPLE ASSIGNMENT (EXCERPT)
Organizing a research proposal
English I: Sandra Jamieson

As we discussed in class, your one-page research proposal should be organized as follows:

1. *Statement of Purpose:* Explain briefly what you hope your research will find or show. State this as a question before you begin your research. After your research you should be able to answer this question in one sentence.

2. *Background:* Explain your interest in and experience with this topic. Include previous research you have conducted on the topic and your reason for being interested in it.
3. *Description:* Describe the kind of research you will conduct—in this case, library research.
4. *Methodology:* Explain how you will conduct the research and how many sources you will use. At least two must be journals and at least two, books.
5. *Significance:* Explain why this topic is worth considering, or this question worth answering; why I should let you select this topic; and what will be learned from it. This is the old "So what?" question again.
6. *Problems:* Describe the problems you expect to encounter and how you will solve them. For example, texts might be unavailable. Your solution will be to visit other libraries or use the ILL service.
7. *Works cited:* List the books you will consider as you draw up your short list—30 is a good number. You can use the list generated by the library computer.

be losing direction or are unsure how to focus their work.

Section 5 also helps them find a focus or research question because it forces them to think of their work as part of a continuing academic endeavor with a larger purpose and wider audience than they might otherwise have considered.

Assigning Library Research Papers

Preconceptions about the research paper

Many students who believe they know how to "do library research" do not. Before assigning a major library research paper, it is therefore helpful to arrange a library tour; to invite a librarian to come to class and provide a brief "refresher"; or to introduce students to major indexes and sources used in the discipline. Many students consider the encyclopedia an appropriate source for a major research paper, so instructors might point out that encyclopedias can be used as a starting point to suggest connections that can then be explored in books and journals. Some students must also be disabused of the notion that newsmagazines such as *Time* and *Newsweek* are standard secondary sources. And many need to have the terms *primary* and *secondary* sources defined for the discipline. A nineteenth-century dictionary can be considered a primary text in a history or cultural criticism course, while its modern counterpart is a secondary source.

Most handbooks and research guides include a section on conducting library research, including advice on taking notes and avoiding plagiarism, but it is beneficial to go over such issues in class so that questions can be raised and answered. A sample research paper, either from the handbook or from a student in a previous course, can provide a model for organization, methodology, and style. Many of the strategies discussed in Chapter 4 are especially applicable to research papers.

Loosely defined research topics

In certain courses, especially those emphasizing general writing skills, it is often appropriate to provide students with a general subject area, or general instructions, and then have the students choose and narrow a topic. Instructors need to consider the pros and cons of this approach. When students are given a general subject, they may spend considerable time deciding on a specific topic. In the process they hone their narrowing and focusing skills; however, they do this at the expense of time spent in actual research. In introductory courses this distribution of time is often appropriate because research time will be at a minimum as students will be expected to use a limited number of sources. Loosely defined topics may also be appropriate for intermediate and upper-level courses, for students in those courses generally have some idea of topics they want to pursue, or they prefer the freedom to select their own, even considering the additional time it takes.

This topic was for an upper-level theory course in which students had read texts representing theoretical positions from a wide range of disciplines. Most students had already formulated strong opinions and welcomed this opportunity to pursue them further.

Notice that although this is a loosely defined topic, Professor Jamieson did provide specific criteria for length, number of sources, and documentation style. She also reminded students of the due date and grade value of the paper.

SAMPLE ASSIGNMENT
Loosely defined research paper
Language and Gender: Sandra Jamieson

Your final assignment is to write a research paper in which you explore a question raised by our readings and discussions this semester.

In order to do this effectively, consider the question, read what at least five theorists have said on the subject, and formulate a thesis that either answers the question or posits that the question is impossible to answer because . . .

The paper should be between 10 and 20 pages long, and may follow either the MLA or the APA format. It is due on Friday, May 6, and represents 70% of your grade for the course.

Many instructors, especially of introductory courses, also require research proposals for papers based on loosely defined topics so that they can determine whether the specific topics students choose are appropriate and reasonably focused.

Tightly defined research topics

Tightly defined research topics tend to be most appropriate in disciplinary courses, in which research assignments are intended to get students to investigate sources and use their findings to support a thesis rather than to learn to select and focus topics.

SAMPLE ASSIGNMENT
Tightly defined research paper
Language and Gender: Sandra Jamieson

---

1. Select a sociolinguistic study of language acquisition (it may be one we have discussed in class, one referenced in one of the essays we have read, or one you find through library research). Find all of the reviews of it that you can, and, if possible, a similar study or duplication of that one. Finally, consider how a theorist from one of the other theoretical frameworks we have explored might interpret these findings.
2. Write a 5-to-10-page analysis of the study using all the information you have gathered. Try to find the unspoken theories and assumptions driving the research and influencing the interpretation of them, and discuss their impact.

For this first writing assignment, Professor Jamieson decided to offer very specific instructions despite the fact that this was an upper-level course. The material was new to students, and its implications challenging, so they needed more guidance for their analysis.

Although the process for completing the assignment was clearly defined, students were free to choose a study whose subject or methodology interested them, or whose tone or assumptions they challenged. In that way they claimed ownership of the project while still meeting the assignment's requirements.

In-class drafting

An effective way to help students focus their research is to ask them to write an in-class draft of the paper without the benefit of notes. This is a variation of the more familiar approach in which students conduct their research, formulate a thesis, and then make an oral presentation to the class. Their peers, often joined by the instructor, orally critique the student's presentation, asking questions and offering suggestions for development. The oral report obviously serves many pedagogical purposes, but some material, as well as responses and suggestions, is inevitably lost. For the in-class draft, in contrast, students conduct their research, determine a thesis, and fully acquaint themselves with the material as they would for an oral presentation. But instead they write a spontaneous draft of the paper during one class period. The activity has many of the advantages of freewriting and it serves many of the same prewriting functions (see pages 48–52).

Writing a draft without benefit of notes compels students to understand and synthesize their material, to formulate an argument about it, and to discuss it knowledgeably without lengthy quotations and paraphrases. The instructor responds to the in-class draft, usually counting it as a portion of the grade for the research paper. It then serves as a first draft. Instructors who use this approach find that students produce a clearer, more focused argument unburdened by a pastiche of quotations and also see a reduction in "patchwriting," which is commonly considered a form of plagiarism. (See pages 217–221.)

This handout has been adopted in all levels of courses in a variety of disciplines. Professor Howard observes elsewhere in her handout, "One of the advantages of writing the first draft without sources [is that] it forces you to a more complete understanding of your sources and your thesis" and thus more closely approximates real research in the academy. Requiring that students read their researched material carefully enough to write the in-class draft makes them conversant with the sources and helps them avoid simply repeating data and quotations.

SAMPLE GUIDELINES (EXCERPT)
In-class draft of a research paper
From "Writing the In-Class Draft of the Research Paper": Rebecca Moore Howard

THE PROCESS
This is the task given you: you are engaging in a research paper assignment that requires you to go through a series of steps designed to bring you to your own idea, a logical idea founded on sound evidence (your sources) and presented convincingly. Among the early steps were examination of sources, which produced your idea (your thesis statement) and your evidence (your sources, listed in a preliminary bibliography). Now you will take another crucial step: using your own words, you will identify and discuss your idea—your thesis—and explain how your sources have led you to believe this thesis.

This step will be undertaken during class. You will have your thesis statement and preliminary bibliography available to you, but you will have neither the sources themselves nor any notes. Careful reading of your sources is therefore an essential preparation for this exercise, or else you will have little to say.

Outlines and revision

Assigning at least two drafts of research papers avoids many pitfalls. Some instructors find assigning a formal outline of the paper after the first full draft (or the second if the students have written an in-class draft) an effective way of teaching students to evaluate their argument and structure. Students write an outline of the paper, listing the thesis and the topic of each paragraph and its evidence, and then analyze the outline to ensure that it reveals a coherent argument with sufficient evidence. (See pages 66–67 on outlining as a revision strategy.)

Citation and documentation

Perhaps the most obvious discipline-specific element of the research paper is the method for citing and documenting sources. Comprehensive handbooks usually explain the MLA and APA styles, and discipline-specific handbooks generally describe the systems favored in particular disciplines. Many instructors also find it helpful to provide a handout for students outlining the preferred citation method.

Instructors sometimes find that students believe that the only thing that matters is "consistency," which generally means that the writer makes up his or her own system and then adheres to it. It may be necessary, therefore, to explain not only the *what* but also the *why* of documentation. It is often helpful to explain that documentation is part of the dialect of the community constituted by the discipline. If one expects to get along in a community, one must learn and use its language, not only for clear communication but also as a sign of respect. That explanation answers another concern that arises from time to time in teaching documentation: "What's so great about this system?" It also addresses the concerns of students who have already become familiar with one system of documentation and wonder why the instructor insists that they use another.

SAMPLE GUIDELINES (EXCERPT)
Documenting sources
"Writing a Research Paper in the Social Sciences: Some Suggestions":
Mary Moran

REFERENCING: THE AAA STYLE
The documentation style you may be most familiar with places references either in footnotes at the bottom of the page or endnotes at the end of the paper, signaled by numerical superscripts within the body of the text. The style I would prefer you to use is that of the AAA (American Anthropological Association). . . . In this style, references are placed within the body of the text, in parentheses at the end of the sentence in which the reference occurs. For example, . . .

Instead of a "Bibliography," a paper using AAA form ends with a page entitled "References Cited." As in a bibliography, all entries are to be arranged in alphabetical order and should contain. . . . The idea is to make it as easy as possible for the reader to return to the exact sources you used to collect your evidence. To this end, "References Cited" contains *only* those sources mentioned in the body of your paper. If you read a book and didn't use it, *don't* include it in "References Cited"! The format for arranging entries is as follows: . . .

Beginning with a description of the style most students learn in high school allows Professor Moran to highlight where the AAA method differs. (In fact, the MLA style has also favored in-text citations since the early 1980s, but the old method is still often taught in high schools.)

Explaining why students must make their reference section easy to follow reminds them that their purpose is not to show what they have read but to join in a discussion with other academics who might be interested in reading their sources, too.

In the course syllabus Professor Hodges specifies the documentation style to be used in the research paper and guides students to two readily available sources.

SAMPLE SYLLABUS GUIDELINES (EXCERPT)
Documenting sources
The Nation on Trial, 1787–1861: Graham Hodges

As the major portion of the grade, you will research and write a 10–15-page, typewritten paper to be handed in on the last day of class. Use the footnote style in the 14th edition of the *Chicago Manual of Style.* This may be found in abbreviated form in Kate Turabian, *A Manual for Writers of Term Papers, Theses, and Dissertations.*

Assigning Laboratory and Field Notebooks

Purpose

Careless note taking or poor writing can seriously reduce the usefulness of laboratory and field notebooks and thus the quality of formal written reports based on the notebooks. A written description of why it is important to keep a notebook followed by a description of how to do so helps students understand and succeed at their task.

These guidelines are both detailed and carefully explained, succinctly conveying both the *why* and the *how* of keeping a laboratory notebook. Although the instructions were written for an organic chemistry course, similar explanation of the role of the notebook in scientific research and the importance of accuracy would help students in other science courses understand fully why they are required to keep a notebook and the serious consequences of carelessness.

SAMPLE GUIDELINES (EXCERPT)
The purpose of keeping a laboratory notebook
Organic Chemistry: John Cochran and Patricia Jue

There are two purposes for keeping a laboratory notebook in research. Usually it is necessary to repeat a given preparation or procedure and the notebook serves not only as a guide to repeating the previous experiment, but also, by virtue of being a record of what you observed during the process, may suggest to you ways in which the procedure can be improved. Ultimately the results of successful research are usually published and the notebook is the basis for your claim to have achieved some specific goal. In case of dispute it is common to require the notebook to be produced in court to establish the authenticity of your claim. Naturally, the laboratory work this year is not likely to lead to such results, but you should learn to keep your notes in such a way that you will be prepared to do original research and record it properly should the occasion arise.

The basic idea of the notebook is that all the relevant data and observations must be entered when they are made and then never altered. Clearly, if the notebook entries have been changed or added to at a later date, the record is worthless as evidence of what you did and when you did it. With this purpose in mind, the following specific procedures describe sound practice. For detail, you may wish to consult *Writing the Laboratory Notebook* by Howard Kanare published by the American Chemistry Society.

Records should be kept in ink (pencil, felt-tip, or erasable ink is NOT acceptable) in a notebook with numbered pages. Black or blue ink is preferred. In research, loose-leaf notebooks are not acceptable and we discourage their use. The type of notebook with duplicating pages available on campus is satisfactory. *The notebook should contain only material related to the chemistry laboratory.* Class notes pertaining to the lab procedures are allowed.

Data and observations must be recorded directly in the notebook when they are made, not transferred from some other scrap of paper. In some cases a tabular arrangement is most convenient.

In addition to explaining how and why to use laboratory and field notebooks, instructors must explain how the notes will be used as the basis for a research report.

SAMPLE GUIDELINES (EXCERPT)
Defining the laboratory notebook
Organic Chemistry: John Cochran and Patricia Jue

While the laboratory notebook is meant to be a DETAILED record of your experimental procedure, observations, data, and results, the formal laboratory report should be a CONCISE summary of the experiment. Since the notebook reminds you of how you performed the experiment and guides fellow experimenters who wish to repeat (and perhaps improve) your work, the entries emphasize the procedure used and the observations/data obtained. On the other hand, since reports are meant to convey your findings to the public, emphasis is placed on the results and interpretation of the data. Remember that outside of the (rather artificial) academic course environment, the readers of laboratory reports generally do not have access to your laboratory notebook or to the laboratory manual. The report must be a self-contained unit.

This general summary of how a laboratory notebook differs from and contributes to a laboratory report helps students form an overall understanding of the project, placing the notebook within the larger framework of the report and of the particular discipline and emphasizing the importance of writing to a specific audience (in this case, those who would seek to replicate the experiment).

Format

Once students understand why they have been assigned a notebook, they need to learn how to keep one using the methodology of the discipline. Although the principles remain the same, the format and style vary considerably across disciplines. Students write more effective entries if they understand how their purpose and chosen methodology influence the style and content of their notebooks.

The examples in these guidelines ensure that students can't misunderstand the professors' instructions or adopt an inappropriate format.

An instructor emphasizing either write-to-learn or disciplinary genres could point out that similar attention to detail is required in all course work. Careful recording of notes can prevent accidental plagiarism, provide evidence of ownership in the event of stolen papers, and serve as the basis for rewrites in the event of computer and disk problems. Similarly, applying a "prelab" procedure to all of their classes will help students be prepared for class and engaged with the material. Writing a brief summary along the lines of the "post-lab," describing what was learned in every class or lecture, helps students assimilate information and allows instructors to assess their progress.

This handout includes a significant amount of discipline-specific language, including abbreviations, terminology, and reference to procedures, all of which should be familiar to students in the course. The reference to a style manual provides an additional source of instruction and information should students need it.

SAMPLE GUIDELINES
Procedures for keeping a laboratory notebook
Organic Chemistry: John Cochran and Patricia Jue

FORMAT

Your name, the course number, and the course title should appear on the front cover of the notebook. It is also a good idea to indicate the time span covered, e.g., Fall 1994. The first page should be the *title page* with such information as your name, the course number and title, the name of your instructor(s), the period of time and the place in which the work was completed, e.g., Fall 1994, Colgate University, Hamilton, NY. The next two to five pages should be reserved for the *Table of Contents* to be filled in as each experiment is performed. Entries should include the title of the experiment, the pages where the work can be found, and the *complete* date on which the work was done.

Each page of the notebook should be numbered. At the top of each page on which an experiment begins, include the full title of the experiment, your name, and the complete date. Subsequent pages should have an abbreviated title, perhaps with some indication that the page is a continuation, e.g., "continued" or "(cont.)," the complete date, and your name.

PRELAB: Before coming to lab, you are required to prepare a brief "prelab" in your notebook that includes the experiment number and title and a brief introductory statement that covers the purpose of the experiment and the type of analysis or synthesis to be performed. A brief outline of the procedure should follow; outline or flow chart format is sufficient.

IN-LAB: Notebook entries should name the book or journal from which any directions or literature physical constants were obtained. It is not necessary to copy extensive directions for experiments if these are given in the original procedure, but deviations from the original procedure or unexpected occurrences should be noted. You should keep a log of the procedure as you do it. Include equations for the reactions. Record the quantities (grams or mL and moles) of all starting reagents used. REMEMBER UNITS. If appropriate, note the grade (technical, reagent) and manufacture of the chemicals used. All original data belong in the notebook. For example, if the amount of a liquid is determined by weighing it in a tared flask, you should record the weight of the empty flask and the weight of the flask plus the sample since these are the direct measurements that you can make. The weight of the sample is then calculated from these figures. If you used the TARE/REZERO feature of the balance, so only the weight of the chemical is obtained, this should be noted. Use the correct number of significant figures in recording numerical data. Take your notebook with you whenever entries will have to be made, e.g., to balances, to the GC. Record the data directly in the book along with any appropriate parameters and comments. Carbon copies should be turned in at the end of each lab period.

POST-LAB: Spectra are to be handed in with the laboratory report; however, since these represent data you should attach photocopies in your notebook or else attach the original copy when it is returned to you. In any case data obtained from spectra should be tabulated in the notebook. After the lab is completed, you should write a brief summary of the data obtained and perform any calculations required. Tabulate data if appropriate, leaving enough room for corrections. This will then serve as a rough draft for the discussion/ conclusion section of your formal lab report. State your final results and whether you completed the objectives of the experiment. Carbon copies are due 48 hours after you finish an experiment.

ERRORS

No entries should be erased or torn out of the notebook. Unsatisfactory data or experiments that did not go well should be noted with appropriate critical comments. Cross out small mistakes with a single line. For larger errors, an "X" may be used. In all cases, one should be able to read the incorrect entry; thus, errors should not be scribbled through!

For a detailed discussion of appropriate writing style, see *The ACS Style Guide: A Manual for Authors and Editors,* Janet S. Dodd, editor.

Some instructors make sample laboratory or field notebooks available to students. Discipline-specific handbooks such as Pechenik's *A Short Guide to Writing about Biology* also include sample laboratory notebook extracts, while others, such as Bond and Magistrale's *Writer's Guide: Psychology,* list the different kinds of data that should be included (31) and quote one-sentence observations typical of those in a notebook in that discipline (140).

Assigning Laboratory and Field Reports

Format for laboratory reports

Students writing laboratory reports benefit from a preliminary explanation of the purpose of such a report as well as of the style and structure they should adopt. Such a discussion can emphasize both disciplinary features of writing and general features of effective prose (such as the need to be precise, to make careful word choices, and to use effective transitions).

The handout's reference to journals in the field helps students to see their work as part of the discipline rather than simply as an assignment in a class. It also reinforces the notion that they can and should immerse themselves in the discourse of the community for which they are about to write. The summary of what constitutes a paper based on those journals is helpful, again grounding the students' work in the field.

The discussion of titles has relevance to more than organic chemistry, and the guidelines provided here could be helpful for a student attempting to compose a title for an English or history paper. Pointing this out in class can help students understand the difference between disciplinary conventions and general writing skills.

In many ways this is true for the advice about writing introductions, writing the discussion section of the paper, and anticipating the expectations of the audience. Students in all disciplines need to learn to evaluate their readers and assess how much information is sufficient. Writing for an audience beyond the classroom also reinforces the students' image of themselves as members of a specific academic community, even as they adopt

SAMPLE GUIDELINES
Organizing laboratory reports
Organic Chemistry: John Cochran and Patricia Jue

A brief glance at some articles that appear in chemistry journals, e.g., *Journal of the American Chemistry Society, Journal of Organic Chemistry,* will illustrate acceptable formats for the formal laboratory report. Generally, these reports contain an introduction, a summary of the experimental procedure, a results section, and a section that discusses the significance of the results. In addition, in a separate section or embedded in the introduction there may be a discussion of the theory behind the experiment. Sometimes the results and discussion sections are combined into a single section.

The *title* may be the most important section of your report. In fact, many readers never get beyond that point of a document. Think about the last time you perused the nonfiction section of the library for a book that was not required reading. The title should be a mini-abstract which allows the reader to ascertain the nature of the investigation. Consider well the title length. If the title is too brief, it will not be informative; however, it should not be a whole paragraph! You should avoid chemical formulas or symbols in the title.

The *introduction* of the report should clearly state the goal for the experiment and provide a brief background to "set the stage" of the experiment. It should convey why the reader should be interested in your work. Remember that while you may be learning or perfecting your laboratory technique, this is rarely the goal of an experiment. More acceptable is that you are synthesizing, isolating, and/or identifying a compound. If you are synthesizing a compound, the introduction might be a good place to discuss chemical mechanisms and reactions. If you are isolating a compound, you could discuss the theory behind the separation technique employed. When identifying compounds, you could discuss classes of compounds and the reactives of functional groups, although it might be easier to discuss this later in the report, especially if you are making chemical derivatives. Since opening paragraphs are introductory in nature, the heading "Introduction" is superfluous. However, some authors include a heading, anyway.

The *experimental procedure* is reported in a section that is often called "Experimental Methods," "Experimental Section," "Materials and Methods," or some equally suitable heading. You should report what you actually did in the laboratory, especially if it deviates from what the laboratory manual asks you to do. Give enough detail about your materials and methods so that others could repeat your work and obtain comparable results. Report the amounts of reagents and solvents used (mass/volume and moles) since these inform the reader of the limiting reagents, and the scale of the reactions. You should assume that the reader is a fairly competent chemist. It is sufficient to state that you refluxed, distilled, washed with some solution, and evaporated without detailing the apparatus used unless it was non-standard and has bearing on your results. Diagrams and flow charts belong in laboratory notebooks. However, you should include the temperatures at which materials were reacted and collected during distillations and the amount of time a material was allowed to react, reflux, and, possibly, dry. Detailed observations usually are included only if they are unexpected, significant, or hint at problems that may affect the results. For example, violent boiling upon addition of a reagent may result in evaporation of product, cloudiness in layers may indicate less than desirable separation, or color in a sample that should be colorless may indicate contamination.

Summarize your data in the *results section*. If you have a lot of data, you may choose to have a separate *data section*. Include only relevant data; raw data and calculations belong in the laboratory notebook. Numerical data may be reported in the text in complete English sentences, or in tables. Using both may be redundant. Avoid phrases such as "X was calculated to be," "Y was measured to be" in favor of a more concise "X was." Also, avoid stating "X = ."

When discussing your experiment, interpret and compare your results. Merely reporting physical constants and the presence of peaks or resonances in spectra is not sufficient. Physical constants obtained for your compound should be compared with values reported in the literature.

If values do not appear in the literature, compare them with values reported for compounds very similar to yours. All literature values should appear with references. Beware of terms such as "actual" or "theoretical" values. The former implies experimentally obtained values, but is often interpreted to mean literature values. The latter implies a value calculated from a theoretical model. Remember that most values reported in the literature were obtained by measuring them from a sample believed to be that compound under conditions that may or may not be exactly the same as the ones you used. The values may not be any more "correct" than those obtained from your presumably pure compound. You may wish to comment on the similarity of your values with the literature values. In analyzing spectra you should identify important features as they relate to the structure or composition of your product(s). You might also comment on features that indicate impurities, side reactions, or remaining reagents in your product. If appropriate, report the results of numerical analysis, e.g., integration of NMR and GC peaks. Finally, you should discuss the implications of your results. Summarize how well the experimental goal was achieved, perhaps with critical comments on how the experiment may be improved. Any conclusions made should be based on the evidence presented; however, do not repeat discussion points or include irrelevant material.

even as they adopt some skills and follow rules applicable to any discipline.

The many examples of specific material to include give students a clear idea of what they are being asked to do, how they should do it, and why. This in turn serves to introduce them further to the discipline and its epistemology. The use of discipline-specific terminology and abbreviations in the handout indicates the degree of specificity required (and indicates which abbreviations are acceptable in the discipline).

Format for field reports

David Hess asserts that while anthropologists are accustomed to teaching students ethnographic fieldwork methods, the *writing* of ethnography is often neglected in pedagogy. He recommends that instructors take undergraduates through guided readings of ethnographies to extract principles of "textual organization, voice, and the politics of metaphor" (164).

For this course, Professor Hess outlines some features of an ethnography and illustrates them with references to fieldwork the students might themselves conduct.

This handout is particularly effective because it walks the students through the stages of preparing to engage in the research process. The subdivisions in each section ensure that they progress logically, first developing a hypothesis, then deciding what constitutes sufficient evidence, and next selecting an appropriate research method. The wealth of examples Professor Hess provides allows the students to visualize each stage of the process and thus develop a satisfying and creative project for themselves. Placing "Style" last corresponds with its place in the writing process.

SAMPLE GUIDELINES
Ethnographic writing
Ethnographic Writing: Describing and Interpreting Social Action: David Hess

---

A GUIDE TO ETHNOGRAPHIC WRITING
I. Research the Ethnography
  A. Developing preliminary hypothesis and research questions
    1. Decide what you want to observe (e.g., turf controversies in the library, sports cuts, teammate or staff squabbles, food fights).
    2. Decide who your readers are (professor, other students, yourself). There are often multiple readers, but some are more important than others.
    3. Decide what your preliminary hypotheses are. For ex.,
      a. Cuts and substitutions not always on the basis of merit
      b. Teammate squabbles (or staff squabbles in dining hall) are linked to internal positions or external roles (race, economic class, school class, etc.)
    4. Decide what would constitute evidence for or against your preliminary hypotheses.
  B. Research Method
    1. Direct observation
      a. As outsider (sometimes using recorder, camera)
      b. As participant (participant-observer method)
    2. Interviews
      a. Decide how much you want to rely on interviews with people you do not know well versus developing a few key informants.
      b. Decide how you will get a representative sample of different points of view.
      c. Decide your mix between informal interviews (conversations) and formal interviews (usually with tape recorder or notepad).
    3. Other sources of information
      a. Written sources
      b. Analysis of spatial organization

      c. Analysis of artwork, graffiti, "material culture"
  C. Field notes
    1. Write down (transcribe) observations, interviews, recordings.
    2. Make preliminary diagrams and illustrations.
II. Writing the Ethnography
  A. Genres: Envisioning a Textual Organization
    1. The Puzzle-Solving Format (e.g., Geertz "Deep Play"). Start with an event (your text) and then examine it from different points of view (your exegesis).
    2. The Time Cycle Format (e.g., Burnett "Ceremony, Rites"). Decide on the time unit (your text—game/evening/work shift, week, semester, or school year) and then examine it from beginning to end (your exegesis).
  B. Framing Devices (Pictures, footnotes, diagrams)
    1. Decide mode: complementary vs. supplementary relationship to text.
    2. Decide tone: serious vs. ironic.
  C. Point of view
    1. Decide the role of the "I."
      a. To establish authority vs. to establish reflexivity
      b. How prominent you wish to make the "I"
    2. Decide how much of your dialogue with informants you want to represent (how close you want to be to a fieldwork report versus an analytical study).
    3. Decide how much you want to represent your point of view versus that of your informant(s).
  D. Style
    1. Decide appropriate metaphors.
    2. Decide how the form of the text relates to its content.

    Handouts can be very helpful when assigning social science reports because if they have no written guidelines students may apply techniques and structures inappropriate to the discipline. The more precise the guidelines, the more effective they will be at allowing the students to enter the discourse of the discipline.

Disciplinary distinctions

Some instructors of introductory courses provide students with a handout explaining the discourse features of their discipline; others rely on published discourse-specific handbooks. (See Chapter 3.) However the information is delivered, students enter more smoothly into the work of a new discipline if they understand some of its discourse conventions.

The specific instructions about the length of each report section and the use of the third person help students to envision their work as part of a discourse community with a specific language and way of thinking. The humor about the effect of the third person helps make students feel comfortable with the style they are being asked to adopt: It is not always logical, and that's all right.

Because the emphasis of the paper is laboratory research, these guidelines save students considerable time by giving examples of appropriate citation methods. The inclusion of several possible methods allows students to develop an active approach to their writing of the report.

SAMPLE GUIDELINES
Presentation of a laboratory report
Organic Chemistry: John Cochran and Patricia Jue

PRESENTATION

Conventionally, reports are not written in the first person ("I did this") nor in the imperative ("Do this"). Rather, reports are written in the third person impersonal—as if the experiment did itself!

Formal reports should be concise and well thought out. Consequently, the maximum limit for each report, not including spectra, title page, and reference page, is set to:

Exp I to IV each	2 pages
Exp V & VI — combined report	4 pages
Exp VII	2 pages

References in scientific articles are usually cited in the text numerically or by the author's name and date:

"was reported previously."[3]
"was reported previously" [3].
"was reported previously" (Cochran, 1990).

A list of all references appears at the end of the article in numerical order if cited by number, or alphabetically if cited by author. The minimum information that references include is:

For journals—author, abbreviated journal title, year of publication, volume number and initial page of article, e.g., for an article by T. R. Fletcher appearing in the *Journal of the American Chemical Society,* Volume 107, pages 2203 through 2212, published in 1985:

Fletcher, T. R., *J. Am. Chem. Soc.,* 1985, **107,** 2203–2212. or
Fletcher, T. R., *J. Am. Chem. Soc.,* **107,** 2203 (1985).

For books—author or editor, book title, publisher, city of publication, and year of publication.

The specific instructions for presenting and citing interview material help students use their research most effectively. Professor Moran requires that students work out for themselves the established format for citation by studying the journal in question. Having done this, they

SAMPLE GUIDELINES (EXCERPT)
Using interview data in field reports
Women, Work, and Family: Mary Moran

HINTS FOR WORKING WITH INTERVIEW MATERIAL

If the interview confirmed your original ideas, try to set up the evidence in such a way that all variables which could be affecting the data are accounted for. This will strengthen your argument and allow you to make *causal* statements about your topic (for example: "A is the way it is *because of* B; and C, D, and E have nothing to do with it").

. . . In all cases, use *verbatim* quotes from your interviews just as you would use quotes from books or articles: to support your argument. Each time you present the reader with a "statement of fact," back it up with a quote to show that you are not just making it up. A strong argument depends on the skillful use of these quotes, so that they build upon each other in a logical way.

Remember to use pseudonyms for all personal names to protect the privacy of your informants. Interview material may be cited by simply using the date on which it was recorded (for example, Interview: April 10, 1985). All other citations and references should be in the *American Anthropologist* style. Look in the journal *American Anthropologist* (in the library) for examples.

are more likely to remember the method than if they were simply provided with a list of rules; and they also practice a strategy for learning conventions in other disciplines. Suggesting that they refer to journals for samples also reminds the students that they are part of a discipline and encourages them to be active and curious scholars.

Handouts describing conventions for different types of writing in the discipline (e.g., research reports, laboratory reports, literature reviews in the sciences) can introduce new students to and remind more experienced students of the conventions of the discipline. (See page 139.)

Assigning Policy Analysis

Policy analysis differs among disciplines, so most instructors like to provide a handout explaining the criteria and method to be used. Handbooks sometimes provide explanations with sample analyses. However, because most policy analysis occurs in political science courses, the best coverage of this type of assignment may be found in political science guides such as Biddle and Holland's *Writer's Guide: Political Science.* The definitions and descriptions in those guides can easily be adapted to the needs of other courses.

SAMPLE GUIDELINES
Generating appropriate topics
Introduction to Economics: Ulla Grapard

OUTLINE
Give me a single page where you indicate what your focus is.

—What question do you want to investigate?

(I want to investigate and analyze the proposals for Workfare. What is Workfare? Where and when has it been suggested or implemented? What are the reasons for Workfare instead of continuing with the usual income support schemes such as AFDC? Who thinks this is a good idea? What evidence is there that it is a good idea, i.e., that it

Although intended to produce a topic for a research paper, the kinds of questions Professor Grapard requires the students to consider policy analysis.

The "brainstorming questions" included in this example (a variation on the Who? What? Where? When? Why? How? questions of journalism) give students a concrete model to follow as they begin to think about a topic. Modeling methods of "prewriting" is an excellent way to teach students the kinds of questions they should be asking. (See pages 48–50.)

does what its proponents want it to do? Who benefits and who loses from this change? Are taxpayers' dollars spent more efficiently? What kind of economic analysis have people conducted? Are there conflicts of equity and efficiency? Are economists able to shed some light on the issue? . . .)

You can structure your thoughts, *formulate your thesis statement, and structure your argument* once you have brainstormed a bit on such questions. The least I will accept on Thursday, July 22 is a page with something along those lines on the topic of your choice.

If students are to select their own topics for analysis, they benefit most from handing in a proposal explaining their topic very early in the process. That way, the instructor or a teaching assistant can ensure that the topic is sufficiently focused and that it will generate an effective piece of writing.

If students are asked to analyze a specific policy, they should be given access to as much information as possible about that policy. Some instructors of upper-level courses prefer to combine training in advanced library skills with such an assignment, helping students find policies to analyze and information to use in their analysis by enlisting the assistance of a special collections or archival librarian if one is available. If the emphasis is to be on learning analytical skills, instructors often hand out detailed descriptions of the policy in question, sometimes walking the students through an analysis of another policy beforehand.

This unusual method of introducing students to policy analysis urges them to consider the policy from the inside and explore its potential impact on all constituencies. Professor Osgood handed out a four-page description of the curriculum (designed by a graduate student in the course) in advance of this assignment. The role playing helped the students evaluate the strengths and weaknesses of the curriculum from different perspectives.

SAMPLE GUIDELINES (EXCERPT)
Writing policy analysis
Seminar in Curriculum Theory: Robert Osgood

The two activities below are based on the curriculum model "Project Society" developed by Jacquie Galler.

1. During the last class period we will hold a mock school board meeting for the Project Society school. Each student will role-play a representative of a different interest group and participate in the "meeting" as that person (parent, student, board member, teacher, curriculum specialist, etc.).

2. The final paper will discuss and critique one or more aspects of the proposed curriculum drawing on the points of view presented at the mock board meeting.

Checklist for assigning research papers

_____ Conduct an in-class discussion of students' assumptions about research.

_____ Explain the purposes of research in the discipline.

_____ Explain the desired outcomes of the assigned research project, both in terms of what the students are to learn and what contributions they are to make to the discipline.

_____ Specify the methodology to be used.

_____ Outline the stages and suggest strategies for developing the research and incorporating it into a paper or report.

_____ Help students focus their topics.

_____ Specify format, length, organization, and other stylistic features of the written report. Provide handouts, or direct students to relevant handbook sections.

_____ Specify expected length of the written report.

_____ Present the method of citation to be used.

_____ Identify what constitutes plagiarism and discuss methods of avoiding it.

_____ Ensure that students have access to sufficient materials.

_____ Ensure that students have sufficient time to complete research and writing.

_____ Explain criteria by which the research will be graded.

For Further Reading

Bazerman, Charles. "Codifying the Social Scientific Style: The APA Publication Manual as Behaviorist Rhetoric." *The Rhetoric of the Human Sciences: Language and Argument in Scholarship in Public Affairs.* Ed. John S. Nelson, Allan Megill, and Donald N. McCloskey. Madison: U of Wisconsin P, 1987. 125–44.

Biddle, Arthur W., and Kenneth M. Holland. *Writer's Guide: Political Science.* Lexington, MA: Heath, 1987.

Bond, Lynne A., and Anthony S. Magistrale. *Writer's Guide: Psychology.* Lexington, MA: Heath, 1987.

Bullock, Richard H. "Athens/Arts: Involving Students in Research on Their Community." *College Composition and Communication* 36 (1985): 237–39.

Cozzens, Susan. "Comparing the Sciences: Citation Context Analysis of Papers from Neuropharmacology and the Sociology of Science." *Social Studies of Science* 15 (1985): 127–53.

Deen, Rosemary. "An Interplay of Powers: Writing about Literature." *Only Connect: Uniting Reading and Writing.* Ed. Thomas Newkirk. Upper Montclair, NJ: Boynton/Cook, 1986. 174–86.

Dowdey, Diane. "Citation and Documentation across the Curriculum." *Constructing Rhetorical Education.* Ed. Marie Secor and Davida Charney. Carbondale: Southern Illinois UP, 1992. 330–52.

Flynn, Elizabeth A., George A. McCulley, and Ronald K. Gratz. "Writing in Biology: Effects of Peer Critiquing and Analysis of Models on the Quality of Biology Laboratory Reports." *Writing Across the Disciplines: Research into Practice.* Ed. Art Young and Toby Fulwiler. Upper Montclair, NJ: Boynton/Cook, 1986. 160–75.

Garfield, Eugene. "Is Information Retrieval in the Arts and Humanities Inherently Different from That in Science? The Effect That ISI's Citation Index for the Arts and Humanities Is Expected to Have on Future Scholarship." *Library Quarterly* 50 (1980): 40–57.

Geertz, Clifford. *Works and Lives: The Anthropologist as Author.* Palo Alto: Stanford UP, 1988.

Gilbert, G. Nigel. "Referencing as Persuasion." *Social Studies of Science* 7 (1977): 113–22.

———. "The Transformation of Research Findings into Scientific Knowledge." *Social Studies of Science* 6 (1976): 262–306.

Gusfield, Joseph R. "Listening for the Silences: The Rhetorics of the Research Field." *Writing the Social Text: Poetics and Politics in Social Science Discourse.* Ed. Richard Harvey Brown. New York: Aldine de Gruyter, 1992. 117–34.

Harris, R. Allen. "Rhetoric of Science." *College English* 53 (1991): 282–307.

Hess, David J. "Teaching Ethnographic Writing: A Review Essay." *Anthropology and Education Quarterly* 20 (1989): 163–76.

Horning, Alice S. "Advising Undecided Students through Research Writing." *College Composition and Communication* 42 (1991): 80–84.

Jeske, Jeff. "Borrowing from the Sciences: A Model for the Freshman Research Paper." *The Writing Instructor* (Winter 1987).

Kalmbach, James R. "The Laboratory Reports of Engineering Students: A Case Study." *Writing Across the Disciplines: Research into Practice.* Ed. Art Young and Toby Fulwiler. Upper Montclair, NJ: Boynton/Cook, 1986. 176–83.

Koen, Billy Vaughn. "Toward a Definition of the Engineering Method." *Engineering Education* 75 (1984): 150–55.

Krieger, Martin. "The Inner Game of Writing." *Journal of Policy Analysts and Management* 7 (1988): 408–16.

Leary, David E. "Communication, Persuasion, and the Establishment of Academic Disciplines: The Case of American Psychology." *Writing the Social Text: Poetics and Politics in Social Science Discourse.* Ed. Richard Harvey Brown. New York: Aldine de Gruyter, 1992. 73–90.

Lorence, J. L. "The Critical Analysis of Documentary Evidence: Basic Skills in the History Classroom." *Teaching History: A Journal of Methods* 8.2 (1983): 77–84.

McCarthy, Lucille Parkinson, and Stephen M. Fishman. "Boundary Conversations: Conflicting Ways of Knowing in Philosophy and Interdisciplinary Research." *Research in the Teaching of English* 25.4 (1991): 419–68.

McMillan, Victoria E. *Writing Papers in the Biological Sciences.* Boston: Bedford, 1988.

Marsella, Joy, Thomas L. Hilgers, and Clemence McLarén. "How Students Handle Writing Assignments: A Study of Eighteen Responses in Six Disciplines." *Writing, Teaching, and Learning in the Disciplines.* Ed. Anne Herrington and Charles Moran. New York: MLA, 1992. 174–88. The six disciplines are biology, education, English, mathematics, psychology, and sociology.

Miller, Carolyn R., and Jack Selzer. "Special Topics of Argument in Engineering Reports." *Writing in Non–Academic Settings.* Ed. Lee Odell and Dixie Goswami. New York: Guilford, 1985. 309–41.

Myers, Greg. *Writing Biology: Texts in the Social Construction of Scientific Knowledge.* Madison: U of Wisconsin P, 1990. Myers presents a theoretical interpretation of "scientific texts in their social context . . . [to] help us understand how texts produce scientific knowledge and reproduce the cultural authority of that knowledge." He discusses journal articles, grant proposals, abstracts, and research reports.

Nadelman, Lorraine. "Learning to Think and Write as an Empirical Psychologist: The Laboratory Course in Developmental Psychology." *Teaching of Psychology* 17 (Feb. 1990): 45–47.

Pickering, Andrew, ed. *Science as Practice and Culture.* Chicago: U of Chicago P, 1992.

Poe, Retta E. "A Strategy for Improving Literature Reviews in Psychology Courses." *Teaching of Psychology* 17 (Feb. 1990): 54.

Price, Derek W. "A Model for Reading and Writing about Primary Sources: The Case of Introductory Psychology." *Teaching of Psychology* 17 (Feb. 1990): 48–53.

Rymer, Jone. "Scientific Composing Processes: How Eminent Scientists Write Journal Articles." *Writing in Academic Disciplines.* Vol. 2 of *Advances in Writing Research.* Ed. David A. Jolliffe. Norwood, NJ: Ablex, 1988. 211–50.

Schmersahl, Carmen B. "Teaching Library Research: Process, Not Product." *Journal of Teaching Writing* 6.2 (1987): 231–38.

CHAPTER 8

Designing and Evaluating Essay Exams

In this chapter:

❏   Choosing an appropriate type of essay exam

❏   Designing exams for accurate evaluation

❏   Designing exams for effective teaching

❏   Responding to essay exams

❏   Grading essay exams

❏   Checklist for designing and evaluating essay exams

❏   For further reading

Choosing an Appropriate Type of Essay Exam

In the familiar exam format, the instructor designs a series of questions on topics derived from the whole course or from the period since the last exam. Some instructors combine short-answer questions with essay questions, generally giving more weight to the essay answer when they grade. The instructor distributes the exam at the beginning of the test period, and students write brief essays in exam booklets ("blue books") for one or two hours. Instructors, however, may want to consider alternatives to traditional essay exams, alternatives that offer rich possibilities for response and evaluation.

Staged and sequenced exams

A variation on the traditional form, the staged essay exam offers a series of questions about a single issue. Building on one another, the questions ask students to approach the issue from different viewpoints or to apply various methods of analysis. On a literature exam, for example, a staged question might ask students to evaluate a single text from a number of theoretical standpoints (e.g., Marxist, feminist, or deconstructionist), or it might ask students to place the text in its historical context in the first question, discuss its literary genre in the second, and analyze its style in the third. Because the first answer informs the second, and the first two answers inform the third, the exam forms a coherent whole. Students may prefer not being required to jump from topic to topic, and instructors may find such essays more satisfying to evaluate.

A sequenced examination focuses on more than one topic but asks questions that build on each other. The most common form of sequenced exam begins with a series of short-answer questions that provide material to be used in answering one or more longer essay questions posed at the end of the exam. In an economics exam, for example, a series of short-answer questions might require students to produce supply-and-demand curves for a variety of fruit crops and to evaluate a production possibilities frontier for an imagined economy, and then an essay question might ask students to use some of the information from the earlier questions to discuss the opportunity cost of a number of possible projects. Alternatively, short-answer questions could be used to influence students' writing style. Economics instructors value short, precise answers, and the most effective economics essay exam elicits a style that avoids all superfluous words and information. A test might begin with a series of questions that students answer in one or two sentences and then conclude with one or two essay questions that prompt longer answers. Having already adopted the mode of concise answers, students might more readily respond to the longer essay questions in the desired tone and style.

Questions distributed in advance of the exam

By distributing exam questions before the test day, instructors encourage comprehensive synthesis of course materials. For a test on which students will answer three questions, for example, the instructor can distribute six questions a week before the test date. On exam day, the instructor specifies which three questions are to be answered.

Giving students the questions in advance allows them to brainstorm, prepare a thesis, and research the material. It also deters them from cramming random course material into short-term memory and then deleting it immediately after the exam.

Students take the timed exam in a classroom, but they usually produce essays with greater depth and fuller development than if they were confronted with the questions only on the test date. Students are still required to demonstrate knowledge and skills learned in the course, but their preparation for writing the essays approximates the prewriting process that academic writers use in out-of-class papers. Instructors who use this testing method report that it allows them to raise their expectations for the quality of students' answers. Because students must learn the material for all of the possible questions, this examination method serves as both a teaching and an evaluative tool.

If the exam is intended to test how students process knowledge rather than how well they memorize it, some instructors allow them to bring note cards with outlines, formulas, or statistics into the exam. These cards are then stapled to the exam when it is handed in.

The take-home exam

Assigning take-home exams gives students more time to prepare and calls for self-monitoring. Students may be asked to bring back the completed exam twenty-four hours later, or they may be given a few days or a weekend to work on it. They may be given a page limit or a time limit. The customary practice is to ask that they write on each question for a limited amount of time (often an hour), although they may spend as much time preparing and outlining their answer as they like.

In practical terms, a take-home exam allows instructors with large classes and heavy course loads to assign writing in courses where they otherwise could not. The time limit on the out-of-class essay exam makes students' responses briefer than assigned out-of-class papers, and grading is thus more manageable. A take-home exam also allows instructors to assign more essays than otherwise might be practical. Giving four carefully prepared questions on a take-home exam allows instructors to ask students to conduct limited research on four questions or to apply class notes to four topics rather than to the single issue or question a term paper would focus on. Moreover, take-home exam answers can be typed rather than handwritten, removing the major frustration instructors experience in grading essay exams: trying to decipher the handwriting. Students may be instructed to write for one hour and then transcribe and edit or, if they have access to computers, to type for one hour and then edit.

The fact that they must do the work outside the classroom makes a take-home exam seem less like a test and thus increases the students' enthusiasm—a factor that may be reflected in the quality of their writing and thinking. The fact that they have a clearly defined time period within which to do the work gives many students a sense of control over the assignment; they cannot procrastinate as they might if they were given two weeks to produce a paper of indeterminate length and scope. Finally, the fact that the exam is being written outside of the classroom, in a writing environment the student has selected, reduces stress and raises the overall standard of the essay.

SAMPLE ESSAY QUESTION (EXCERPT)
Take-home exams

Don Quixote: *Interpretation and Viewpoints:* Robert L. Hathaway

A Manchegan gentleman, who has read deeply in chivalric chronicles, decides to ape the wondrous deeds of the heroes of knight-errantry, thus to re-introduce their ideals and to gain fame and glory in like historic manner: "Scarce had the rubicund Apollo spread o'er the face of the broad spacious earth the golden threads of his bright hair . . ."

Dorotea, with little more to go on than a name and the recollection of the chivalric tales she has read, creates for herself an identity and ancestry as the Princess Micomicona of—naturally—Micomicón, even to the extent of stoutly defending that identity in the face of Sancho Panza's claim that she is really a private lady.

The innkeeper Juan Palomeque the Left-Handed denigrates the veracious deeds of the Great Captain and of Diego García de Paredes, preferring instead to believe the extravagant feats of Felixmarte of Hircania and Cirongilio of Thrace whose histories are printed "by license of the Royal Council, as if they were people who would allow a lot of lies to be printed. . . ."

Seeking a solitude wherein to escape from importuning suitors, Marcela leaves home and hearth to take up the shepherdess' crook and the pastoral mode of life, but unfortunately a number of aspirants—Grisóstomo chief among them—also adopt the pastoral style in their pursuit of the damsel.

In like manner Eugenio and a legion of fellow sufferers create their own Arcadia wherein to bemoan the loss of the capricious Leandra. Cardenio seeks in the wilderness, awaiting Heaven's intervention on his behalf (whether for salvation or condemnation), rigorous punishment for having failed in his duty to Luscinda.

The grave and compassionate Canon of Toledo has never finished a novel of chivalry but has nonetheless been tempted to create a "proper" example of the genre—to the extreme of having written more than a hundred sheets.

A priest and a barber wall up a library, the disappearance of which is attributed to a malign enchanter.

Each of these has had his or her life affected by literature, to varying degrees. Three evidence what may be called aberrant behavior: Grisóstomo in his suicide, Cardenio in his fits, Don Quixote in his posturings. But only the last of these three is, it is generally agreed, "mad." What is the difference between Don Quixote's case and those of the other characters cited herein for whom imaginative literature has provided a model for dealing with life?

Clearly this question would be inappropriate for an in-class essay examination, not only for its sheer length, but also for its complexity. As a take-home exam, however, it has many merits. Chief among them is that it does not prompt students to repeat information that has been given them; instead, it prompts them to apply practiced methods of analysis to a new problem. As is often the case with a take-home exam, the problem itself is a highly developed argument of the instructor's own construction. The students are being invited into that argument, and Professor Hathaway provides plenty of explanation and data for their consideration.

Designing Exams for Accurate Evaluation

In his chapter on tests and examinations in *Teaching Tips,* Wilbert McKeachie observes, "Unfortunately, it appears to be generally true that the examinations that are the easiest to construct are the most difficult to grade and vice versa" (89). Quickly formulated essay topics tend to produce essays that are difficult to read and evaluate, while carefully crafted questions whose possible answers are thought out in advance produce clearer essays that are more easily graded.

Writing specific questions

Short, very specific topics are usually most effective for in-class essay exams. Students should be able to understand immediately what is required of them so that they can focus their energy and intellect on preparing and writing their responses. Questions that call for broad synthesis or abstract thinking are more appropriate for take-home exams.

The successful question for an in-class exam should deter students from resorting to generalities and instead demand that they provide discrete blocks of information for a specific purpose. It may take a little longer to write questions that will produce specific answers, but it is well worth the effort.

Professor Grapard believes that this question worked because if her students didn't know the meaning of "opportunity cost," they couldn't fake it. The question also required a thoughtful answer that considered the interaction of economics and cultural values, applying materials from the textbook. It gave her students the freedom to structure their own answers, but it also required that they demonstrate knowledge of specific economic and religious considerations.

SAMPLE ESSAY EXAM QUESTION
Testing for specific knowledge
Economic Issues: Methods of Inquiry: Ulla Grapard

To a Hindu farmer with a large field, what is the opportunity cost of killing a cow for its beef?

Writing clear, comprehensible questions

Essay exam questions are most effective when they are succinct. Although too much brevity can be misleading—especially in exams for courses that do not traditionally require essay answers—

SAMPLE ESSAY EXAM QUESTION (EXCERPT)
Critical and Qualitative Thinking: Kenneth G. Valente

1. Consider the graphs $y = x^{-1/2}$, $x^{-1/3}$, and $x^{-1/4}$. Why didn't Mathematica draw these graphs for values of x between -5 and 0 (as instructed)? Was it right to do this? If not, sketch in the appropriate graphs for values of x between -5 and 0.

2. Describe (in words) the behavior of today's graphs as the values of x get close to zero. Can you explain your observations?

3. Consider the graphs $y = x{-}4$ and $y = x^{-1/4}$. Which "goes to zero" faster as x gets large in a positive sense? Explain why this is so.

Professor Valente reports that the second part of question 2 ("Can you explain") was a complete failure. The students adequately described the graphs, satisfying the first part of question 2, but they completely overlooked the second part of the question. In retrospect, Professor Valente realized that for many math students "describe" and "explain" mean the same thing; they assumed that they had completed the second part when they wrote their answers to the first, or they simply did not understand what the second part of the question was asking. He observes that explaining the distinction between these two terms in class prior to the exam would have reduced confusion and helped the students understand the process of mathematical thought.

The problem was confounded by the phrase "Can you," which appears to give students the option of answering "yes" or "no" rather than offering an explanation. Revising question 2 to read "Explain this behavior" would solve that problem.

questions accompanied by lengthy or complex instructions waste valuable time as students struggle to interpret them. Instructors have observed that students who carelessly read extensive explanations often misunderstand what is asked of them. Redrafting and shortening the question can make it clearer without shrinking its scope.

Essay exam questions should be phrased in language already familiar from the course. Unexpected phrasing can leave students unable to say anything, even when they know the answer. A linguistics instructor, for example, may have conducted class sessions on ways in which speakers use different language varieties in different social situations. If such behavior was not labeled "code-switching" in class, the term should not be introduced for the first time on an exam—even if it is accompanied by a definition. This does not mean that exams must ask only for material that has been rehearsed in class; on the contrary, many successful exams ask students to consider new materials using methods that have been practiced in class.

This question succeeded because students were asked to apply a carefully defined structure. First they had to study the reaction and predict the results in (a); then they had to study their answers and offer an explanation in written form in (b). The wording of (b) provides a framework for the answer by using key terms such as *explain* and *account for,* which suggest strategies for students.

Once the students are used to the predict-explain-account-for strategy suggested here, they will be able to write one-part answers that include both the chemical predictions and a discussion of them and so approximate the kind of writing expected of chemists.

SAMPLE ESSAY EXAM QUESTION
Structuring students' answers
Organic Chemistry: John Cochran

---

a. $SbCl_5$ reacts rapidly with A and B. Predict the organic products of the reaction shown below.

b. Explain briefly why these reactions take place so readily and account for the stoichiometry in each case (i.e., the molar ratio of RCl to $SbCl_5$).

Wording exam questions to suggest strategies for answers

It is particularly hard to grade students' essay answers when they are poorly structured or poorly developed. Assigning exam questions that suggest strategies for information retrieval and organization can produce better essays and teach students to be more effective exam takers. Some instructors like to give a series of essay exams early in the term with questions structured to prepare students for less "helpful" exams later in the term. This strategy is especially effective in disciplines that do not routinely assign essays and essay exams.

Questions using key terms such as *analyze, predict, describe* and *explain,* and *evaluate* tend to produce more effective essays than questions using the vaguer *discuss* or *comment on,* unless the students have learned what those terms mean in the discipline in which they are working. Similarly, instructions such as "Pay close attention to the structure of the argument," "Include specific references to the literature," or "Support your argument with a detailed discussion of the text" remind students what is expected in an academic essay.

Including a quotation in a question can focus the students on one passage and demand that they consider the whole text through that quotation. On essay exams, though, the quotation must be short and specific. Otherwise, students may be forced to read it too quickly and, without time to ponder it, may misunderstand what the question asks. If students are responding to a quotation or a complex problem, it can be very helpful to ask a series of questions to help them structure their answers. These questions should not limit the

---

SAMPLE ESSAY EXAM QUESTION
Using quotations
World Literature: Walter Jacobsohn

"Modern industry has converted the little workshop of the patriarchal master into the great factory of the industrial capitalist. Masses of laborers, crowded into factories, are organized like soldiers. As privates of the industrial army they are placed under the command of a perfect hierarchy of officers and sergeants. Not only are they the slaves of the bourgeois class and of the bourgeois state, they are daily and hourly enslaved by the machine, by the overlooker, and, above all, by the individual bourgeois manufacturer himself. The more openly this despotism proclaims gain to be its end and aim, the more petty, the more hateful, and the more embittering it is."—*Karl Marx*

What does this passage reveal about Marx's attitude towards the "bourgeois manufacturer" and the laborer? What is the impact of the military metaphor? Are the terms "petty," "hateful," and "embittering" appropriate? Explain whether this description fits the experience of the characters in *The Jungle* and *Life in the Iron Mills.*

Although the quotation is long, this assignment worked because the four-part question established a structure for the answer.

The purpose of the question was not to test how well the students knew Marx's work, but to make them synthesize the course material, including Marx and two works of fiction they had read. The instruction to consider the terms "petty," "hateful," and "embittering" helps students focus their answers and use specific examples.

answer so much as limit the focus or suggest a practical order in which to consider ideas and information.

Essay questions are most successful when they prompt students to reconsider material from different perspectives and to use critical thinking skills. By carefully suggesting the structure of the essay as part of the question, instructors can help students remain focused on the question.

Writing questions that demand focus

Vague examination questions allow students to "waffle" on topics they may know little about; the resulting content-free "bull" too often earns good grades in the academy, according to William Perry. More unfortunately, such questions often make even knowledgeable students sound as if they are rambling. Frequently it is impossible for students to write a good answer to general questions—although it may also be extremely difficult for them to write a "wrong" answer.

This question did not work because it is too general. In their essays students could say anything at all, and thus they said very little of substance. The highest grade that Professor Jamieson gave for this question was a B+, to a student who argued that Moses fit all three categories and who gave one example of each. Most students selected one category and then proceeded to use plot summary to justify it—and they had few other options.

SAMPLE ESSAY EXAM QUESTION
Providing sufficient specificity
Roots of Western Civilization: Sandra Jamieson

3. "Some are born great, some achieve greatness, and some have greatness thrust upon them." Discuss the life and character of Moses based upon this quotation.

The problem with the preceding question, as the professor noted, is that while it tests the students' knowledge of the plot of Exodus, it does not ask them to go beyond that. In a five-page out-of-class paper assignment, students might have carefully considered the implications of each assertion and drawn on close textual analysis to explore various interpretations of Moses' life. In an examination situation, however, students tended to retell the story of Moses' life as their evidence for choosing any of the three possible categories. The high percentage of very boring essays taught the instructor an important lesson about designing exam questions—unfortunately at the expense of the students. Had the instructor taken the time to map out some sample answers and list the material she hoped to see included in the answers, she might have been able to predict the problem and revise the question:

> "Some are born great, some achieve greatness, and some have greatness thrust upon them." It could be argued that Moses illustrates this principle. Select three incidents from Exodus that support or contradict this assertion and use them to describe the life and character of Moses.

This revised question demands that students know specific incidents well rather than having a general knowledge of the plot. As she designs the exam, the instructor can make a list of the main events in the life of Moses, noting the elements that successful answers will discuss. Such a checklist will reveal whether there is sufficient material to write a satisfactory answer and thus indicate whether the question needs revision. It will also serve as an aid to grading the exams.

If students do not have time to finish their exams, they will be frustrated—and so will the instructor who grades their answers. A one-hour exam may be constructed to allow students twenty to thirty minutes for answering each essay question. But if the scope of the questions is then narrowed to elicit answers written in fifteen to twenty minutes, students will have time to plan and proofread their answers.

Designing Exams for Effective Teaching

Using essay exams to teach study methods

Although essay exams can be used solely to test whether students have learned material from the course and can synthesize it, they can also be used as a teaching tool. Students study differently as they prepare for essay exams that ask them to apply rather than simply repeat what they have learned. (See, for example, Marton and Säljö.) If students know they will have to be able to apply the formulas and concepts they learn, they will develop study methods to help them do this; students who are required only to memorize and repeat formulas and concepts will learn to do only that. Wilbert McKeachie therefore suggests giving the first essay exam early, "after the third or fourth week of a fourteen-week semester" (88). Such a practice prompts students to start reviewing material almost immediately rather than waiting until the midterm exam; helps the instructor identify any comprehension problems and make necessary adjustments or suggest tutoring; and familiarizes students with the style of learning expected in the course—understanding and application rather than memorization (88).

McKeachie suggests making all tests cumulative rather than simply covering material taught since the last test. In this way students learn to make connections within all the course material and increase their overall comprehension of the subject.

Using essay exams to monitor the course

Students can use essay exams as a self-evaluation of what they have learned and retained from the course material. Giving an exam in the first few weeks of the course (ideally worth a smaller percentage of the final grade than later exams) helps students evaluate whether they are studying effectively and comprehend the material fully. The early exam might be the most important one for the students because it can help them decide to seek help or drop the course rather than wait until the midterm when it is often too late. For this reason it is helpful if possible to return the exams during brief conferences with students so that advice, praise, and encouragement may be given and so that students do not procrastinate on signing up for extra help or for tutoring. (Teaching assistants can also hold these conferences.)

Instructors, too, can learn from essay exams how effectively they are teaching and how well students are grasping the material. Instructors can revise the syllabus and offer review classes if necessary or recommend that students visit a writing center or form study groups. If these resources are not available, instructors might recommend that the department hire and train tutors.

Responding to Essay Exams

Writing comments on exams to explain what the students did well and how they might improve on the next exam is an important pedagogical device. In classes whose only writing activity is on exams, instructors can use their written responses to encourage students to engage the material, to ask questions during lectures, and to avail themselves of office hours.

Praise

Most college students can describe their weaknesses as writers, but few can name their strengths. Instructors tend to notice errors that impede the reading process and mark or correct them on students' papers. The exchange of written materials thus customarily focuses on error. Yet it is equally helpful for instructors to focus on well-developed ideas, effective word choices, and smooth transitions. Students need to know what skills and strategies work—and why—so that they can effectively replicate them. Noting why an answer received a good grade, why an essay's structure is effective, or why a sentence or paragraph is particularly pleasing has a profound effect on students, reinforcing their positive writing traits in a way that a high grade alone does not. Laudatory comments accompanying a high grade also help to wean students away from grade dependency, from working for grades rather than for learning.

Even on unsuccessful papers it is important for instructors to point out what works well. Otherwise students may think of themselves as "hopeless" writers and give up the effort entirely; or they may try to change their writing style and strategies completely, throwing out the good with the bad. If instructors always include some praise and acknowledgment of effort, students are more likely to be interested in all the comments on the paper. Praise should be specific; it should not be a brief generalization such as "good idea," nor should it be followed by the word *but*.

SAMPLE INSTRUCTOR'S RESPONSE TO AN ESSAY EXAM ANSWER
Giving praise
Roots of Western Civilization: Tom Howard

Question 1—This is a very interesting discussion—I'm particularly pleased that you found a connection to the issue of responsibility. It has got one serious problem, though. What about the execution of "some of the servants"? You deal with the suitors extremely well, but the servants are never mentioned. Whether you're going to argue that the same elements that endorse slaughtering the suitors apply to the servants or that the servants deserved death for different reasons, you must deal with those servants explicitly. This grade is too low for the quality of what you did here; unfortunately, what you *didn't* do is also involved.

"B"

The question on this exam said, "In *The Odyssey,* Homer seems to set up a social and moral framework within which it is right for Odysseus to slaughter all the suitors and some of the servants. Describe and comment on this framework." Professor Howard's comments to this student begin with general praise ("a very interesting discussion") and then move to specific praise ("you found a connection . . ."). Although a description of what the student does well is followed by the negating word *but*, the comments conclude with a reminder of what the student did well.

Comments explaining specific errors

In many cases a computational or interpretive error leads a student to write an unsatisfactory essay exam answer. An explanatory comment in the margin helps the student understand the grade and also communicates the correct answer. The more specific the comment, the more helpful it will be. To minimize the time spent writing comments—and to save students from the discouragement of reading excessive corrections—many instructors adapt some form of trait analysis: identifying one or two key errors in an essay and explaining them in a sentence or two. These can be errors of style, structure, or content. The instructor's comments will prove most helpful if they suggest how the student might have avoided the problem or explain how to prevent it from occurring again.

Professor Howard's comments on this student's answer explain how she strayed from answering the question. He describes what she said that was pertinent to the question; what she said that was tangential to it; and how the latter obstructed the former. Such comments encourage the student to be more attentive to the question itself on future exams. Howard's comments also help this first-year student make the transition from high school to college exam writing: They specify that giving information related to the topic is not of value in college writing. Instead the student must directly answer the question.

SAMPLE INSTRUCTOR'S RESPONSE TO AN ESSAY EXAM ANSWER
Commenting on errors
Roots of Western Civilization: Tom Howard

Question 1—Only part of this answer is directly responsive to the question. You start off by explaining why you feel Odysseus was justified in what he did. Now, I don't deny that I'm interested in that, but the question asked you to talk about how Homer justifies the killing. You do get around to that, but you don't develop that aspect of things far enough. And the end of the answer is a discussion of the differences between the ancient and modern worlds, which certainly isn't anything the question asked for. Nothing that you say is wrong, but not enough of it is to the point to be completely successful.

"C"

If the first essay exam answers contain many grammatical errors, stating that these features will count on the next exam may produce significant improvement. McKeachie remarks, "Apparently my students can speak, punctuate, and write clearly if they need to, but don't bother if it isn't expected" (97). Students sometimes believe that instructors who do not comment on or grade for style and mechanics do not care about these issues. A word of caution, though: Attention to style and grammar is for most writers a matter for revision. If these elements are to be counted on an essay exam, the instructor should leave students enough time in the exam period for reading over and revising their prose and should consider allowing them to consult a dictionary and writers' handbook.

In determining criteria for grading essay exams, many instructors elect not to grade for style and grammar unless errors are so rife as to interfere with their understanding of the answers. (See Chapter 11.)

McKeachie observes that poor answers arise more often from students not recognizing "relationships, implications, or applications of material" than from lack of data, and he suggests that instructors "look for cues" that indicate where such a breakdown occurs and then write appropriate comments (104). This strategy of not merely identifying errors but analyzing why they recur is much more valuable to students, for it enables them to see patterns of error rather than random errors. An overall comment at the end of the exam can explain overall skills, strengths, and error patterns, even encouraging students to go over the exam themselves looking for specific examples of those features (both the good and the bad).

Grading Essay Exams

Establishing criteria

Some instructors like to write out their own answer to each exam question as a way of evaluating the question and listing what they expect from students. This practice can also provide a good estimate of how long it will take students to write an answer. (Students will need more time than the instructor to evaluate what the question is asking them to do and then plan and organize their answer—something the instructor already did when writing the question.) From this exercise the instructor can generate a checklist for use in grading the exams. Remembering that even the most accomplished students are unlikely to achieve the comprehensiveness and subtlety of the instructor's answer, the instructor can appropriately scale down his or her expectations in the checklist. When the examinations are graded and returned, the instructor's sample answers can be given to the students as a model of what a good answer might look like (and as an indication of how seriously the instructor takes exams).

Once criteria have been established, the instructor can skim over all of the answers to each question, select one to represent each grade range, grade these answers, and write comments on them. The instructor may then find it useful to refer to those answers while grading the remaining exams. Choosing and referring to "touchstone" answers help the instructor maintain consistency, especially when grading answers that are difficult to evaluate. It also helps prevent the phenomenon that William Perry describes wherein students with a good prose style and a sense of the discipline's conventions can succeed by writing generalities backed by little more than an authoritative tone.

Some instructors like to make anonymous A and B answers available to the class to help them understand the expectations of the course. (Before students' work is copied and distributed, the instructor should always obtain the students' permission.) Reproducing copies of poor answers does not have sufficient pedagogical import to justify its humiliating effect on the writers of those answers, even though their names may not be attached to the samples and even though they may have agreed to have their answers distributed. Samples of good answers should be sufficient for making the instructor's points.

An alternative to grading each question and using those grades to calculate an overall grade is to grade the entire exam as one unit, assessing the overall skill and knowledge it reveals. Proponents of holistic grading, as this practice is called, claim that it provides a more accurate reflection of students' abilities and that holistic grades are more consistent than grades calculated from averages. This method prevents one bad answer from pulling down the grade of an otherwise excellent exam or one good answer from "saving" an otherwise poorly prepared set of responses. It also takes considerably less time to evaluate than does assigning a separate grade to each answer.

For this exam the instructor handed out five questions a week in advance. When the students came to the test, Professor Howard told them which questions to answer. Her holistic response to this student's entire exam speaks to the general strategies used by the student rather than responding to each answer. This gives the student a strong sense of himself as a test taker, knowledge on which he can build for his next exam.

The fact that the questions were distributed in advance allows Professor Howard cer-

SAMPLE INSTRUCTOR'S RESPONSE TO AN ESSAY EXAM
Making holistic comments
Sociolinguistics: Rebecca Moore Howard

What I like about this exam is your using personal observation to back up your linguistic analyses. The third question, by asking you to apply your linguistic knowledge to a hypothetical situation in which a classmate would be teaching bilingual students, certainly opened up that possibility, and I like your having used personal observation in your answer to the first question, as well.

Given that you had the opportunity to consider your answers in advance of test day, I think you might have done a better job of organizing your materials. At times your prose becomes a bit too sweeping and breezy. Your response to #2 in particular would benefit from a much tighter attention to your data.

What makes this exam strong, though, is your confidence with your materials. You synthesize Hudson and Ellerbroek, two very disparate sources, very convincingly. You not only explain Berlin and Kay's research on color terms, but you also offer your own observations concerning its shortcomings.

In sum, this exam indicates that you have come to think of sociolinguistics as a way of looking at and understanding your world; and when you talk about sociolinguistics, you keep your data straight and make new things of it. That strikes me as an "A" exam.

tain expectations that would be inappropriate in a traditional essay exam; thus she can comment on the student's style as well as the content of his answers.

Checklist for designing and evaluating essay exams

DESIGNING ESSAY EXAMS

_____ Decide whether a traditional, staged, sequenced, or take-home exam will best fit your course goals.

_____ Decide whether the chief purpose of the exam is to measure what students have already learned or to prompt them to make new connections.

_____ For in-class exams, make sure the questions are specific, demanding precise knowledge.

_____ Write questions that are brief, clear, and easy to understand.

_____ Word questions to suggest strategies for answers.

_____ Write out your own answers to the questions to determine whether they can be answered satisfactorily in the allotted time.

EVALUATING ESSAY EXAMS

_____ Use your own answers as a basis for grading criteria (scaled down for students' level of expertise in the discipline).

_____ For each question, choose a touchstone answer to represent each grade range—A, B, and so forth—and then evaluate the remaining students' answers.

_____ As an alternative to grading the answers to each question, consider a holistic approach, in which you grade the exam as a whole.

_____ When returning exams, hand out copies of your own answers and of good student answers. (Remove names and secure permission first.)

For Further Reading

Aubrecht, Gordon J. II. "Is There a Connection between Testing and Teaching?" *Journal of College Science Teaching* 20 (Dec. 1990): 152–57. Aubrecht suggests strategies for writing effective examination questions that reflect the overall goals of the course and traces patterns of error in essay answers to poorly written exam questions.

Cook, Thomas H., Steven E. Dyche, and Samuel Hubbard. "Bonus Homework, Study Group, Pair Test, and Test Retake." *Journal of College Science Teaching* 16 (May 1987): 520–23. These pedagogical strategies were studied over a ten-year period and proved beneficial to students.

Fleming, P. R. "The Profitability of 'Guessing' in Multiple-Choice Question Papers." *Medical Education* 22 (Nov. 1988): 509–13. Strategic guessing significantly improved students' grades over a two-year period.

Gronlund, N. E. *Constructing Achievement Tests.* Englewood Cliffs: Prentice, 1982.

Lederman, Marie Jean. "Why Test?" *Journal of Basic Writing* (Spring 1988): 38–46. Lederman encourages the use of essay tests for overall student development.

McKeachie, Wilbert J. "Tests and Examinations." *Teaching Tips: A Guidebook for the Beginning College Teacher.* 8th ed. Lexington, MA: Heath, 1986. 86–109. The author offers a general discussion of benefits and strategies for effective use of examinations, with most emphasis given to essay exams. He discusses when to test, how to structure exams, and how to administer exams (with a long discussion on preventing cheating), as well as scoring, grading, and returning exams. His is a useful discussion for both novice and veteran teachers.

Marton, F., and R. Säljö. "On Qualitative Differences in Learning: I—Outcome and Process." *British Journal of Educational Psychology* 46 (1976): 4–11.

———. "On Qualitative Differences in Learning: II—Outcome as a Function of the Learner's Conception of the Task." *British Journal of Educational Psychology* 46 (1976): 115–27.

Mehrens, W. A., and I. J. Lehmann. *Measurement and Evaluation in Education and Psychology.* New York: Holt, 1973.

Norman, G. R., et al. "Factors Underlying Performance on Written Tests of Knowledge." *Medical Education* 21 (July 1987): 297–304. Comparing multiple-choice and modified essay questions, the authors find the latter more labor-intensive but also more informative.

Perry, William G. Jr. "Examsmanship and the Liberal Arts." *Examining in Harvard College: A Collection of Essays by Members of the Harvard Faculty.* Cambridge: Harvard UP, 1963. By mouthing generalities, students can too easily succeed on examinations without offering much concrete information.

Popken, Randall L. "Essay Exams and Papers: A Contextual Comparison." *Journal of Teaching Writing* 8 (Spring–Summer 1989): 51–66. Popken compares essay exams and papers in history and sociology and finds that their different pedagogical and rhetorical functions complement each other.

Posner, Richard. "Life without Scan-Tron: Tests as Thinking." *English Journal* 76 (1987): 35–38. Improvements in critical thinking and writing result from replacing objective tests with written tests.

Rabinowitz, Howard K. "The Modified Essay Question: An Evaluation of Its Use in Family Medicine Clerkship." *Medical Education* 21 (Mar. 1987): 114–18. Rabinowitz explains the benefits of using modified essay questions rather than multiple choice, based on his twelve years of experience with the former.

Scannell, Dale P., and Jon C. Marshall. "The Effect of Selected Composition Errors on Grades Assigned to Essay Examinations." *American Educational Research Journal* 3 (Mar. 1966): 125–30.

White, Edward M. *Assigning, Responding, Evaluating: A Writing Teacher's Guide.* New York: St. Martin's, 1991. White offers a discussion of the uses of essay exams and writing portfolios in writing assessment. He explains designing and assessing essay exam questions; teaching students to write effective in-class essays; and designing and evaluating writing portfolios. The book includes a chapter on responding to student writing.

CHAPTER 9

Assigning and Evaluating Collaboration

In this chapter:

- Creating an environment for collaboration
- Leading class discussion
- Small-group discussion
- Assigning collaborative writing
- Responding to collaborative work
- Grading collaborative work
- Collaborative student dialogues
- Peer response to writing
- Checklist for collaborative learning and writing
- For further reading

Creating an Environment for Collaboration

Collaboration is often the norm in business and scientific writing, but only recently has the pedagogy of collaborative learning gained currency in the undergraduate curriculum. Instructors are finding that collaborative writing and discussion enable students to learn more than they would working alone. John Trimbur explains that collaborative pedagogy helps students "reach consensus through an expanding conversation" (602).

Three types of collaboration occur in undergraduate classrooms: class discussion, as a whole class or in small groups; collaborative writing groups, in which a group of students plans and completes a written project; and peer response, in which groups of students meet to respond to one another's individual writing.

Choosing groups

The most effective collaboration occurs among people who feel comfortable with one another. Students tend to be insecure about their writing and seldom find it easy to sit down and share it with others, particularly those whom they do not know well. Students who have never experienced collaborative or small-group learning can learn from those who have but may also feel insecure in their presence and have trouble, at least initially, contributing to the effort. Allowing them to select their own groups may decrease some insecurity, but it may also produce some groups that need extra attention as they learn how to collaborate.

If the instructor selects collaborative groups, it is helpful to provide a classroom environment that allows students to feel comfortable as part of the larger group (calling everyone by name, for instance) and makes them feel at ease when voicing opinions and discussing writing issues. (See pages 166–168 for suggestions on involving students in class discussion.) If students get to know one another in the public setting of the classroom, they will have an easier time settling in to private, instructor-selected groups.

Class discussion

To succeed in engaging students in constructive class discussion, whether in small groups or in the whole class, the instructor may need to counteract the traditional classroom environment, in which learning occurs as a result of students' listening to and taking notes in lectures. Students are assumed to come to the classroom for "information," the "facts"—and the instructor is the font of such knowledge. Students may also believe that class discussion is a gift that a beneficent instructor occasionally bestows as a respite from the rigors of fact gathering; or they may view their role in class discussion as simply demonstrating to the instructor that they have acquired transmitted facts. Persuading students that class discussion can be an engagement in collective problem solving is a challenge that instructors can meet by demonstrating the benefits of collaborative learning.

Collaborative writing groups

Once groups have been selected, instructors usually allow a few minutes for participants to get to know one another and overcome shyness and uncertainty. A brief discussion of the purposes of collaboration can help students learn to work together more effectively. Educated in a society that views writing as a solitary effort to produce "original" texts, students may not readily perceive how collaborative all their writing is. James Porter has observed that writers cannot, in fact, identify the myriad and usually untraceable sources of their ideas (35). Thus, it's a good idea, at the beginning of collaboration, to discuss plagiarism and the difficulties of defining what needs to be attributed and what does not.

Collaborative assignments also engage students in types of writing that they may be involved in after college. In graduate school in the natural and social sciences and in the workplace, much of their writing will be done in cooperation with others. Many instructors who assign collaborative writing ask students for confidential evaluations of the process. Students thus have the opportunity to express the natural frustration that inevitably arises from the process as well as to report more serious problems (e.g., if one person is not completing a fair share of the work). The evaluations may lead to further conversation between instructor and collaborators, with perhaps different grades given to the members of the group. This evaluation procedure can be conducted during the writing process or just at the end, when the paper is handed in.

Peer response groups

Some students may have had experience, pleasant or unpleasant, with peer response. If they have taken classes in which the instructor allowed or encouraged negative "critiquing" or did not train students in productive methods of peer response, they may view the activity with fear or disdain. (Pages 184–189 offers suggestions for a more positive peer-response pedagogy.) All students need to be reassured, therefore, that they will not be subjected to fault-finding and that the instructor will provide concrete guidelines for peer response.

Instructors may encounter some students who question the validity of peer response, especially because many students are accustomed to writing solely for the instructor who will assign the grade. They may question their classmates' authority for grading their writing. Instructors can perhaps explain the value of peer response from their own experience with peer review of scholarly work, explaining that responses and suggestions from their colleagues—and their responses to their colleagues' work—substantially enrich the revising process by providing the author an active audience with whom to converse. The peer review stage is the last opportunity for the author, text, and readers to engage in direct conversation that affects the text.

Leading Class Discussion

At the heart of collaboration is conversation, and the first conversation students will have in a course will be class discussion among all members of the class with the instructor as leader.

Usually, a few well-prepared and well-socialized students will raise their hands in response to all of the instructor's questions while the rest of the class sits in silence. Instructors can encourage more class members to participate by acting as scribe and moderator rather than as judge, asking open rather than closed questions, calling on individuals rather than merely waiting for raised hands, and requiring students to listen to one another and address their comments to other students rather than the instructor.

In one successful method for leading class discussion, the instructor acts as facilitator and scribe, eliciting comments from students and writing their ideas on the board. Accustomed to the idea that "correct facts" are written on the board, students will feel their own ideas validated and will be inclined to take their classmates' contributions seriously. While writing students' remarks on the board, the instructor can organize them into columns or categories, draw lines to show links or disunities, or ask questions to clarify and then revise statements.

Eliciting comments is best accomplished by calling on individuals rather than by addressing questions to the class in general and waiting for hands to go up. The enthusiasm of those raised hands can be consoling to the instructor, but it often causes feelings of resentment and inferiority among the other class members. Calling on individuals, in contrast, ensures that everyone will eventually have an opportunity to speak—even those who haven't the courage or motivation to volunteer. The instructor must take pains to ensure that, as the weeks go on, all the students in the class are called on with approximately equal frequency.

It may be difficult, especially at first, to prompt useful comments from every student. In response to "I don't know," the instructor's next best question may be "Have you read the assignment?" If the answer is negative, the instructor can call on another student who has. If the original student has read the assignment, the instructor can challenge "I don't know" by helping the student recall what he or she has read. The simple question "What do you remember? Tell me anything" allows even the most nervous student to provide some information. The instructor can write it on the board and ask another student to validate the first student's contribution—"Is this your memory of what the author said?"

And as soon as a student offers an opinion about the issue at hand, the instructor can turn to another and ask, "Do you agree?" Asking one student to respond to what another has just said encourages students to listen to one another and consider others' ideas rather than sit unhearing while they await their turn to perform. A question as simple as "Do you agree with what she just said?" is guaranteed to spur discussion, provided it is followed by a second question: "Why?" Without that follow-up question, students may simply resort to bland affirmation of statements that they didn't even hear. Another all-purpose strategy for jump-starting class discussion is to ask one student whether he understood what another just said. If the answer is "no," the instructor can ask for repetition of the original statement. And if the answer is "yes," the instructor responds, "Great. So tell me what she said." Once the student has done that, the instructor can go on to ask the "Do you agree?" question. After a few such episodes, the class members can usually be relied on to listen to one another.

Another strategy for engaging students in class discussion is to avoid asking questions that have only one right answer. Most students can spot questions to which the instructor has determined the answer, and very few of them will venture to respond. A "closed" question is of the type "What are the three ways to . . . ," where the three ways have already been determined. An "open" question is of the type "What ways can you think of to . . ." or "What do you consider an effective way to . . . ," where students can propose possibilities that even the instructor may find enlightening. Open questions about texts can be "What do you consider to be the chief point?" or "How convincing did you find the argument?"

Of course, closed questions may be necessary to clear up misunderstandings. Yet even these can be posed in ways other than the standard "What does the text say about this?" where the student must supply the correct information. Instead, the instructor can ask, "How much of the text's discussion on this do you remember?" Students can answer this question correctly, even if they remember very little. The instructor can then fill in the gaps or, better yet, invite other members of the class to do so or direct their attention to the crucial passages that they have misunderstood or forgotten. If many students have trouble remembering a specific passage or theme, asking them to speculate on why they think this happened can generate productive discussion.

Whole-class discussion works well for classes of thirty or fewer students, but as enrollment exceeds thirty, small-group work will be a more productive means of involving students in active learning.

Small-Group Discussion

Exploiting the connection between writing and talking, the in-class small-group discussion is one widely used means of collaborative learning. In William Sweigart's research, twelfth graders demonstrated greater comprehension of course materials through small-group discussion than through whole-class discussion or lecture.

To facilitate small-group discussion, the instructor divides the class into groups as small as three or as large as nine and assigns them a task, preferably one that is written on the board or handed out in written form. (If directions are given orally, the students can too easily forget or misunderstand them.) They might be asked to summarize a class activity such as a laboratory experiment or field research. Or they might be asked to respond to an assigned reading or a class lecture: to evaluate the argument, to put it in the context of other course material, to discuss the students' personal responses to it, or to summarize its chief points.

Assigning Study Questions

Class discussion in any format can be facilitated by giving students discussion questions with each reading assignment. Students can use these questions for directed reading that can lead to content-rich class discussion. Effective questions should do more than ask students to look for certain facts; they should be phrased to help explain the text and suggest reading and note taking strategies. They can focus on whatever the instructor wishes to emphasize in the text: understanding and interpreting content; evaluating evidence, assumptions, and biases; making connections and comparisons with other texts and lecture material; and so on.

SAMPLE STUDY QUESTIONS (EXCERPT)
Generating small-group discussion
Racism, Sexism, and Social Darwinism: Mary Lynn Rampolla

1. According to Gould, what is the theory of recapitulation, what is its relationship to Darwin's theory, and what role did it have in the development of new "scientific" theories about race and gender?
2. What is "neoteny," and how is it different from recapitulation? After reading Vogt's first lecture, can you detect the impact of Darwin's theory on Vogt's ideas?
3. On p. 9, Vogt says that male and female skulls diverge more sharply in the "civilized races" than in "inferior races." What is the significance of this "fact"?
4. What, according to Vogt, is the relationship between humans and other mammals? How is his view different from that of Gobineau? How do his views on this relationship reflect the impact of Darwin?
5. Vogt, like the other figures we've studied in this course, believed in racial ranking. How is his ranking system different from that of the pre-Darwinian thinkers we've looked at, and how does it reflect the impact of evolutionary theory?

Professor Rampolla used these questions in a writing-intensive first-year seminar in the history of science. Questions 1 and 2 focus on specific concepts from the course that students must know to comprehend the text and engage in analysis or evaluation.

The succeeding questions ask students to *connect* this text to other readings in the course; *analyze* and interpret the source, paying specific attention to the significance of the author's views in the discipline and in the outside world; *compare* this author's conclusions with those of other authors from the course; and *describe* specific aspects of the content of the text.

The tight focus of these questions helps students practice a variety of academic skills, including honing their mastery of academic thinking.

6. What, according to Vogt, is the impact of religion on science?
7. According to Vogt, how do male and female skulls compare?
8. Vogt compares female skulls to those of "infants" and people of "lower races." What is the significance of this comparison? What role does evolution play in this comparison?
9. According to Vogt, the inequality between the sexes increases with civilization. How does Vogt explain this correlation? What are the implications of this theory?
10. What is the significance of Vogt's assertion that "woman preserves primitive forms"?

Having assigned study questions, instructors can stimulate discussion by asking the students to write out their answers and present their answers in their small groups. Or a discussion leader can be charged with leading each group through the questions using his or her own notes. Each group can then present a five-minute summary of its discussion to the entire class or lead class discussion on one question.

For an assigned reading of substantial length, another approach to small-group discussion is to assign the first part of the reading and then in class have the students collaboratively generate their own study questions based on their understanding of the selection. Afterward, these questions can guide the students' reading of the remainder of the selection, and their answers can provide the substance of subsequent class discussion and small-group work. This strategy works best if the instructor has distributed his or her own study questions for at least two previous readings to familiarize students with how study questions are asked and the types of issues they address.

Setting up small groups for discussion

Methods for designating membership in small groups vary. Students can simply be told to gather in groups of a designated size, which will enable them to choose peers with whom they feel comfortable—but which may also make wallflowers feel conspicuous and uncomfortable, much like the last child on the playground to be picked for a team. The alternative is for the instructor to choose groups. The instructor may do this deliberately, putting students with similar (or different) skills or inclinations together. Or it may be done at random. The benefit of random selection is that it puts together people who might not otherwise be listening to each other and thereby broadens the experience of the groups. At first group members may feel uncomfortable if the group crosses racial, gender, age, class, or ability lines and if members are unused to working with people from other social backgrounds; however, the demands of a tightly focused task can help them overcome their uncertainty. Instructors who predict or observe tension or discomfort often find it helpful to assign a specific task to each group member in preparation for collaboration, perhaps asking each to write up and hand in both their individual work and the work resulting from the collaboration. Though asking all group members to write up results of the collaboration may seem redundant, it can help students who are new to discussion groups get a better overall sense of what collaboration accomplishes. It also helps ensure that all group members participate.

If the groups seem to gel, many instructors choose to keep these same groups for the term. Constant membership has the advantage that a group learns to work together and accomplishes each new task with increasing ease. Sometimes, though, personal conflicts arise or some students find themselves carrying the load while others coast. Changing group membership has the asset of bringing fresh and unfamiliar perspectives to new tasks; it broadens the students' scope of experience.

During and after small-group discussion

Once the groups begin work, the instructor should facilitate and monitor the pragmatics of group discussion. Participants should sit close together so that they can talk readily to one another in low voices. Proximity promotes confidence among the students, particularly in early sessions, when they may be self-conscious about having other groups listening in. As the groups are getting established, the instructor must be sure that every student remains physically within the group. Then the instructor should observe the types of activity taking place within the groups. Have the students fallen silent? Have they begun reading their texts or writing notes to themselves? Are they engaged in seemingly irrelevant discussion? Walking around the classroom, the instructor may overhear a group engaged in intense conversation about yesterday's football game instead of today's assigned topic. It is usually a mistake to charge in and upbraid the group. Irrelevant discussion often serves important purposes: Students may, without realizing it, be using irrelevant discussion as a way of stalling while they figure out what they want to say about the assigned topic, or they may be in the process of becoming more comfortable with each other before returning to the difficult and perhaps intimidating task at hand. The instructor's best approach may be to allow digressions for a brief time and then, if necessary, intervene and help the group focus on the task. Usually, students will return to the task on their own, when they have had time to think about it and space to get to know each other. Each group can elect a secretary who takes notes, gets discussion back on track when it is periodically derailed, and reports the outcome of discussion to the class. (The instructor should make sure that groups don't habitually designate the same student for this job or automatically choose a woman.)

While the small groups work, the instructor may elect to take part in one of the groups, to move from group to group, or to stay out of the way and let the students take charge. Allowing the groups autonomy may at first feel strange to those who are accustomed to thinking of the instructor as the source of classroom truth. But instructors and students alike soon learn to appreciate the intellectual activity of small groups, and students come to realize that there is no one "right" answer owned by the instructor, transmitted through a lecture, transcribed in class notes, memorized, and returned to the instructor on tests. If the instructor does elect to take part in small-group discussions or even to monitor them, it is therefore crucial that he or she refrain from the impulse to supply answers or to leap on incorrect information.

Many instructors leave time at the end of class for each group to report, so that all students can hear the outcome of their peers' discussions. It is important that the reporting of group activity not blur differences among participants. The reporter for each group can be charged with summarizing all the opinions of the group; or the reporter can be charged with summarizing the dominant ideas, and then the instructor can ask group members for dissenting or alternative opinions. Another way of disseminating the work of small groups is to ask for a representative to write up the findings and then photocopy them for distribution to the entire class or put them on reserve in the library.

Assigning Collaborative Writing

Collaborative writing can take many forms. In each one, the students work together to develop ideas and commit them to paper. Although instructors are probably most familiar with the collaboratively written report, article, or book, the principles of collaborative writing can also be used to produce statements, arguments, and summaries.

Collaboratively written academic papers

Johanna W. Atwood differentiates two types of collaborative writing: hierarchical (dividing tasks) and dialogic (writing together).

Writers in hierarchical collaboration produce an outline together and divide it into sections. Then each member drafts a part of the text. Next the writers gather together to construct a complete paper out of the separately authored pieces.

Hierarchical collaboration teaches cooperation, as the students divide the work and fulfill their separate roles. This model tends to be effective for writers who do not know one another well or have not come to trust one another as writers; and for long student papers it may be the only practical way of writing collaboratively. It is also particularly appropriate to courses in the natural and social sciences that focus on disciplinary genres (see Chapter 1), for it engages students in writing activities typical of professional work in those disciplines.

SAMPLE WRITING ASSIGNMENT (EXCERPT)
Hierarchical collaborative writing
Introduction to Quantitative Social Research: Robert Elgie

ASSIGNMENT 12: THE BIG ONE

A few weeks ago, Susie, Gary, and their editor wrote the introduction and conceptualization sections of a research report focused on "environmental activism" which they defined as the willingness to make personal sacrifices in support of environmental objectives. They created a conceptual model which incorporates a number of hypotheses concerning the anticipated patterning of this willingness among Colgate students. I have placed a printed copy of their work on the lab bulletin board, and the document itself is in the STATVIEW folder of every lab Macintosh, labeled ENVIRON(SPR93)PAPER. Print out a copy for yourself and *read it carefully.* Study most carefully the flow chart which summarizes their hypotheses.

You are now joining their research team to complete their research report by writing the "Research Design," "Findings," and "Conclusion" sections of this paper. You will analyze the data file ENVIRON (SPR93)DATA to do so. It is also in the STATVIEW folder (in the GEOG225 Data Sets folder) on the Macs in Lawrence 14. Please copy this data onto your own disk and use your own version so that you don't accidentally corrupt the files on the lab Macs.

In the "Research Design" section you should describe *briefly* the nature of the survey research design we used, including our sampling procedures. Aim to do this in no more than one page (single spaced, double spaced between paragraphs).

In the "Findings" section you should seek to accomplish the following objectives. . . .

I strongly suggest that you test these hypotheses *in two stages.* . . .

I would like you to close this "Findings" section with a revised flow chart that summarizes the findings from the set of multiple regression models.

Professor Elgie has designed his syllabus to include staged assignments. (See pages 58–60.) This assignment, twelfth in the series, follows an earlier task of dialogic collaboration. From the dialogic collaboration Professor Elgie chose one group's work and asked the entire class to conduct hierarchical collaboration, building on Susie and Gary's work. His assigning hierarchical collaboration engages the students in a form of writing common among professional geographers: building on work begun by others as well as turning one's work over to others for completion.

His intention in this assignment is not only to teach students how to work in the kinds of relationships typical of professional geographers, but also to prompt them to produce materials that will serve as a template for future work. Elgie's directions provide the student writers

with a discipline-
specific outline for the
presentation of data.

Finally, in the "Conclusions" section of your report, give a brief summary of your findings and their implications and perhaps the usual suggestions for future research.

Hand in the entire report including both a clean copy of the first part that was done by Susie and Gary and the sections you have written. This way you will have a complete quantitative research example (from problem statement to conclusion) for future reference. In fact, I suggest you simply add your name as a third author to the first page of Gary and Susie's section to reflect the fact that you have now joined their research team. You will be paid later.

Helpful Hints

I cannot stress too strongly that I don't want you to perform every analysis imaginable or to throw a lot of raw STATVIEW tables into your "Findings" section. Create a careful but simple game plan that suggests what analyses would be most appropriate. Prepare your own tables that summarize the findings produced just as you have been doing over the past few weeks. Number those tables and integrate them into the body of the paper. Don't slavishly use my cryptic STATVIEW variable names for questions. Think up short phrases that will mean something to the reader of your paper. Reorder variables in a table whenever the revised ordering will help to make a point.

Final Suggestion

I am making the final three class periods open labs with me available as a consultant for a reason. Use them wisely to develop your plan of attack, perform analyses in the lab, and discuss findings that you find confusing with me. If you simply ignore this project for the next week and don't seek my help, I guarantee that you will regret it.

In the dialogic model, writers compose one text together, debating and discussing content and style at the sentence level as they produce the text. Dialogic collaborative writing teaches cooperation by engaging students in extended conversation and collaborative problem solving and decision making. It is therefore especially appropriate for a course focusing on write-to-learn genres. (See Chapter 1.) As the preceding sample assignment indicates, some collaborative writers use both hierarchical and dialogic models at different stages of the writing process. For example, writers might divide up tasks and separately research and write first-draft text (hierarchical) but then revise and construct subsequent drafts together (dialogic); this book was written using that method. Or, as Professor Elgie's assignment demonstrates, they might do the reverse, with dialogic collaboration coming first.

Collaborative position statements and arguments

Another fruitful use of collaborative writing is the drafting of position statements or arguments on topics that have proven controversial in class discussion. Students can be grouped according to their opinions, with each group charged with writing a position statement that asserts its point of view, presents the evidence for its beliefs, and explores the counterevidence (the doubts that the students have about their positions, or alternative interpretations that they deem plausible). The resulting documents can be distributed to the entire class. Or the group can be charged with oral presentation, after which the class can respond and ask questions. Such an assignment is most frequently given toward the end of the term, when students have had an opportunity to get to know one another and when the premises of disputed topics have had the entire term to become established.

SAMPLE ASSIGNMENT
Hierarchical and dialogic writing combined
Rhetoric: Sandra Jamieson

1. I will hand out a list of about twenty of the debatable statements suggested in class.
2. Each student will write at least five arguments for and against four statements of their choice from the list.
3. They will give me those arguments, with the statements ranked in order of preference as a discussion topic. I will then attempt to compose groups of four people for each topic—with the understanding that students can trade places and change topics if they are uncomfortable with either, but that they will try to work with the group they are placed in.
4. *Each group* will collectively compose a list of at least ten arguments for and ten against the selected statement using their own lists and discussion within the group.
5. *Each student* will individually write rough drafts of two papers (one for and the other against) using those arguments. I will collect and keep copies of these to ensure that each student's voice appears in the final piece.
6. The group will read and carefully critique the papers each member writes. When the group of four is entirely cognizant of all the possible arguments for and against, they will divide into two groups of two, one group to argue in favor of the statement, the other against it.
7. Using the pieces already written, and aware of the arguments that the other pair will make, each pair will collaboratively write a five-page argument. They can research individual points and

This assignment was collaboratively drafted and executed and was designed at the students' request when they learned that Professor Jamieson was herself engaged in a collaborative writing project. The students modified the final assignment so that it could be accomplished collaboratively.

The first drafts of the position papers were written hierarchically, with each student taking responsibility for half of the arguments. Then the students dialogically combined and revised the drafts. By the end of the process almost no sentences remained in their original form.

The students worked on the papers both in and out of class, and the entire project took two weeks to complete. (Only two entire class periods writing process, and these took place at the later, dialogic stage.)

On their course evaluations the students overwhelmingly declared that this was their favorite writing assignment, the one that had taken the most work, and also the one from which they had learned the most. It also produced the best papers any of them had written.

statistics if they feel their paper requires it, and they can also include anecdotes and quotes to add to the power of the piece. This work must be done both in the classroom and outside of it, and will comprise the last paper of the course.

8. We will then return to our discussion of presentations and pairs will work on reformulating the arguments so that the papers can be presented orally to their fellow students.

9. The last class of the semester will be three hours long and will be a formal debate in a lecture hall with an invited audience. One person from each pair will present their adapted paper, while the other is responsible for the two-to-five-minute responses/summing up speeches, which will also be prepared collaboratively, but can be modified to respond to specific points raised by the audience during the question period. Either member of the pair can answer questions and comments from the floor during discussion. Each class member in the audience will be required to write a series of notes on, and comments about, each presentation and then mark the comment sheet with his or her decision in favor of or against the statement. Guests should be encouraged to do this also.

Whole-class collaborations

As the preceding sample illustrates, even an assignment can be drafted collaboratively by the entire class. The instructor can become scribe as well as participant, writing on the board the ideas the class generates for an upcoming paper. Together the class (including the instructor) selects and refines the assignment, which the instructor may designate to be completed individually or collaboratively. The process of designing a writing assignment requires that students know the course material well, because they will be called on to offer and explain suggestions. It also teaches students how to analyze future assignments to understand the writing task thoroughly.

If the assignment-design process is productive, some instructors elect to engage the entire class in the process of drafting a paper. The procedure is generally to produce an outline collaboratively, with the instructor again adopting the role of scribe and writing on the board the ideas the class generates. Often the instructor also has to play a role in the decisions about organization. Once class members have produced what they deem a satisfactory outline, they divide its sections among the class. Depending on the size of the class, more than one student may be assigned to a single section. Regardless of how many students are assigned to each section, though, the individual students write a draft of their section for the next class session.

The instructor again becomes scribe. (An overhead projector or networked computer classroom facilitates this task.) The entire class

---

SAMPLE WRITING ASSIGNMENT
Whole-class collaboration
Writing from Sources in the Social Sciences: Tom Howard

Ken Kesey taught a graduate creative writing seminar in which he and his students co-wrote a novel, which was later published by Viking Press. We will adapt his idea for "Writing from Sources." The only major modifications of Kesey's plan are that the group writing project will consist of a research paper rather than fiction, and we will work on networked computers rather than with pen[cil] and paper.

The research topic will be chosen by the class. Research for the paper will be conducted outside of class, but all writing will be performed in class time, with all students participating. The networked computers will make it possible for everyone at the same time to see what an individual is writing, and to be able to superimpose suggested changes, also visible to the entire class.

Professor Howard says that two caveats are necessary for computer-networked dialogic collaboration. First, unless this is the only class activity, it is not tactically possible to complete a full-length paper in a semester using this method. It is the process of writing rather than the final product that is the goal of such pedagogy. Second, the instructor must have override capability on the network so that screens can be blanked or frozen to make a pedagogical point. This particular class was conducted in a classroom equipped with DOS computers linked by a Robotel network and also projected onto a large screen through an overhead projector. This approach worked well for the class of eighteen students. Yet it was the process itself rather than the finished product that was pedagogically valid. Although working together on the research paper consumed weeks of labor without producing a finished product, the students were excited by the experience, and several chose to continue the project as independent study in the succeeding semester.

revises the individually drafted sections, sets an overall style, and puts the parts together, with students conducting additional research and drafting outside of the classroom as necessary.

Collaborative summaries

Summarizing an assigned reading takes on a new dimension when authorship is collaborative. The task of summary might seem a closed question—to reproduce accurately the content of a text—but it is in fact open-ended. Texts have meaning only insofar as people read and understand them. Assigning a group summary can help students respond to texts more critically, recognizing that they can be interpreted in a variety of ways. In addition, group summary makes students active intellectuals who must engage with the text and with other students to establish meaning. The product of group summary is far richer than summaries of students working alone or of the instructor explaining the text, with students as passive listeners. Students also come away from the exercise with a good model for out-of-class studying.

One valuable method is to have small groups work on a preliminary draft of the summary. The class then revises that draft, usually with the issue of conflicting interpretations surfacing. Another method of collaborative summarizing is to begin the process not with small groups but with the entire class. The instructor calls on one student to relate what he or she can recall from the assigned reading. Other students make additions, deletions, and revisions. (Calling on individuals in such an exercise is important; otherwise, the discussion may be monopolized by those who are habitually well prepared for class and comfortable with contributing. And when an instructor calls upon a student, it is important not to let others leap in and supply answers before that student has had an opportunity to ponder the question and formulate an answer.) The instructor serves as scribe, recording the students' observations on the board, an act which lends validity to student contributions (for the habits of schooling tell us that what is on the board is important information). The members of the class therefore tend to take their work more seriously and treat their classmates' statements with greater respect. In addition, the instructor can step in at crucial junctures to ask questions that will lead the class to deeper analysis or to clarify difficult points that the class cannot decipher.

Responding to Collaborative Work

Some instructors respond to drafts during the process of collaborative writing; others wait until they see the finished product. Both the timing and the nature of the comments will depend on the method students use to write their papers.

Responding to drafts from hierarchical collaboration

Each student engaged in hierarchical collaboration (see pages 172–174) can provide the instructor with a record of his or her contribution to the project. Most instructors provide final comments to all of the authors of a paper written through hierarchical collaboration. Asking for all drafts, writing comments in the margins or holistic comments at the end, and then copying the whole package for each student is one method of response.

The exit interview is a less labor-intensive method in which the instructor writes a holistic comment on each draft (see page 62) and then meets with the students together to discuss the process. This method can give the students a greater sense of closure and provide the instructor with valuable insight into the process of student collaboration and collaborative assignments.

Responding to drafts from dialogic collaboration

Dialogic collaboration produces one draft from the entire group, and participants will probably be unable to distinguish individual members' prose. To grade this type of collaboration the instructor has several options. Perhaps the easiest is simply to respond to the assertions rather than the style of the final product, addressing the paper on the basis of the research or the strength of the argument. The instructor would provide copies of his or her response to each contributor. It is tempting to expect more research from a collaborative paper than from an individual assignment, but this expectation must be tempered by the knowledge that collaborative papers require more time and effort than individual ones because the writers must work around one another's schedules, study habits, and prose styles.

Responding to collaborative drafts: coherence and cohesion

If the assignment was designed primarily to teach students how to collaborate, it is particularly helpful for the instructor to respond to interim drafts and comment on style, since collaborators typically experience difficulty in melding different prose styles. To encourage collaborative ventures, an instructor should comment on the cohesion and coherence of the prose and offer suggestions for smoothing out style and tone.

If the paper is composed hierarchically, the finished product may particularly lack cohesion, jumping from one author and idea to the next without consistent style or effective transitions. The instructor can offer suggestions for smoothing it out and in the process teach some valuable editing skills.

Dialogic papers tend toward a lack of coherence. As collaborators struggle on the sentence level, they often forget to look at the overall paper for clearly stated ideas and well-developed arguments. Again, the instructor can teach important editing skills.

Whatever method is adopted, to encourage student collaboration instructors should write comments articulating and affirming the process. Especially pleasing prose, effective structure, or well-developed reasoning should be noted, as should passages that do not show the marks of disparate voices.

Grading Collaborative Work

If the students have used a hierarchical approach and each has identified his or her contributions, or if they have written self-reports about the process of collaboration, the instructor can collect all drafts and comments and evaluate each student independently. The model generally adopted for this method of grading is to assign a grade to the finished paper that constitutes a percentage of each student's final grade (50–75%) and assign the remaining percentage of each student's grade to his or her individual work. This method is particularly effective with first-year undergraduates and with groups in which the collaboration has not been entirely smooth.

When collective grades are given, the instructor evaluates the final product and assigns the same grade to each student who worked on it. Many instructors assign a collective grade to collaborative work as a way of reinforcing the model of cooperation established by the nature of the assignment. If all of the students involved in a collaboration are graded only on the basis of the final product, they have greater incentive to work on that product and thus truly collaborate. This grading method is especially effective for juniors and seniors with fairly equal writing skills and motivation who can thus be expected to contribute equally to the paper. If it is used for first-year students, it is especially important to monitor their work, perhaps devoting one or more class periods to the writing process.

Collaborative Student Dialogues

Written student-to-student dialogues

One of the most exciting academic writing assignments is written student-to-student dialogues, which can be accomplished through E-mail or through exchange of papers. Intensity builds as students write back and forth to one another and learn to communicate in writing about academic issues and problems. Sometimes in the early stages of written dialogues the instructor can make some written or oral response to the exchange. Usually, though, the instructor's participation becomes unnecessary; the students are propelled by their written conversation. One result is that students tend to speak much more readily in class discussions. In situations where class discussion is constrained by class size, sensitive reading material, or classroom dynamics, written student dialogues can be a valuable forum.

SAMPLE WRITTEN STUDENT-TO-STUDENT DIALOGUE (EXCERPT)
Talent, Society, and the State: Tom Howard

OK! OK! I seem to have been wrong in an interpretation of Bohr's words that "original work is inherently rebellious" (Rhodes, 95). As a first response, I know now that I was in too much of a hurry to find the answers to my overwhelming questions about truth and fact. I realize even more so now that in order to find the real and satisfying answers, much more time and thought was going to be needed. As a large portion of the class pointed out to me, rebellion does not warrant a negative connotation. I address all of you who wrote to me, you are all right. Rebellion in the form about which Rhodes is speaking deserves a pat on the back. Too many people today are too easily influenced by societal rules and regulations. Although many times it is necessary [to] conform, at other times it would only be dangerous to all of mankind. Thought processes should not be influenced, but all people should be able to form their own thoughts and opinions, of course. But even more importantly, new thoughts and ideas should be congratulated and encouraged to find more continuous ideas to back up those new ideas. I now understand the word "rebellion" under a different light; not as a wrong and negative descriptive, but as a necessary radical way of life. Although it is not the correct characteristic for everyone, in the hands of the right people, it is a positive and exciting characteristic.

Kristin Cardin, a junior chemistry major, was participating in a student-to-student dialogue in an interdisciplinary general education course.

By the time this entry was written, the instructor had long since ceased to take part in the dialogue and he did not grade the exchange. He had become simply the facilitator who collected, selected, and distributed the students' writing.

The professor reports that exchanges of this intensity are the norm rather than the exception in student-to-student dialogues. The product of such dialogues is intellectual electricity. Students are in control, writing to one another rather than to the instructor. They are writing about—and developing—their beliefs about the intellectual content of the course. They tend to be enthusiastic about the dialogues, sometimes continuing them even after the course is over and asking the professor to participate.

Some instructors require them for the first few weeks of the course until the students feel comfortable with one another or during a part of the semester when provocative reading materials or sensitive issues are likely to need additional discussion and analysis.

Often the dialogue begins with a response paper or journal assignment. (See Chapter 10.) Students are asked to write informally in response to a class discussion, lecture, or assigned reading. The instructor reads these papers and selects several that represent a range of responses, duplicates them, and distributes them to the class or makes them available on library reserve. The students read all of the papers and respond to one or more of them. From these responses the instructor again selects representative samples, and the procedure begins again.

Less labor-intensive dialogue can also take place in a collaborative journal held in the library reserve room. Students can be assigned to write an entry in the journal once a week (or less often if class size makes that frequency impractical). Topics can be assigned or students can be asked to read all of the entries written since they last looked at the journal and respond to one or more. Some instructors read the entries after each cycle and write a brief synthesis, analysis, or comments on specific points. Students may then respond to the instructor's comments in their next entries. After the first four cycles, individual students or groups of students can be assigned to write the overall comment imitating the form adopted by the instructor. Groups of students can write collaboratively or divide the total number of entries among themselves (the most practical response in large classes). The other students can then respond in their next entries.

If students wish to write anonymously, they may elect to adopt pseudonyms or identify themselves by ID number; however, social markers of class, race, and region are often still apparent in writing in the form of regionalisms and nonstandard grammar and usage. Because many students have learned to see nonstandard grammar and terminology in writing as "errors," some may find it difficult to respond to the content of such work and may tend to dismiss it because of perceived errors. Instructors can stress that informal writing is acceptable in the dialogues and journals, or they may discuss issues of nonstandard usage in making the assignment. (See pages 78–79 for a discussion of nonstandard dialect interference.) The desire to remain anonymous can encourage students to adopt standard English forms and thus practice what linguists term *code-switching*—the shift from one dialect to another, depending on circumstances. Discussing the practice may help students be more attentive to language and word choice as indicators of one's identity. Instructors who encourage such a discussion observe that at first it may constrain the writing of students who have never consciously code-switched but that it reassures students to know that the practice is widespread and serves many purposes. Other instructors do not raise the issue in class because, while most of us can identify spoken dialects, few students are able to connect the written interferences of dialect to any ethnic group unless they themselves are members of that group. Other instructors argue that a discussion of code-switching diverts students' attention from the content of the dialogue and encourages them to try to guess the identity of each writer as they read.

E-mail student-to-student dialogues

As campus computing facilities improve and more students become familiar with word processing, many instructors incorporate computer networks and electronic mail (E-mail) into their classes. Both systems allow student-to-student dialogues to occur with very little work for the instructor. Dialogues can follow the method described in the previous section, with the students sending their work to the instructor via the network or over E-mail and the instructor sending selected responses back to all of the students (using a "broadcast" function on the E-mail or network). In some classes, students carry on course-specific E-mail conversations with peers on other campuses.

Computer networks also allow for electronic class journals and anonymous discussion groups. Each method uses a discussion group model that is available on E-mail. All the students in the class are members of an electronic group. When they send a message to the group, every member receives it. All of the students can record responses to class discussions, lectures, readings, or the responses of other students. This provides the class members and the instructor with a running commentary on the course and on student reaction to it. Comments can be signed or written under a pseudonym. The instructor may choose whether to participate in the discussion, anonymously or as facilitator. Cynthia L. Selfe describes an E-mail discussion group that allowed students in a graduate English class at Michigan Technological University to talk anonymously. Although participation in the group was optional, students took part eagerly and discussion was animated. Selfe attributes the success in part to the anonymity made possible in the electronic forum: all extratextual social markers of class, race, and gender had been rendered invisible. Though social markers may still be apparent in texts (see pages 183–184), they are less obvious than when students communicate face-to-face. As Selfe's comments suggest, such methods are especially useful in classes where the material is sensitive or where the class dynamics are too volatile for open, easy discussion. They are also valuable for classes that are too large to allow everyone to participate in discussion: No one has to sit with a hand in the air, waiting in vain to be called upon. Everyone has a chance to speak on E-mail.

Instructors who have never set up an electronic discussion group can seek help from the computer center on campus, and many elect to devote some class time to having a computer consultant explain the procedure to the students. Differing degrees of computer literacy and resistance tend to be overcome quickly if the students send their first message from the computer lab under the supervision of the instructor and/or a computer consultant.

Professor Howard set up the E-mail component to her course so that all students—even those who didn't want to be identified by their real names—could receive credit for their contributions.

SAMPLE WRITING ASSIGNMENT
Procedures for an E-mail dialogue
Language and Race: Rebecca Moore Howard

Ten points of your grade will be derived from your participation in the electronic conference for SOAN/COMP 244. Your grade for this activity will be more quantitative than qualitative. I am not urging you to glut the conference with verbiage in order to get an "A" for this activity; rather, I am urging you to drop in on the conference from time to time and say what you think about any aspect of sociolinguistics. If you wait until late in the semester to begin contributing, I will doubt your sincerity.

You must always sign your contributions to the electronic conference, but you may use a pseudonym, if you wish. At the end of the semester you will need to tell me your pseudonym so that I can credit your contributions to you; but your pseudonym(s) will be secret from the rest of the class unless you choose to reveal it.

Peer Response to Writing

In peer response a student writer receives feedback on his or her drafts from other students, either individually or in groups. Like collaborative writing, peer response presupposes that students can learn from one another and work together without an instructor's intervention. Peer response to writing not only produces improved revisions of essays but typically produces improved first drafts, for students tend to work harder on writing that they know their classmates will read and analyze.

General guidelines

From the many successful systems of peer response that have been developed, a few general guidelines emerge. The instructor should give peer reviewers concrete tasks rather than asking them to respond generally to another student's paper. One way to structure response to an argumentative essay is to ask readers (1) to state what they believe the thesis or main point of the paper is; (2) to point out places where they were particularly persuaded by the argument; (3) to point out places where they had difficulty understanding or believing the argument; and (4) to offer suggestions for revision. Many other and more detailed ideas are offered in the sources listed on pages 191–192.

Before peer response pairs or groups set to work, the instructor should model the process in class so that students have a positive framework for conducting their own peer responses. Otherwise, students may fall into patterns of error finding and hierarchical evaluation ("This is a really good paper"; "This is a really bad paper"); or they may simply fall silent, unable to think of anything to say.

The instructor must steer students away from making a negative evaluation and toward offering a description of what works in the paper as well as suggestions for revision. While some suggestions will point out weaknesses, students should be discouraged from adopting the negative tone that they may think the terms *critique* and *evaluation* imply. Peer response is an exercise in community, not in judging. In *Writing without Teachers* Peter Elbow calls successful peer response the "believing game" and negative evaluation the "doubting game." The reader in the believing game accepts the authority and authenticity of the writer's assertions, becomes a member of a cheering squad, and strives to help the writer develop his or her point even more convincingly, whereas the reader in the doubting game looks for the writer's errors and a pattern of flaws. Peer reviewers need to set their sights on the believing game, the approach to writing that assumes a friendly relationship with the writer.

One-to-one peer response

One-to-one peer response characteristically occurs in a two-person exchange of drafts in progress. In the most common version, each writer first explains what he or she is trying to accomplish in the paper and identifies any passages that are proving troublesome or are not yet fully developed. Then each writer becomes the reader of the other's draft and writes a response. It is important that the reader write a response before speaking, because the writing process gives him or her time to think through the features of the text and contemplate possible responses, which increases his or her thinking-in-writing skills. Written comments are also vital in helping writers revise their papers, because of the impossibility of recalling everything said in a peer review and the difficulty of taking notes while listening. Some instructors provide a response sheet and ask the reader to fill it out and give it to the writer along with the draft of the paper. Others ask the writer to make a report of the results of the peer response.

These guidelines, used for peer response in English classes, help peer reviewers focus their reading and pay close attention to details. The order of the questions listed in sections 1 and 2, and their terminology, follow the organization and subject headings of the handbook Professor Steiner assigned to her class, enabling her students to refer to the handbook with ease during the discussion as a means of clarifying rules or checking explanations.

Discussing the introduction first requires that the students think carefully about the purpose of the paper and the direction it promises to take. Steiner's decision to have her students consider the conclusion immediately after the introduction invites them to consider whether the paper ends as it promised it would in the introduction. It also reduces the risk of the conclusion's simply repeating the introduction rather than reflecting on the analysis or propelling it toward further examination and discussion.

By placing grammar last, Professor Steiner deliberately imitates the writing process: Readers observe surface-level errors first, but writers should try to postpone focusing on them until last.

SAMPLE GUIDELINES
Peer response, emphasizing introductions and conclusions
From "Some Questions to Guide Editing": Joan Steiner

ORGANIZATION
1. Does the introduction present the general subject of the essay? Does the writer provide a "bridge" leading to a specific aspect of the general subject? Does the introduction create interest? Does the last or next to last sentence of the paragraph sufficiently introduce the thesis to be supported or question to be investigated? Does the introduction anticipate the main divisions of the essay by stating the major points to be discussed? (optional) Is the tone established consistent with that in the rest of the paper?
2. Does the conclusion (whether sentence or paragraph) give a sense of completeness? Is it emphatic, leaving the reader with an idea to remember through the use of a strong comment? Does it present a final comment? Does it echo the introduction without repeating it?
3. Are the materials as a whole arranged in a logical and readable order? Is the organizing principle clear and well focused? If not, how could the organization be improved?
4. Are the topic sentences of the paragraphs indicative of a coherent order? Are they parallel in form?
5. Are there sufficient transitions from paragraph to paragraph so that the paper flows without noticeable gaps or unexpected turns of thought?
6. Are the individual paragraphs unified and coherent?

CONTENT
1. Does the writer have something to say?
2. Is his/her chosen subject worth writing about, i.e., is it a suitable choice and is the treatment of some substance?
3. Does the writer discuss the subject with relative completeness and in sufficient detail?
4. Does he/she project "authority" (i.e., a grasp of the material)?
5. Does he/she convince the reader?
6. Does he/she engage the reader's interest?

STYLE
1. Is the writing smooth and clear?
2. Are the words aptly and accurately chosen with a sensitivity to denotation and connotation?
3. Has the writer skillfully used such devices as parallelism, coordination and subordination, sentence variety, etc.?
4. Has the writer avoided unnecessary repetition, clumsy phrasing, jargon, clichés, wordiness, passive verbs?
5. Has the writer observed the rules of good grammar?

Small-group peer response

Small-group response works the same as one-to-one pairings, except that every member of the group reads the work of every other member of the group. (Sometimes the process takes place over the entire semester.) Usually the readers do not respond individually, but as a group. Readers talk over together—and with the writer—their responses to and suggestions for the paper. The process may begin with each reader making an individual comment, but the purpose of the group is for readers to provide more than one perspective on strengths and weaknesses of the draft. Some instructors hand out a feedback sheet or ask the group to appoint a scribe to record their suggestions. Group discussion heightens the writer's sense of audience and underscores the idea that the writer always writes for readers. It also helps the student writer to see which passages pleased or confused the majority of readers, providing a more complete picture of the writer's skills and weaknesses.

Because instructors may not be able to monitor all of the groups, some hand out a feedback sheet for each writer to fill out at the end of the session. This sheet offers the instructor valuable information about what to expect on the revised paper. It also encourages students to be self-reflective. Evaluating the session helps them to see what they learned from it and to plan ways to use the group time more productively in the future.

SAMPLE GUIDELINES
Feedback sheet for small-group workshops
Critical Reading and Writing: Margaret Flanders Darby

ROUGH DRAFT WORKSHOP ANALYSIS
Name _____
Date _____

1. Brief description of kind(s) of help requested of the group in the workshop.

2. Notes from listening to group discuss draft.

3. Next steps to be taken with draft.

4. Analysis of outcome: in what ways exactly was the workshop helpful or not?

Professor Darby focuses the writers' responses to peer review by first asking each one to describe what she or he had hoped to gain from the workshop. Then she asks the writer to record his or her notes from the group discussion. This prompts the writer to take notes, and it also allows the instructor to evaluate the success of the workshop.

By asking the writer to follow the discussion notes with a summary of how he or she will revise the drafts, Darby ensures that those notes will be fully utilized in the revision process.

Peer response groups can be assigned to work out of class, but they are more successful in class or in study sessions with teaching assistants, where the instructor or teaching assistant is available to answer questions and where the structured time eliminates distractions. Even if response groups work outside of class, it is essential to have one or more in-class or T. A.-facilitated study session to model techniques for the group sessions.

Whole-class workshops

Whole-class peer response sessions have several advantages. They are the most structured form of peer response and the one in which the instructor retains greatest control. Thus they allow the instructor to teach the entire class while also encouraging students to read and respond to one another's papers as part of the revision process. In whole-class workshops, all students take part in responding to the work of one class member at a time. A student's work is distributed (either as photocopies or through E-mail or a computer network), and other students respond to it in a class session, with the instructor acting as moderator. Whole-class workshops are particularly effective for working on specific areas of writing such as the thesis or introduction. The process of reading and evaluating twenty to thirty introductions written by class members makes students very aware of what a good introduction looks like and what should be avoided as they revise their own. Once they have participated in two or three whole-class workshops, students may be more inclined to speak in subsequent class discussions, and the overall tone of those discussions may be more precise and more text-based.

An enrollment of more than thirty students is not conducive to whole-class discussion of any kind, including whole-class peer response. Classes with large enrollments will be characterized by both chronically silent and chronically vocal members. Whole-class peer response in large classes is therefore best employed as a model for small-group work rather than as a regular activity of the course.

Professor Sotol uses a typical creative writing workshop model as a way of increasing her students' analytical and editing skills and introducing them to the benefits of peer response.

SAMPLE GUIDELINES
Preparation for peer response workshops
Specialized Writing and Research Skills: Katherine Sotol

Reading:
By five o'clock of the day you have turned in your drafts they will be organized in folders in the Reserve Reading Room of the library and available for you to critique. You cannot remove work from the folders or remove folders from the library (so don't ask).

To prepare for the workshops on these drafts, read *all* of the papers in the folder labeled for that day of workshopping. Read each paper through once to get a general idea about the content, then go back and read more critically. As you read, make notes, using the criteria we have been discussing in class: Mechanics, Material, Organization, and Expression. Your notes do not have to be extensive, but should be substantive, consisting of praise for what is done well, criticism for what is done poorly, and advice for revision. Be honest, but not cruel. Fair, but not wimpy.

Workshopping:
In class, the student facilitator will have that day's folder so that if we have difficulty with a significant point in an argument, s/he can look it up and read the passage aloud. The student facilitator will state the title, give a brief summary of the argument to refresh everyone's memory, and then begin workshopping the paper. The facilitator may call on individual students, may conduct a large group discussion, or may systematically question each student in the class. No matter which method the facilitator chooses, everyone in class is obligated to help her or his peers become better writers, and so everyone is obligated to participate in the workshop.

The facilitator will respond to students with follow-up questions and comments: "What can the author do to strengthen the support in this argument?" "Why do you think the conclusion is weak?" "I enjoyed the author's sense of humor." The facilitator will make sure the discussion keeps moving forward, going over each of the four criteria. When the class has thoroughly discussed the evaluative criteria, the facilitator will ask for suggestions for revision.

While the class workshops the paper, the author will take notes on the discussion, but will not participate. When the class has finished workshopping, the author may ask the class to clarify any unclear criticism and to advise on revision.

After the class has answered the author's questions, the facilitator will move on to the next paper.

Revising:
Once your draft has been discussed, you will have one week to revise it and turn it in to me *along with the first draft and the notes you made during the workshop.*

Grading:
I will grade the student facilitator on how well s/he conducts the workshop and I will grade the quality and coherence of each student's comments.

This model is not limited to small classes; Professor Sotol regularly uses it in classes of thirty or more. The key is to prompt students to read each draft and make notes. At the beginning of the semester they need to learn how to be succinct and give coherent oral explanation; but once they have practiced these skills, the class progresses at a good pace. Assigning grades to the responses ensures that the quality remains high.

It is very helpful for student writers to hear multiple responses to their prose because the similarity among responses gives them a heightened sense of audience and helps them to see both error patterns and strengths.

By using student facilitators, Sotol increases the students' sense of responsibility to one another and encourages them to become more active, questioning learners.

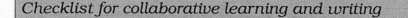

Checklist for collaborative learning and writing

FACILITATING SMALL-GROUP DISCUSSIONS

_____ Seat students very close together.

_____ Provide discussion questions or issues.

_____ Direct groups to elect a secretary to record the discussion and keep it on track.

_____ Allow students to take charge of their own discussion; do not monitor them too closely.

_____ Intervene only if a group falls silent or digresses for too long.

_____ Ask each group to report to the class (orally or in writing) after small-group discussion.

_____ Include dissenting opinions in the group report.

FACILITATING STUDENT-TO-STUDENT DIALOGUE

_____ Encourage courtesy (and perhaps keep dialogues anonymous).

_____ Consider specifying that informal usage is allowed.

_____ Provide a topic or question to begin the discussion.

_____ Model the process by responding to the dialogues.

_____ Monitor the dialogues and intervene in case of personal attacks.

FACILITATING PEER RESPONSE

_____ Model the process in advance.

_____ Give peer response groups concrete tasks.

_____ Discourage negative feedback.

_____ Require written feedback.

OPTIONS FOR DESIGNING COLLABORATIVE WRITING ASSIGNMENTS

_____ Assign dialogic projects for write-to-learn courses in which the objective of collaboration is greater understanding of the materials.

_____ Assign hierarchical projects in disciplinary courses to model the ways in which professional writers collaborate.

For Further Reading

Atwood, Johanna W. "Collaborative Writing: The 'Other' Game in Town." *The Writing Instructor* 12.1 (1992): 13–26. The author differentiates dialogic collaboration (writing together) from hierarchical collaboration (dividing tasks) and concludes that writers get more satisfaction from dialogic collaboration.

Bruffee, Kenneth A. "Collaborative Learning and the 'Conversation of Mankind.'" *College English* 46 (1984): 635–52. Bruffee, the foremost proponent of collaborative learning, describes thought as internalized conversation and writing as that internalized conversation made external again. Teachers, he says, can help students by putting them in conversation with each other and by helping them turn that conversation into writing.

Duin, Ann Hill. "Implementing Cooperative Learning Groups in the Writing Curriculum." *Journal of Teaching Writing* 5 (1986): 315–24. Duin's suggested guidelines and procedures for English classes are readily adaptable to courses throughout the disciplines.

Elbow, Peter. *Writing without Teachers.* New York: Oxford UP, 1973. This volume remains important in composition studies, for it describes and models positive ways for writers to work together in peer response groups.

Flynn, Elizabeth A., George A. McCulley, and Ronald K. Gratz. "Writing in Biology: Effects of Peer Critiquing and Analysis of Models on the Quality of Biology Laboratory Reports." *Writing Across the Disciplines: Research into Practice.* Ed. Art Young and Toby Fulwiler. Upper Montclair, NJ: Boynton/Cook, 1986. 160–75. Peer critique of laboratory reports improved the quality of the reports. Results from a comparison of exercise physiology laboratories revealed that peer critiquing produced a greater awareness of the structure of laboratory reports and also encouraged students to revise.

Garrett, Margaret, and Ashton Nichols. "'Look Who's Talking': Dialogic Learning in the Undergraduate Classroom." *ADE Bulletin* 99 (Fall 1991): 34–37. Team teaching combined with whole-class discussion produced satisfying pedagogy.

Graybeal, Jean. "The Team Journal." *The Journal Book.* Ed. Toby Fulwiler. Portsmouth, NH: Boynton/Cook, 1987. 306–11. In an introduction to religion class, Graybeal assigns permanent teams who for each class session generate materials such as "lists of 'big questions'" (306). The benefits of team journals are dissent, deep confusion, self-awareness and self-criticism, safety in numbers, affirmation and reinforcement, and community building.

Grimm, Nancy. "Improving Students' Responses to Their Peers' Essays." *College Composition and Communication* 37 (1986): 91–93. The author offers the guidelines for peer response that she gives her students.

Herrington, Anne J., and Deborah Cadman. "Peer Review and Revising in an Anthropology Course: Lessons for Learning." *College Composition and Communication* 42 (1991): 184–99. The success of peer review depends not just on the students but also on the instructor. Case studies of two students in an upper-level writing-intensive anthropology course demonstrate the value of peer response in promoting active learning. Included in the article are the procedures for peer response that the anthropology professor used.

Holt, Mara. "The Value of Written Peer Criticism." *College Composition and Communication* 43 (1992): 384–92. Holt offers a sequence of assigned activities, derived from the work of Kenneth Bruffee and that of Peter Elbow and Pat Belanoff, to promote successful peer criticism.

Maimon, Elaine P. "Collaborative Learning and Writing Across the Curriculum." *Writing Program Administration* 9.3 (1986): 9–16. Collaborative projects can expand and make concrete the readership for students' writing while holding down the instructor's workload. Students rather than instructors can be the readers of students' work. With collaborative learning, instructors also have the opportunity to assign papers that have not a hypothetical audience but a real one—the members of the class.

Porter, James E. "Intertextuality and the Discourse Community." *Rhetoric Review* 5 (1986): 34–47. The author asserts that writing is by definition collaborative rather than solitary.

Selfe, Cynthia L. "Technology as a Catalyst for Educational Reform in English Classes: Computer-Supported Writers' Conferences." *Constructing Rhetorical Education.* Ed. Marie Secor and Davida Charney. Carbondale: Southern Illinois UP, 1992. 150–70. Arranging an anonymous electronic discussion group for a class can empower students to speak without the extratextual markers of class, race, and gender. Students—even the graduate students of Selfe's case-study graduate English course in grammar and editing—who are otherwise quiet in class speak more readily in the E-mail discussion. The E-mail discussion, in turn, engenders more in-class discussion.

Sweigart, William. "Classroom Talk, Knowledge Development, and Writing." *Research in the Teaching of English* 25.4 (1991): 469–96. Twelfth graders demonstrated greater comprehension of course materials through the vehicle of small-group discussion than through whole-class discussion or lecture.

Trimbur, John. "Consensus and Difference in Collaborative Learning." *College English* 51 (1989): 602–16. Collaborative learning is not just group work; it involves "a process of intellectual negotiation and collective decision-making. The aim of collaborative learning, its advocates hold, is to reach consensus through an expanding conversation." Some critics charge that consensus can involve "potentially totalitarian practice that stifles individual voice and creativity, suppresses differences, and enforces conformity" (602). Others worry that the attention to discourse communities implicit in social constructionist pedagogy will fail to examine the reproduction of power in the larger society. Trimbur argues that consensus can be used to explore rather than eradicate difference and to interrogate authority (603).

Ventis, Deborah G. "Writing to Discuss: Use of a Clustering Technique." *Teaching of Psychology* 17 (1990): 42–44. In an introductory psychology class, whole-class discussion was precipitated by students' presentation of key vocabulary and was followed by end-of-class journal-writing.

CHAPTER 10

Assigning and Evaluating Journals

In this chapter:

- The purposes of academic journals
- Assigning journals
- Responding to journals
- Grading journals
- Checklist for assigning and evaluating journals
- For further reading

The Purposes of Academic Journals

Whereas many students write their academic papers to "please the teacher," they can think of journals as a place to please themselves. "Pleasing the teacher" can involve saying things one does not believe, but journal-writing involves figuring out and saying what one does believe. Assigning academic journal-writing, therefore, suggests to students that their writing for college might involve not just performance but also belief formation. By reading students' journals, moreover, instructors expand their understanding of how the course is progressing for students and can then better respond to their needs. Academic journal-writing serves other purposes as well: Students can review their journals to select ideas and topics for developing formal papers; students can see the journal as a record of their learning process in the course; most students find journal-writing a pleasurable way to discover and develop their ideas free of worries about how their writing might be judged.

Using journals to incorporate class material

Journal entries can be assigned as an in-class or out-of-class activity asking students to analyze or to respond to readings or class discussion. At the end of class, for example, ten minutes can be set aside for students' written reflection. They can be asked to explain something they learned, to pose a question that they would like to have addressed, or to make a statement of their own choice. Or the instructor can require that students use the journals outside of class to reflect on their reading, perhaps prompted by directed questions. The instructor has several options for reviewing either type of journal entry: He or she can periodically collect the entries and read them at home and return them; collect them at the end of class, read them, and return them at the beginning of the next class; or ask a few students to read their entries aloud at the beginning of a class— an option particularly useful to instructors whose class size prevents them from reading every student's response. The latter two methods provide immediate feedback on the intellectual products of the class session and can help focus the lecture or discussion and address areas of confusion. In addition to assigning out-of-class or in-class journal writing, many instructors encourage students to engage in

---

Professor Rampolla requires students to keep a journal to help them understand and think about the readings in her writing-intensive first-year history seminar. Her careful instructions for preparing for class— combined with questions in her syllabus (see pages 195–96)— inevitably provoke responses and ideas that students can immediately express in a journal entry while the ideas are fresh.

Combining journal-writing with class preparation also helps students make efficient use of the journal instead of recording shallow "knee-jerk" responses.

SAMPLE GUIDELINES
Using journals to incorporate class material
Racism, Sexism, and Social Darwinism: Mary Lynn Rampolla

FSEM 005: PREPARING FOR CLASS

The following suggestions might be useful in preparing for class discussions:

1. Read the assignment at least twice. The first time around, read for general understanding of the content. At this point, it might be useful to write summary note cards, particularly of passages that are complex or confusing.
2. Once you are sure you understand the content, read the assignment critically. Be sure you can identify the author's purpose and thesis, and note the evidence she uses to support her thesis. Examine the argument for logical errors, and identify any assumptions — statements of "fact" that the author doesn't prove — that underlie the argument.
3. Think carefully about the questions suggested for discussion in your syllabus.
4. *Write a thoughtful response in your journal to one of the questions, or to any other issue of interest that was raised by the homework assignment.*
5. If possible, discuss the text with other members of the class.

periodic self-sponsored journal writing in which they write in response to a topic or topics raised in the class.

Using journals to generate paper topics

In classes where students have been encouraged to explore relevant issues in their journals throughout the semester, the journals can provide material for formal papers. Students can be asked to browse through their accumulated journal entries and pick one idea to develop into a formal, graded paper. Instructors can assign some journal entries on course-specific issues; some on examples, events, or issues to be examined using the intellectual tools provided by the course; and some on connections observed in accumulated journal entries.

SAMPLE JOURNAL ASSIGNMENT
Generating personal responses and observations
Gendered Voices: Margaret Flanders Darby

LANGUAGE NOTEBOOK

Throughout the course, you will keep a language notebook, handing it in on Fridays roughly every other week: Sept. 18, Oct. 2, Oct. 16, Oct. 30, Nov. 13 and Dec. 4. In the notebook you should record heard/observed/read instances of language use that have relevance to our topic and your response to them. Although it is required, there are no restrictions on this project, including length, and it does not have to be typed. It will not be graded. My emphasis here is on your personal response to the flow of language around you. It is also an opportunity to talk to me in the privacy of the written page, without the judgment of a grade. Matters of language and gender can be surprisingly fraught with emotion, and I often find that students like to write down things for me to read and respond to that they do not want to say in class. You will get back my informal written response to your entries and credit for handing them in.

While this assignment does not make an explicit connection between journal entries and paper topics, Professor Darby has found that the informal observations and suggestions recorded in the notebook provide students with rich material for paper topics.

SAMPLE JOURNAL ASSIGNMENT
Exploring issues and generating paper topics
Racism, Sexism, and Social Darwinism: Mary Lynn Rampolla

Reading assignment: Carl Vogt. *Lectures on Man*, Lecture VII, pp. 194–202; Lecture XVI, pp. 461–469; and Dr. J. Langdon Down, "Observations on an Ethnic Classification of Idiots."

DISCUSSION/JOURNAL TOPICS

1. Where do developmentally disabled people fit into Vogt's views on human evolution?

These very focused questions guide the journal responses of the students in Professor Rampolla's first-year seminar; however, they do not limit the ideas that the readings could stimulate. Any of these questions has the potential to produce thoughtful journal entries that could easily be expanded into paper topics.

2. What does Vogt mean by "arrested development"? How is this related to the theory of evolution?
3. According to Vogt, are humans derived from simious groups? What "evidence" does he supply to "prove" his views about the relationship between humans and apes? What problem in the theory of evolution does the existence of "idiots" solve for him?
4. Are all human groups derived from the same "simian" stock? What are the implications of Vogt's answers to this question?
5. What condition is J. Langdon Down describing? What is the relationship between his classification system and the theory of evolution?

Asking specific questions in the syllabus, in handouts, or in class can also prompt journal entries that may suggest paper topics.

Using journals to encourage critical thinking: the dialectical notebook

Journal entries have traditionally been used in writing courses to stimulate critical thinking and to encourage students to develop an active relationship with their readings. One typical approach is to have students respond informally to their reading in the journal directly after they finish reading rather than waiting for class discussion, when the immediacy will have been lost. Perhaps the best-known and most widely adopted method of such journal-writing is the "dialectical notebook" or "double-entry notebook" described by Ann Berthoff. In this model the students divide the page in half vertically and use one side to summarize the assigned reading and the other to respond to or annotate it. Some instructors couple this notebook with more traditional journal writing by asking students to use their responses and annotations as starting points for formal or informal journal entries. A similar strategy can be adopted with field or laboratory notebooks: the observed material is placed on one side of the page, the student's responses, musings, and questions on the other. The dialectical notebook lets students interact with their research without leaving the traces of that interaction on the research material itself. It also provides a record of students' states of mind during each stage of the project as well as their feelings about each stage. Encouraging students to perceive themselves in dialogue with their course material helps them remain focused and reminds them to continually explore, evaluate, and question.

Research at Cornell University found that "engineering students keeping laboratory notebooks should 'examine the adequacy of and the reliability of the data as the measurements are made' and that a necessary part of this examination is being 'required to write a summary of [their] work in the laboratory notebook following completion of each experiment.'" A dialectical notebook would achieve this end, ensuring that students "think as well as record" (Gottschalk 400).

SAMPLE JOURNAL ENTRY
Keeping a double-entry (dialectical) notebook
Cultural Literacy: Sandra Jamieson

READING NOTES	RESPONSE
E. D. Hirsch, *Cultural Literacy: What Every American Needs to Know* (Boston: Houghton, 1987). *Preface:* Explains that cult. lit. is "the only sure avenue" (xiii) for "disadvantaged" Americans to succeed, but to achieve it we must return to education theories of 50 yrs ago and reject Rousseau and Dewey (xiv–v) and return to a model of learning through the "piling up of information" (xv). Plato was right that "we have an obligation to choose and promote our best traditions" even if he was wrong about the superiority of philosophers (xvi). C.L. is about "accumulating shared symbols" (xvii) and gaining access to communities formerly closed to people who didn't share them (xv).	Well he's right that there is a problem in education and that it is connected to social class—Kozol shows us that—but he really annoys me in his insistence that everyone must learn "*OUR* best traditions." *WHOSE* best traditions? Who gets to decide what is best? His tone makes it sound as if all *reasonable* people must agree on this, as if there's some standard we can apply as test. But the standard is the norms of the people whose world the "disadvantaged" must enter to be advantaged. He uses important sounding phrases like "needs of a modern nation," "the modern world," "opportunity," and "thrive" but he doesn't define them—why will acculturation satisfy those "needs"? Why not change dominant culture to make it "ours" rather than change "us" through "acculturation"?

Professor Jamieson offered this model dialectical notebook to a writing-intensive first-year seminar on culture and education. The double-entry method allows the student to vent her anger and frustration at the material in the right-hand column while keeping the left-hand column focused on content. Comments on word definition will also help the student in writing a fuller analysis later.

Using journals for writing unconnected to the course

Some instructors invite students to use the journals to write about their lives outside of class, on the premise that this promotes fluency in writing and allows students to write about something familiar. These entries can be responses to current issues or personal life details and they can help students see an intimate connection between living and writing. Some instructors believe that requiring students to write about personal issues is an inappropriate invasion on the part of the instructor; they argue that students should always have the option of refusing such an assignment and replacing it with less personal material. In writing in the disciplines, journal-keeping customarily focuses on assigned readings or class activities, and "personal" entries are simply discussions of course-related events from the student's point of view.

Assigning Journals

Designing journal assignments

When journals are assigned, students should receive specific written guidelines explaining what is required and how the work will be evaluated. The instructor must choose whether to specify the topic to be written about in the journals (directed writing), whether to let each student decide what to write about (undirected writing), or whether to assign a combination of the two. In any case, both the students' and the instructor's use of the journals will be facilitated by a requirement that the entries be dated and arranged in chronological order, with the pages numbered.

Professor Jamieson begins by explaining her rationale for assigning a journal in this first-year writing course. If students can be encouraged to see regular journal writing as beneficial to their own development, they are more likely to expend the effort to do it well. For many students, journal entries often feel like "busywork" if they are not somehow incorporated into the course. Others become frustrated because writing does not come easily and does not seem to flow any better after one or two weeks of journal writing. An oral or written reassurance that this is

SAMPLE GUIDELINES
Journal-writing
English I: Sandra Jamieson

THE WRITER'S JOURNAL
Because writing every day has the same impact on a person's writing as working out has on his or her body, every student will keep a writer's journal as part of this class. You will be required to write in your writer's journal at least four times a week. (Every day is the ideal, but is not always realistic.) While you will not be graded on the content of the journal, you will be graded on the seriousness with which you address the issues raised and the frequency with which you write. (I will give extra consideration to people who write an entry every day.) Therefore, it is important that you read the following instructions carefully and ask questions if they are not clear.

Rather than a daily record of events, a writer's journal is a place for you to practice thinking-in-writing, the fundamental skill for you as a member of the academic community. Your entries should quite literally be mental workouts, and, like physical workouts, they demand that you do them when you are awake. If you try to write when you are tired, you will not help yourself, nor will you produce an interesting entry. If you try to do a week's worth of entries at once, you will be wasting your time (just as doing five hours of exercise one day a week does not help your body as much as doing 30–45 minutes a day). Students who cheat might fool me, but ultimately they only cheat themselves because they will waste the opportunity to become better writers. . . .

Sometimes I will require that you write on a specific issue as homework for the class. This will generally take the form of a continuation of discussion started in class, a topic we did not cover in class, or an issue raised in class but not discussed. I may also ask you to consider a particular topic in writing, to prepare you for discussion the next day (in which case I will collect that entry then). At other times I will ask you to select a story from *The New York Times* and summarize, analyze, and respond to it. Writer's journal entries may also take the form of "dilemmas" where I ask you to consider a particular dilemma I have identified in class. The structure for these entries will be as follows:

1. State and explain the dilemma.
2. Describe the two (or more) opposing positions one could adopt on this issue.
3. State your position (or adopt one if you have not thought about this issue before).
4. Defend your position—explain in as much detail as possible why you consider it to be the better response to the dilemma. (Imagine you are attempting to persuade a person holding the opposing opinion.)

Finally, your writer's journal entries may be written in response to an event, class discussion, reading, film, or conversation which inspired, angered, or otherwise aroused your interest. You may analyze and respond or summarize and respond; however, you may not simply summarize—you must say something ABOUT the issue you raise (preferably something which you have not already worked out and drawn conclusions upon).

You may revise journal entries as part of your individual writing program, and you will be asked to revise five entries for inclusion in your final portfolio.

normal because journals build skills over time can make a significant difference in student attitude. Professor Jamieson observes that the physical "workout" metaphor worked very well in this regard.

This handout explains exactly what is and is not appropriate material for a journal and outlines the different kinds of journal assignments the course will involve—both directed and undirected writing. As a result, the students have a clear sense of what is expected of them.

Collaborative journals

Usually journals are individual tasks, but some instructors may want to assign permanent teams who, in or out of class, discuss issues and record a collective response in a journal. Jean Graybeal has developed a successful method for collaborative journals in an introduction to religion class. For each class session, teams generate materials such as "lists of big questions" (306). The benefits of team journals, she says, are dissent, deep confusion, self-awareness and self-criticism, safety in numbers, affirmation and reinforcement, and community building (308–09).

Team journals might function as part of ongoing discussion groups (see page 170), which could work together at regular intervals (each Friday, for example) for part of a class period. The instructor will collect the journals from time to time and help the group see the ways in which their collective problem-solving and discovery strategies are developing.

As Graybeal observes, team journals might also fuel class sessions. Teams can be assigned in rotation to work out of class, generating topics and issues for the whole class's attention and discussion.

Responding to Journals

Methods of responding

How instructors respond to journals varies greatly. Some read journals and return them without comment. Journals may serve a better pedagogical role, however, if the instructor comments on them—even if that comment is only one or two sentences. One useful mode of response is to point out passages that the instructor finds particularly insightful and also to help clear up any inaccuracies or misunderstandings recorded in the journal.

Instructors should keep in mind, though, that students' journals may not always be comprehensible. The expectations of clarity and development that might be appropriate on formal papers are not applicable to student journals: the instructor cannot demand that the journal provide expository satisfaction. It is appropriate, though, for instructors to remark that they do not understand a passage and to encourage the student to consider the matter more fully. Considerations of style, organization, and mechanics are also irrelevant to student journals, which are successful in part because the writing is admittedly informal. Instructors' comments on style, organization, and mechanics only constrain the student writer and inhibit future entries. They are also time-consuming, although many instructors do take the time to praise especially enjoyable style or content.

Instructors' comments are best presented on a separate sheet of paper. For maximum pedagogical effectiveness, journals must be "owned" by their writers, and instructors' annotations on the journal entries themselves might diminish that sense of ownership. If the entries are dated and arranged chronologically with pages numbered, it is relatively easy for the instructor to respond on a separate paper, making references to page numbers or dates. Responding on a separate paper also allows the students space to record reactions to the instructor's comments. Some instructors require students' response to their comments to ensure that they read and think about the observations (and to give students the opportunity to clarify or correct the instructors' misunderstandings).

Instructors of large classes often skim each journal and comment on only one or two entries rather than trying to respond to all of them. Staggering the timing of collection and teaching students to respond to their own entries can also reduce the labor involved in assigning journals to large classes.

Timing of journal collection

There are several effective ways to time and structure responses to journals. The instructor may collect journal entries as they are written, respond to them, and return them to the students—a method that may be excessively labor-intensive. More practical is to schedule journal submission at intervals in the semester, much as one would schedule the submission of formal papers. The instructor also has the option of an end-of-semester review or a combination of periodic and end-of-semester reviews, but the former option requires considerable time at a point in the semester when time is generally quite limited.

SAMPLE GUIDELINES
Journal review procedure
Language and Race: Rebecca Moore Howard

RESPONSE JOURNALS[1]

Throughout the semester, you will keep a journal in which you respond to assigned readings, to class discussions, and to your own observations about the interaction of language with ethnicity/race. At the end of each class I will make suggestions for topics to explore in your journal; or you can develop topics of your own. On September 17, October 27, and December 14, I will ask you to submit your response journal, accompanied by analysis. I will then respond to and grade your journal, together with your analysis. Whenever you submit a journal, please be sure that the pages are numbered.

Response journal 1:

1. Reread all of your journal entries.
2. Use a highlighter pen to mark passages that you find "especially surprising or thought-provoking or well-written."

Professor Howard uses this method of journal-keeping for a junior-level course, offering the students the choice of writing directed or undirected entries.

The pressure of deciding what to write about can spoil some students' experience with journals and waste time they might have used writing if the instructor had suggested topics. Often, a suggested topic reminds students of an issue that an assigned reading raised for them. Yet the undirected option allows them the freedom to stray from the suggested topic as they are writing, once again increasing the possibili-

---

[1]This method of journal keeping, and the quotes in this handout, are taken from Trudelle Thomas's "Restless Minds Take Stock: Self-Evaluation of Student Journals," *ATAC Forum* 4.2 (1992): 10–16.

ties of their engagement in the course.

The carefully explained and numbered instructions walk the students through the process of evaluating their own entries, suggesting review questions and helping them to see patterns and to trace connections between their entries. This process could also generate paper topics.

The organization of the final journal into a "book" with a preface and formal appendices helps students to see the academic journal as an important part of their work, which in turn impels them to work hard on their self-evaluation.

3. Give each entry a title.
4. Use the margins to jot down any questions or comments you have for yourself or for me. Imagine yourself a "kindly editor" who is "trying to ferret out what is most valuable in them thus far." Trudelle Thomas recommends that you ask the following questions:
   —What is surprising?
   —What is most interesting here?
   —What is working well?
   —What changes do you observe?
   —Do you see any ideas developing or changing?
   —Do you see any patterns emerging?
   —What are the obstacles or pitfalls for you in writing your journal?
   —How is the journal working for you?

5. Write a 150–300-word progress report. Summarize what you are doing well; plan for what you want to change. Plan how you might use the journal more effectively, "perhaps through a wider focus, greater honesty, a more relaxed tone, more regular entries, etc."

Response journal 2:
Follow the same procedure as for response journal 1, but you may limit yourself to the period September 18–October 27; you are not required to review your entire journal. Please use a different-colored highlighter to differentiate these analyses from response journal 1 analyses.

Response journal 3—book presentation:
Please use a third highlighter color for this analysis. Review your entire journal, following previous procedures, but instead of writing a progress report, prepare a book framework for your journal. Provide the following materials:

1. Incorporate your formal papers as Appendices to your journal.
2. Organize your journal into whatever sections you choose. You may want to consider chronological or thematic formats. Provide a one-page Table of Contents that presents your journal according to your organizational plan.
3. Write a Preface that provides a "factual background" for the journal. You may want to give information about the author and/or about the context in which the journal was prepared.
4. Write a Conclusion or Afterword in which you reflect upon the significance of the journal.
5. Provide any illustrations that may be appropriate.
6. Ornament the cover in whatever manner you consider appropriate.

A variation on this method of response, perhaps most appropriate for first-year students, uses a combination of response from the instructor and student self-evaluation. In this model, which is practical only for classes of forty students or less, the instructor collects entries for the first two weeks and, on a separate sheet of paper, responds to each one individually, to model appropriate responses and to suggest ways for students to expand their thinking. Leaving a space at the end of each comment for the students to respond encourages them to read the comments carefully. At the end of the fourth week, students re-read their entries for the last two weeks and respond to them in the same way as the instructor did at the end of week two (leaving a space for the instructor to respond). Weeks six and nine repeat the process, with the instructor simply making one overall comment at the end of the students' self-evaluations but not necessarily reading the journals. In larger classes a variation of this model can be worth the time if students are not assigned papers in the class but are evaluated by examinations or if the instructor staggers journal collection and comments on several entries at a time.

Responding to personal revelations

Sometimes students make personal and occasionally disturbing revelations in their academic journals, even when only class-related journal entries have been assigned. How the instructor responds depends very much on the instructor, the student, and the relationship between them. It is helpful to remember that students writing in a course-related journal that is to be submitted in a class are very aware that they are writing for an audience, the instructor. Personal confidences, therefore, can be interpreted as being made to that audience, no matter how surprised the instructor may be. Perhaps the instructor is the only trustworthy adult available to the student at the time; perhaps the student believes that the instructor will be able to suggest a solution; or perhaps the student simply wants to know whether his or her situation is sufficiently dire that it will provoke a response.

Most instructors of writing in the disciplines choose to respond to such a student's revelations. For the response to be useful, it should be personal; approaches like "Come see me during office hours" or "Have you talked to a counselor?" do little to encourage the student to make the big step of initiating face-to-face interchange. Much more promising would be to stop the student at the end of class, express concern and a willingness to help, and then invite the student to lunch or to the snack bar that day or to a stroll across campus at that moment—or, if these options are not possible, to schedule an appointment at a specific time.

In the interchange, the instructor must maintain a mentoring relationship. If it is his or her belief that the student needs counseling, the instructor's most helpful response will be to encourage the student to seek professional services (available on most campuses) and reassure the student that those services are specially qualified to help. If, in contrast, the instructor begins counseling a student who is resistant to seeking professional services, that instructor not only falls into the role of an amateur doing a professional's job but also enables the student to postpone consulting a professional.

Grading Journals

Journals can be integrated into the syllabus as either graded or ungraded activity. Since their primary purpose is self-sponsored intellectual exploration, their grading must be handled carefully. The National Council of Teachers of English recommends a quantitative rather than qualitative emphasis in grading journals (see Fulwiler 7), and many instructors, instead of attaching letter grades to journals, use a system wherein journal-writing adds points at the end of the semester. Quantitative considerations literally focus on quantity— on the frequency and volume of writing. A variety of qualitative considerations, though, are often also applied to grading journals. In these cases the instructor generally does not attach letter grades to individual journal entries but instead grades a collection of entries periodically during the semester or once at the end. Letter grades in these cases can be assigned not only for the quantitative features but also for a speculative, questioning spirit; seriousness of purpose; sense of completeness; and intellectual initiative.

Checklist for assigning and evaluating journals

TOPICS FOR JOURNAL ENTRIES

_____ Response to assigned reading.

_____ Response to lecture/class discussion.

_____ Self-sponsored writing about the course.

_____ Self-sponsored writing outside the course.

OPTIONS FOR READING STUDENTS' JOURNALS

_____ Collect entries as they are written.

_____ Collect journals at scheduled intervals during the semester.

STRATEGIES FOR RESPONDING TO JOURNALS

_____ Write on separate paper, not on the students' entries.

_____ Ignore issues of style, organization, and mechanics.

_____ Point out valuable insights or pleasing style.

_____ Straighten out misconceptions or misunderstandings.

_____ In cases of personal confidences, maintain a mentoring rather than a counseling relationship.

GRADING JOURNALS

_____ Don't grade journals as you would a formal piece of writing for style, clarity, or organization.

_____ Grade groups of entries, not single entries.

_____ Consider whether you want to do quantitative grading, which measures frequency and volume of entries, or qualitative grading, which rewards a speculative, questioning spirit and intellectual initiative.

For Further Reading

General bibliography

Berthoff, Ann E. "Speculative Instruments: Language in the Core Curriculum." *The Making of Meaning: Metaphors, Models, and Maxims for Writing Teachers.* Upper Montclair, NJ: Boynton/Cook, 1981. 113–26.

Enos, Theresa. "Gender and Journals: Conservers or Innovators." *Pre/Text* 9 (Fall/Winter 1988): 209–14.

Flitterman-King, Sharon. "The Role of the Response Journal in Active Reading." *The Quarterly of the National Writing Project and the Center for the Study of Writing* 10 (1988): 4–11.

Fulwiler, Toby, ed. *The Journal Book.* Portsmouth, NH: Boynton/Cook, 1987.

Gannett, Cinthia. *Gender and the Journal: Diaries and Academic Discourse.* Albany: SUNY UP, 1992.

Gottschalk, Katherine K. "Writing in the Non-Writing Class: 'I'd Love to Teach Writing, But . . .'" *Teaching Prose: A Guide for Writing Instructors.* Ed. Frederick V. Bogel and Katherine K. Gottschalk. New York: Norton, 1984. 393–415.

Graybeal, Jean. "The Team Journal." *The Journal Book.* Ed. Toby Fulwiler. Portsmouth, NH: Boynton/Cook, 1987. 306–11.

Perry, Donna M. "Making Journal Writing Matter." *Teaching Writing: Pedagogy, Gender, and Equity.* Ed. Cynthia L. Caywood and Gillian R. Overing. Albany: SUNY UP, 1987. 151–56.

Thomas, Trudelle. "Restless Minds Take Stock: Self-Evaluation of Student Journals." *ATAC Forum* 4.2 (1992): 10–16.

Discipline-specific reports

CHEMISTRY

Meese, George. "Focused Learning in Chemistry Research: Suzanne's Journal." *The Journal Book.* Ed. Toby Fulwiler. Portsmouth, NH: Boynton/Cook, 1987. 337–47.

ENGINEERING

Selfe, Cynthia L., and Freydoon Arbabi. "Writing to Learn: Engineering Student Journals." *Writing Across the Disciplines: Research into Practice.* Ed. Art Young and Toby Fulwiler. Upper Montclair, NJ: Boynton/Cook, 1986. 184–91.

ENGLISH

MacDonald, Susan Peck, and Charles R. Cooper. "Contributions of Academic and Dialogic Journals to Writing about Literature." *Writing, Teaching, and Learning in the Disciplines.* Ed. Anne Herrington and Charles Moran. New York: Modern Language Association, 1992. 137–55.

FOLKLORE

Sweterlitsch, Richard. "The Honest Voice of Inquiry: Teaching Folklore through Writing." *The Journal Book.* Ed. Toby Fulwiler. Portsmouth, NH: Boynton/Cook, 1987. 239–45.

FOREIGN LANGUAGES

Sandler, Karen Wiley. "Letting Them Write When They Can't Even Talk? Writing as Discovery in the Foreign Language Classroom." *The Journal Book.* Ed. Toby Fulwiler. Portsmouth, NH: Boynton/Cook, 1987. 312–20.

GEOGRAPHY

Baltensperger, Bradley H. "Journals in Economic Geography." *The Journal Book.* Ed. Toby Fulwiler. Portsmouth, NH: Boynton/Cook, 1987. 387–90.

HISTORY

Mulholland, Bernadette Marie. "It's Not Just the Writing." *The Journal Book.* Ed. Toby Fulwiler. Portsmouth, NH: Boynton/Cook, 1987. 227–38.

Steffens, Henry. "Journals in the Teaching of History." *The Journal Book.* Ed. Toby Fulwiler. Portsmouth, NH: Boynton/Cook, 1987. 219–26.

INTERDISCIPLINARY COURSES AND GENERAL EDUCATION

Thaiss, Christopher. "A Journal in the Arts." *The Journal Book.* Ed. Toby Fulwiler. Portsmouth, NH: Boynton/Cook, 1987. 246–53.

MATHEMATICS

BeMiller, Stephen. "The Mathematics Workbook." *The Journal Book.* Ed. Toby Fulwiler. Portsmouth, NH: Boynton/Cook, 1987. 359–66.

Selfe, Cynthia L., Bruce T. Petersen, and Cynthia L. Nahrgang. "Journal Writing in Mathematics." *Writing Across the Disciplines: Research into Practice.* Ed. Art Young and Toby Fulwiler. Upper Montclair, NJ: Boynton/Cook, 1986. 192–207.

MUSIC

Ambrose, Jane. "Music Journals." *The Journal Book.* Ed. Toby Fulwiler. Portsmouth, NH: Boynton/Cook, 1987. 261–68.

Larson, Catherine M., and Margaret Merrion. "Documenting the Aesthetic Experience: The Music Journal." *The Journal Book.* Ed. Toby Fulwiler. Portsmouth, NH: Boynton/Cook, 1987. 254–60.

PHILOSOPHY

Kent, O. T. "Student Journals and the Goals of Philosophy." *The Journal Book.* Ed. Toby Fulwiler. Portsmouth, NH: Boynton/Cook, 1987. 269–77.

North, Stephen M. "The Philosophical Journal: Three Case Studies." *The Journal Book.* Ed. Toby Fulwiler. Portsmouth, NH: Boynton/Cook, 1987. 278–88.

PHYSICS

Grumbacher, Judy. "How Writing Helps Physics Students Become Better Problem Solvers." *The Journal Book.* Ed. Toby Fulwiler. Portsmouth, NH: Boynton/Cook, 1987. 323–29.

Jensen, Verner. "Writing in College Physics." *The Journal Book.* Ed. Toby Fulwiler. Portsmouth, NH: Boynton/Cook, 1987. 330–36.

POLITICAL SCIENCE

Brodsky, David, and Eileen Meagher. "Journals and Political Science." *The Journal Book.* Ed. Toby Fulwiler. Portsmouth, NH: Boynton/Cook, 1987. 375–86.

PSYCHOLOGY

Hettich, Paul. "Journal Writing: Old Fare or Nouvelle Cuisine?" *Teaching of Psychology* 17 (Feb. 1990): 36–39.

Jolley, Janina M., and Mark L. Mitchell. "Two Psychologists' Experiences with Journals." *Teaching of Psychology* 17 (Feb. 1990): 40–41.

SOCIOLOGY

Allen, Henry, and Lynn Fauth. "Academic Journals and the Sociological Imagination." *The Journal Book.* Ed. Toby Fulwiler. Portsmouth, NH: Boynton/Cook, 1987. 367–74.

CHAPTER 11

Grading Student Writing

In this chapter:

❐   Assigning grades to papers

❐   Coping with plagiarism

❐   Dealing with ideologically objectionable papers

❐   Using writing portfolios for evaluation

❐   Checklist for grading student writing

❐   For further reading

Assigning Grades to Papers

In the last twenty years the once-widespread notion that grading and responding to student writing meant correcting every error and writing copious notes has been replaced by more sophisticated grading strategies. Faced with extensive error correction, students become overwhelmed and cease to read the comments (Hairston; Shuman). Moreover, the writing of students whose instructors make extensive comments does not improve significantly more than that of students whose instructors write only brief summary statements and discuss a few errors (Arnold). In addition to comments about the paper, instructors should plan to write a sentence about why they have assigned the particular grade. A handout that explains what each grade represents can also be helpful for students as well as for instructors confronting a pile of papers to be graded.

Approaches to grading papers for grammar, usage, punctuation, and mechanics

Papers containing intelligent thought and logical argument but excessive errors in grammar, usage, punctuation, and mechanics, as well as stylistic problems, present a difficult dilemma for instructors of writing in the disciplines. If papers are graded for content alone, students will conclude that the grade overrides any comments on sentence-level problems. On the other hand, if grammar and usage are taken fully into consideration, a paper with interestingly developed ideas but with many surface errors may receive a lower grade than others demonstrating good grammar and usage but uninspired thinking. Many instructors resolve the dilemma by returning a paper with a lot of surface errors to the student for revision. This is an effective way to direct the student's attention to such errors, but it should be accompanied by some form of trait analysis (see the next section) and information about where to seek help in revising the paper (see Chapter 3). The instructor should adopt specific strategies for responding to the prose of learning-disabled students, speakers of nonstandard English dialects, and nonnative speakers of English (see pages 78–81).

The sociolinguistic perspective that Standard Written English is one dialect among many (see pages 78–79) rather than the "best" or "pure" form presents quandaries for instructors grading papers. If Standard Written English is not "correct" or "pure," can one assert it as a criterion for determining grades? Some instructors respond in the affirmative, saying that because Standard Written English is the dialect of the academy and because the college course is taught in that context, it is appropriate to insist that students master the language of the community—and to reduce their grades if they do not. Other instructors respond in the negative, saying that because some students' dialects are relatively close to Standard Written English and others are not, one would be grading the students' home environments and penalizing those whose home dialects do not closely accord with the preferred form. When grading papers, the latter instructors take one of two approaches: Either they let students know where they are handling Standard Written English well and where they need more work but do not reduce their grades for errors, or they ignore usage entirely.

The latter option—ignoring usage entirely—can do great damage: Students may read the instructor's lack of comment as a message that usage does not matter or that the instructor does not care about it. The other option, in contrast, emphasizes the importance of Standard Written English in many contexts (including the academy) and helps students master its intricacies.

Both options are exercised in a variety of ways. Some instructors mark every error in a paper in the belief that students need to know just how far they are from the ideal. Other instructors mark just major or prevalent errors. Either way, the message about errors is important. If students mistakenly believe that their prose accords with the standard, they will have no impetus for studying the standard and changing their usage.

One way to acknowledge grammar, usage, and mechanics is to assign two grades to papers, one for sentence-level features and another for organization and development, preferably giving students the chance to revise. (See pages 69–70.) Although obviously related, the two areas are usefully treated separately if the paper is to be revised to avoid the possibility that errors caused by dialect interference will bring down the overall grade. (See page 78.) Comments, however, should respond to both areas. The paper can then be resubmitted and revised for a single final grade. A variation of this method involves the instructor assigning a grade to each element or cluster of elements and then averaging the overall grade at the end—a method that is successful only if the instructor explains each grade.

This method of grading and explaining grades allows the instructor to weight whatever elements of student writing she or he considers most important. For Professor Jamieson, this form focuses her attention as she writes comments and determines grades. She can give credit to students who have conducted sufficient research but have failed to use it to support an effective thesis, thus helping them see the importance of a thesis. She can also differentiate between write-to-learn elements of academic literacy and specific disciplinary conventions.

SAMPLE GRADING SHEET
Assigning grades to separate elements of a paper
English I: Sandra Jamieson

GRADE EXPLANATION
Name:
Date:
Title of paper:

Your final grade for this paper is an average of the grades listed and explained below. Please feel free to discuss any aspect of this process with me during my posted office hours.

1. Thesis and development of argument: GRADE:
   EXPLANATION:

2. Use of evidence: GRADE:
   EXPLANATION:

3. Use of academic discourse conventions: GRADE:
   EXPLANATION:

4. Style, grammar, usage, and expression: GRADE:
   EXPLANATION:

   OVERALL GRADE:
   FINAL COMMENTS:

The advantage of the preceding approach is that students who receive widely disparate grades for different elements of a paper will come to understand which aspect(s) of their writing they need to work on, even if the present course does not actively address those writing skills. Many theorists object, though, that the practice of assigning several grades to one piece of prose rests on a fallacious belief in the analytic separability of the components of prose. From this perspective, content, usage, mechanics, and organization are inextricably interrelated, and holistic grading (see pages 213–215) is most appropriate.

Trait analysis

The results of composition research discourage teachers from marking and explaining each error in a student's paper. Richard H. Haswell asserts that students can correct 61% of their errors simply in response to seeing marks on the page, without any explanation of the errors. The other 39% of students, however, may be daunted by seeing their papers covered with red ink unaccompanied by explanation. They may conclude that they are so far from the standard that it would be hopeless to undertake improvement and that their best option is to sign up for classes taught by instructors who don't care about grammar and usage.

Other research suggests that marking every error probably wastes the instructor's time. Students generally fail to read most of the comments (Harris), become overwhelmed by them (Hairston; Shuman), misinterpret what they mean (Rankin), or simply use them to "fix" errors without understanding why (Butler).

In trait analysis, the instructor responds only to what he or she considers the most important or most frequently occurring errors in the paper. Developed for placement tests in composition by scholars such as Richard Lloyd-Jones and refined most recently by Liz Hamp-Lyons, trait analysis is a principle easily and constructively adapted to paper grading in the disciplines. Defining one or more specific realms in which the student can improve his or her application of Standard Written English gives the student a concrete and manageable perspective on his or her writing. The instructor can also cross-reference the handbook adopted for the course (see page 32) or suggest that the student seek assistance from the instructor or a tutor (see pages 35–39).

Trait analysis allows the instructor to determine which aspects of the paper deserve the most emphasis and assign a grade accordingly. Explanations of the grading criteria can be written on a separate sheet and keyed to numbers written in the margins; or global comments can be made under particular headings. After reading the comments, students should know how well they handled the specific elements being graded and how those elements contributed to the overall grade.

In especially large classes, a checklist like those described by Joyce MacAllister can be useful. She suggests listing the priorities for the paper and analyzing them on a scale of 2 through 10, perhaps (after Cooper) gathering those priorities under larger topics such as "General Merit" and "Mechanics" (62) and weighing some topics more

By grading six different elements, Professor Jamieson makes it clear which elements she considers important and allows the student to see which areas of the paper are particularly effective or weak. This sheet was used midway through the course. Earlier writing in the course was not graded for organization or originality of thought because initial writing samples revealed that the students needed to learn these skills before they could be graded on them.

Separating the grade for the thesis from that for evidence encourages students to appreciate the importance of developing and supporting arguments.

SAMPLE GRADING SHEET
Using trait analysis
Roots of Western Civilization: Sandra Jamieson

Name:_____ Date:_____
Paper Title:_____
Your final grade for this paper is an average of the individual grades for the following elements.

ELEMENT OF YOUR PAPER	GRADE
1. Clarity, strength, and expression of thesis:	
2. Quality and quantity of evidence supporting the thesis:	
3. Organization:	
4. Originality of thought:	
5. Effectiveness of the overall argument:	
6. Style and usage (grammar, punctuation, word choice, etc.):	
FINAL, OVERALL GRADE FOR THE PAPER:	

than others. Another method, called a *dichotomous scale,* involves checking "yes" or "no" beside a list of elements considered important in the paper and determining a certain amount of "yes" votes per grade point.

This method does not encourage additional comments, although it does not preclude them. It does give students some understanding of the rationale for their grades and indicates what areas of their writing students should strengthen.

SAMPLE GRADING SHEET
Using a dichotomous scale
Developed from "Responding to Student Writing" by Joyce MacAllister (59)

		YES	NO	
Content	I.	____	____	Ideas themselves are insightful. Ideas are creative or original.
Organization	II.	____	____	Each paragraph has a controlling idea.
Mechanics	III.	____	____	There are many misspellings. There are serious punctuation problems.

Trait analysis can also help instructors design assignments. Having identified in advance what will be important for a given paper, the instructor can list on the assignment the major criteria by which he or she expects to grade.

SAMPLE ASSIGNMENT (EXCERPT)
Listing traits for grading
American English: Rebecca Moore Howard

Your paper will be acceptable only if it exhibits the following features:

1. All pages (except the title page and the first page of the manuscript) numbered in the upper right-hand corner
2. Typed manuscript
3. Double-spaced text

Your summary will be graded according to how well it covers all the main points in your own language. It should contain neither quotations nor plagiarism. It should contain no typographical or spelling errors.

In this linguistics seminar for first-year students, Professor Howard assigns a summary early in the term and determines in advance that she will grade features such as manuscript preparation, coverage of the main points, and the writers' use of their own "voice" and style rather than those of the source. She does not grade features, such as documentation, that she will teach later in the term.

As the preceding sample illustrates, some instructors emphasize different skills at different points of the semester, placing little emphasis on skills they have not yet taught and greater emphasis on issues already covered. Instructors who assign only one paper might require a draft a week in advance of the final due date, identify specific features for each student to revise, and then assess the grade partly or wholly on the success of this revision of specific "traits." Such a practice gives all students a fair chance to show improvement and does not penalize students whose writing skills may not be as developed as those of their classmates.

Finally, if the instructor does not want to determine the specific aspects in advance, a checklist like the one described by Reising might be appropriate: a four-part form on which instructors describe three strengths and three weaknesses; write miscellaneous comments; and make recommendations (MacAllister 62). As with the dichotomous scale, this grading method ensures that students learn to assess what they do well in addition to what they do poorly—an essential part of improving one's writing (Edwards; Elbow; Zak).

Holistic grading

Holistic grading requires instructors to put away the pen until they have read over the entire paper once and then read it a second time more slowly (but still without marginal comments) to assess deeper meanings and patterns. The final comment (which can be as little as one or two sentences) speaks to the paper as a whole, focusing mostly on content but also commenting on stylistic features if they are particularly effective or ineffective. The grade also addresses the paper as a whole rather than averaging the grades for components.

Holistic evaluation is much quicker than other methods of evaluation. Considering papers as a whole mimics the way we typically read professional essays, and it encourages students to pay attention to topic, overall structure, and organization during revision and redrafting, instead of surface-level errors and isolated paragraphs. Michael Janopoulos's work suggests that holistic grading of nonnative speakers requires particular care, however, because surface-level errors may distract the instructor from the content. The instructor can reduce this risk by slowing down the reading process and writing guidelines beforehand.

In formulating this guide, Professor Jamieson allowed students' input into the grading process. They identified what they considered to be elements of a "good" paper and evaluated some sample papers (from another class) on the day they handed in their first paper. Professor Jamieson designed this guide on the basis of that discussion. The explanation of each grade discusses sample papers as a whole and makes suggestions for revision. Professor Jamieson believes that without guides like this one her grades would be much less constant, influenced by personal taste more than clearly identifiable features of the paper as a whole.

The guide helps the instructor decide between grades and reminds her of her general criteria for evaluation. Including a dis-

SAMPLE EXPLANATION OF GRADES
Holistically graded papers
Ethnicity and Identity in the U.S.: Sandra Jamieson

GRADES FOR ANALYSIS PAPERS

Based on the analysis of your peers' papers that you presented in class Wednesday, I have assigned grades according to the criteria described below:

A: An "A" paper addresses the assignment carefully and thoughtfully, and then goes a little beyond it to say something original. In this case that means the paper identifies a clear and focused thesis about the text and follows it in a well-organized manner, presenting a clear and persuasive argument to support the thesis and adequate evidence to back it up. The writer paid close attention to the text, citing specific passages and discussing them in relation to the thesis by carefully considering what they reveal about Hirsch's project, his assumptions, and his conclusions. Such a paper maintains a consistent style, presents quotations effectively, avoids repetition and digression, and is proofread to catch all grammatical errors and create smooth and effective transitions. In addition to a clear introduction setting up the thesis, an "A" paper also has a thoughtful conclusion discussing the implications of the argument and encouraging the reader to consider the issue further.

B: A "B" paper addresses the assignment but does not go beyond it in any significant way. It may also lack a clear structure. In this case that means the paper identifies a thesis but does not fully explore the way the issue plays itself out in the text nor consider its implications. The paper may make some intelligent connections but not explore them fully, or it may have a thoughtful thesis which is not fully developed. Some "B" papers have the feeling of being unfinished, as if they could have been placed within a larger framework (such as U.S. society, world issues, or the overall socioeconomic system within which education occurs). Many "B" papers have the capacity to be "A" papers with one more draft. Perhaps the thesis needs to be more clearly articulated, or more textual evidence needs to be cited. Sometimes they need to be more effectively organized or more carefully proofread; indeed, sometimes working on the grammatical and organizational structure allows the writer to see how to strengthen the overall argument.

C: A "C" paper may somewhat address the assignment but seems to miss its essential point or go off on a tangent that never connects back to the thesis. In this case the paper often does articulate an interesting thesis but then either contradicts itself or simply moves off in another direction. Some "C" papers are the result of the writer's unfamiliarity with the text; however, more often they result from the writer's having too much to say on an issue about which he or she has strong feelings. This excess of emotion gets in the way of a purely rational argument and may produce strong but unsupported (or even insupportable) assertions. It frequently produces an excess of grammatical errors, as well. Many "C" papers have the capacity to be "A" papers with one or more careful drafts. If they lack a clear thesis and thus do not present their arguments strongly, the writer can return to the introduction and carefully state what the paper will prove, then reorganize the paper around that. Papers that earn a "C" because of the strong emotions they aroused in the writer often become truly excellent papers because the writer's feelings provide incentive for the necessary revisions. On the other hand, papers that earn a "C" because the writer did not know the text well enough should generally be abandoned and started from the beginning after the writer has reread the text.

D: A "D" paper does not seriously address the assignment. It may raise some issues that connect with the assignment, but for the most part it reveals a lack of understanding of the assignment or, in some cases, a writer who was simply not yet ready to begin the paper and needed more time to carefully consider the issues. In this case the paper may address a question outside of the text, using the text as a jumping-off point to discuss something raised in it rather than analyzing the text itself. Or the paper may simply be an elaborate plot summary of the text which raises important issues and maybe makes relevant connections, but doesn't say anything about them. These papers may have occurred because the writer

cussion of what could be done to improve the paper also helps her determine an appropriate grade, because it returns her attention to the paper as a whole.

The students find this guide helpful, too; it allows them to see what they might do to revise a paper and helps them to think of even "D" papers as having some potential. It also helps them revise drafts of future papers for the class.

was not sure how to write analytical papers or because the writer felt strongly about an issue raised in the book and allowed those feelings to get in the way of the real assignment. In either case, the paper should be used as "research notes" towards another paper rather than a first draft of a paper to be revised. Reading over the paper carefully often reveals an issue which could become the thesis of another paper, and much of the summary in the paper can be used to support the argument. The existence of strong feelings can lead to an exploration of why the text provoked such a strong reaction, and this, in turn, produces effective analysis.

+/–: The plus or minus part of the grade represents the top and bottom range of the letter grade rather than a different set of concerns. These grades often reflect grammar and style issues which mar an otherwise good paper or which raise the reader's appreciation of a paper whose content needs work. Stylistic and grammatical revisions rarely raise a paper grade more than one of these subdivisions (e.g., from a "C" to a "C+").

Writing comments and explaining grades

Nancy Sommers's research reveals that most marks and comments on papers simply explain the grade without offering suggestions for revision or for future papers. Sommers proposes that instructors' comments should help students engage the issues raised by their writing and should point out the extent to which their compositions achieve their apparent purpose. Marginal comments, holistic evaluations, and checklists serve both these ends. Concrete responses and suggestions delivered in a personal tone—that of a reader responding to a writer rather than the cold voice of authority—are the most effective (Connors and Lunsford).

When writing comments and assigning grades, instructors should focus on elements already covered in the course, to deter students from feeling overwhelmed. Using trait analysis, even instructors with fairly large classes can write comments referring to previous papers by glancing back at their grade records. This not only helps students see where they still need to concentrate their attention but also serves another important function that is harder to articulate and measure. By responding to the student as a writer of previous papers rather than as the author of discrete and unconnected pieces of writing in response to externally defined assignments, a teacher of writing in the disciplines helps that student to see himself or herself as engaged in a process of strengthening skills and becoming a more effective writer.

SAMPLE RESPONSE TO A STUDENT PAPER (EXCERPTS)
Using trait analysis
Language and Race: Rebecca Moore Howard

It seems to me that this paper exhibits a problem similar to that I identified when discussing your previous paper: you are making each paragraph coordinate with the others, so that the evidence for your thesis appears to be a list of examples. Actually, that's not what's happening. Look at paragraph 4: it is an explanation of its predecessor, not a second example. Yet your use of parallel language (both paragraphs begin with the words "Marckwardt ignores the contributions of") suggests that they are items in a list. (See section 7c of *The Bedford Handbook for Writers* for an explanation of how parallel language works this way.)

Your use of counterevidence (or, more accurately, your nonuse of it) is also an issue in this paper. The absence of counterevidence would prevent this from being an "A" paper. But before you tackle this issue, I think your attention would be best focused on your development of evidence for your thesis, learning ways to demonstrate its complexity rather than simplifying it, which is what these coordinate lists accomplish. As you take increasingly advanced courses, simple coordination of your evidence is increasingly inappropriate, and it may cause you to continue to earn "C's" in the future.

Come see me as you work on your revision.

"C"

Professor Howard begins her response to this student in an upper-level linguistics course by referring to his last paper and thus placing this one in the context of his history as a writer of linguistics papers and his overall development as a writer. This helps the student define his perception of himself as a writer. It also reminds him to look back at that previous paper as he revises this one. Finally, by mentioning that there are other errors but urging the student's attention to the primary issue, Professor Howard gives the student a manageable agenda for revision and for future writing: one thing at a time, rather than everything at once.

Coping with Plagiarism

Identifying plagiarism

Just one advantage of assigning more than one paper in a term or of using portfolio evaluation (see pages 223–27) is that the instructor can gain a general sense of each student's prose style. And aberrations from the usual style often alert instructors to the possibility of plagiarism. In one type of plagiarism, the writer inserts unattributed, extended passages of source material into the paper. Such plagiarism is textually evident when, for example, passages of the paper fail to differentiate *their* from *there* and *cite* from *sight* and *site* and contain a variety of punctuation problems, while other passages have flawless sentences and also exhibit high style and vocabulary typical of published scholars. Most institutions also classify *patchwriting* (see page 220) as plagiarism. Patchwriting is often evidenced in flashes of high-level, discipline-specific vocabulary that is syntactically mangled. A third variety of plagiarism, sometimes apparent when the entire paper is of a style quite different from the student's previous work or when a well-written research paper does not respond to the assignment, is the theft or purchase of an entire paper. Instructors should be aware of the commercial research paper industry described by Gary Galles, an industry that sometimes even places commercial ads in college papers.

Instructors who suspect the possibility of plagiarism must proceed with great caution. All of the signals listed in the preceding paragraph can have other, innocuous interpretations. The well-written research paper that does not respond to the assignment can result from a competent student's having misunderstood the assignment. The paper containing passages of disparate style can result from a cut-and-paste writing process with insufficient revision. And high-level vocabulary in mangled syntax can characterize the work of a student who is well read but inexperienced in writing or a student with a learning disability (see pages 80–81).

As a first step in learning how to identify plagiarism, instructors might consult their college's definitions, which are usually reproduced in the student handbook or college catalog. Instructors may also find the perspectives of Bond, Kibler, et al., and Mawdsley illuminating. If the syllabus lists a comprehensive writer's handbook as one of the texts for the course, instructors will find it useful in defining some types of plagiarism.

Identifying plagiarism also usually involves instructors in time-consuming and often frustrating library detective work or in tricky conversations with students. These conversations are best not begun by announcing the worst-case scenario, plagiarism. In fact, they might best be conducted without recourse to the word at all. Instead, the instructor can address style and sources: "I was puzzled by the difference in style between these two paragraphs. Can you tell me a little about your writing process for them? What sources did you use?" Conversations conducted in an interactive, nonaccusatory manner frequently render a clear, satisfying account of the composing process, from which the instructor can make judgments about whether plagiarism was involved. Sometimes, though, the student has plagiarized intentionally and denies vehemently any irregularities. In such cases, the instructor must decide whether to undertake library detective work. If the college library does not own the works cited by the student or if its circulation staff cannot account for their current whereabouts, the instructor has cause for renewed conversation with the student. Teachers of writing in the disciplines may also need to consult works with which they are familiar that are not listed in the student's works cited and which they believe may be the source of suspect prose.

Responding to plagiarism

Having ascertained that a student has plagiarized, the instructor has several options for response. Some choose to deal with plagiarism directly rather than submitting themselves and the student to the campus judiciary system. This option leaves control entirely in the hands of the instructor; he or she will determine the immediate outcome and will probably be satisfied with it. This option also protects the instructor from the much-feared possibility that the campus judiciary system (or the student plagiarist) will somehow criticize the instructor.

Limiting response to the instructor and student, though, allows for the possibility that a student may plagiarize again and again in his or her college career, accepting the risk of occasionally having to rewrite a paper for a persnickety instructor. Being subjected to the campus judiciary process, in contrast, acts as a powerful deterrent to plagiarism, and those who plagiarize again after such a confrontation and are caught at it are suspended or expelled from most institutions. In determining whether to mount an individual or judicial response to an incidence of plagiarism, instructors—even experienced instructors—are well advised to consult their department chair, the director of the writing program (often a member of the English faculty), or the campus official charged with adjudicating plagiarism.

Many composition theorists endorse an individual rather than judicial response to patchwriting, a composing phenomenon commonly categorized as plagiarism. In an article on plagiarism, Rebecca Moore Howard defines patchwriting: "Copying from a source text and then deleting some words, altering grammatical structures, or plugging in one-for-one synonym-substitutes (233)". Although at most institutions patchwriting, like the purchased paper, can subject the offender to punishments as severe as expulsion, composition theorists have argued that it results not from an ethical lapse but from students' inadequate knowledge of citation conventions. Alice Drum urges instructors to adopt pedagogical strategies that teach students how to write from sources using acceptable paraphrase and proper documentation. For Drum, these strategies include sequenced assignments. (See Chapter 6.) Susan H. McLeod advises writing program administrators to act as disciplinarians for intentional plagiarism (such as purchased papers) but as communication facilitators between teachers and students in cases of unintentional plagiarism (such as patchwriting).

Howard agrees that inadequate knowledge of citation conventions may prompt the student to try patchwriting, but she asserts a cause even more compelling for instructors of writing in the disciplines: Students patchwrite—they glue together bits of a source's language into new sentences, with or without documentation—because they are inexpert not so much with citation conventions as with the language of the discipline. They must work "monologically," with only the source's language at their disposal, because both the ideas and the words of the source are new to them. Patchwriting in this situation is inevitable, even healthy, for it signals the students' efforts to appropriate and manipulate the language of the discipline as represented in the source prose.

Patchwriting is not, of course, a desirable final product for students' writing. Yet it may not be a signal of an ethical lapse or of an inadequate knowledge of citation conventions, but rather of an unfamiliarity with the language of the discipline, an inability to write in anything but the language of the source. Instructors wishing to make an individual rather than judicial response to patchwriting, as Drum, McLeod, and many others advocate, must discover which pedagogical response is most appropriate: to teach citation conventions, to guide students to a deeper understanding of the concepts about which they are writing and the vocabulary to express that content, or a combination of the two. Particularly if a significant number of students in the course engage in patchwriting (as in the case reported by Howard), the instructor should look to a lack of facility with the language of the discipline as the probable cause.

Deterring plagiarism

Although the cause of patchwriting is often an unfamiliarity with the vocabulary or concepts of the discipline, an ignorance of citation conventions can also cause not only patchwriting but also the form of plagiarism in which a writer copies but does not attribute extensive passages of prose. It is comforting but pedagogically useless to declare, "Teaching citation is not my job. They should have learned that in freshman comp." On the contrary, there is no better place than a discipline-based course for learning how to write from and cite sources. The instructor of writing in the disciplines will therefore perform an important service by at least outlining citation conventions in class.

Simply referring students to a printed source such as a style manual is insufficient, for it does not provide in-class conversation, questions, and answers. Most first-year undergraduates (not to mention many advanced students), for example, are astonished—and dismayed—to learn that patchwriting is *verboten*, for they have labored in the belief that if they make grammatical changes, substitute synonyms, and/or cite the source, they are at liberty to do what they will with another's prose. Showing them samples of unacceptable patchwriting is usually a galvanizing pedagogical moment. (In "A Plagiarism Pentimento," Howard provides extensive examples of patchwriting.) To the realization that they must use their own prose to talk about the ideas of another, using quotation exactly and sparingly, students typically react with a horror that requires approximately twenty minutes' class time to examine and discuss. Usually at least one student exclaims, "But that means I've been plagiarizing every paper I've written!"—and other faces in the classroom become drawn and ashen. The instructor should be firm but understanding: "Yes. Most writers patchwrite when they are inexperienced at writing from sources. One of the biggest tasks facing you in college is learning how to speak in your own prose voice about unfamiliar and difficult ideas."

Students leave the classroom chastened, burdened by the task before them. They return complaining, text in hand, pointing to a culprit passage: "But how can I say this any other way?" The instructor must hold his or her ground in insisting that this is the wrong question to ask. As long as a writer is staring at a prose passage trying to figure out alternative wording, that writer is skating on the thin ice of patchwriting. The solution is to put the source text away, wait a while, and then write about its ideas. That way the writer forces himself or herself to understand the passage. After writing about it, the writer can return to the text and if he or she discovers duplicated key phrases, he or she can quote them.

As important as teaching students how to cite quoted material and avoid patchwriting is teaching them how to document paraphrased material. In many high schools, students are assigned research papers for which they are taught to footnote quotations. They are then required to incorporate a certain number of quotations—properly footnoted—in their papers. From such instruction students erroneously draw the conclusions that research papers are characterized by a certain proportion of quotations and that only "research" papers need documentation and citation; as a further consequence, they do not learn to document material that has been paraphrased.

Teaching citation and showing students alternatives to patchwriting, then, are important components of a pedagogy that deters plagiarism. Another primary component is the instructor's involvement in the students' writing process, which entails either assigning more than one paper during the term or assigning one large paper in stages. (See pages 110–111.) Instructors who get involved in students' writing processes (pointing out tendencies to patchwrite in early drafts, outlines, and so on) may not only deter patchwriting and use of extensive, unattributed passages but also foreclose the purchase of term papers. Margaret Kantz believes that one reason for students' submitting purchased papers is that "they know they are supposed to say something original but have no rhetorical problem to solve and no knowledge of how to find problems that they can discuss in their sources" (84). But if the instructor assigns the paper in stages (see pages 110–111), mentors students in individual conferences (see pages 35–37), or engages the class in peer response (see pages 184–189), the chances that students will feel insufficiently confident to write their papers are greatly reduced.

Dealing with Ideologically Objectionable Papers

The offensive paper—whether racist, sexist, homophobic, or "politically correct"—looms as a challenge for instructors across the political spectrum, not least because it calls into question the limits of a instructor's intellectual, moral, and ethical responsibilities. Issues of freedom of speech compete with those of fair play and citizenship in the classroom. David Rothgery describes the instructor who "sat the student down and set him right" in response to a racist paper (241); others return such papers ungraded, with a written explanation. Prejudice of any kind is intellectually limiting—whether it is racist, sexist, or "liberal"—and in papers it tends to result from a failure to consider evidence and research in the field or to incorporate or deal fairly with counterevidence to one's argument. Clearly defined grading criteria (see pages 18 and 211–213) allow such papers to be graded on the basis of their use of evidence and counterevidence, quality of argument, and logic of interpretation. To ignore content entirely, though, does not help the student understand the nature of advanced literary and academic writing and simply passes on the problem to his or her next instructor.

The problem of objectionable content is easiest to deal with if it has been accounted for in course planning and syllabus development. Some instructors hand out guidelines in the syllabus or as they assign papers. Many include in their syllabi a "class behavior" section that can be expanded to include the content of papers. A corollary guideline explaining what is and is not acceptable in academic papers helps students understand their audience and purpose and gives the instructor a framework for response. Explaining that this is less a political issue than one of intellectual development can help reduce the personal affront that students might otherwise feel when their values and prejudices are challenged.

Professor Jamieson reports that she has never actually asked any student to leave her class; but neither have her students engaged in discriminatory comments in class discussion, on papers, or on comments on papers. Some have made such comments to her in private, but such one-on-one overtures do not pose the potential damage that they might if introduced in the classroom.

SAMPLE SYLLABUS (EXCERPT)
Guidelines regarding objectionable behavior
English I: Sandra Jamieson

Ground rules:
A seminar is only as strong as its laziest member, so it is essential that each member of the seminar accepts her or his responsibility to the other members. Thus:

. . . .

2. You must respect your fellow writers. This means that you must take them and their ideas and writing seriously and comment constructively with sensitivity to their feelings. Failure to do this will result in a collapse of the trust necessary for a workshop and you will be asked to leave (and marked as absent). Lack of respect ranges from discriminatory comments (homophobia, racism, sexism, etc.), to yawns, the pulling of faces, drumming fingers, laughter, asides to other members of the seminar, and so on.

This trust can also be destroyed by racist, sexist, homophobic, or otherwise discriminatory comments in the papers you will share with your peers or about those papers as you respond to them. Please refrain from such comments.

In a write-to-learn context, ideologically biased papers indicate that students have not learned to think critically or to consider evidence or new ideas with an open mind. In such situations, prejudicial comments are just that: judgments made prior to a consideration of the evidence. Like clichés, their effect is to shut down thought. They are thus out of place in write-to-learn classrooms. Instructors may elect to deal with the student's critical thinking skills by requiring one or more revisions and conducting individual conferences to discuss the student's difficulty in making the ideological or conceptual shifts that the paper prompts. When the issue touches the student's a priori religious beliefs, instructors may choose to direct the student to a different topic that the student can explore without strong beliefs getting in the way.

In the context of disciplinary genres, bias is clearly out of place. Since most disciplines require authors to make their assumptions and premises clear and to explain their basis, requiring students to do the same in academic papers promotes professionalism. Regardless of one's personal politics, professional journals simply do not accept openly biased articles and are becoming increasingly sensitive to the unspoken prejudice in premises that limit objectivity. Some journals publish articles reflecting specific political positions. Those journals are recognized as political, though, and they address a limited audience—unlike discipline-based journals, which seek to address all intellectuals pursuing research in the area they cover. Explaining this distinction can be very helpful to students as they struggle with the tension that they may feel between free speech and writing in the disciplines.

Using Writing Portfolios for Evaluation

The writing portfolio, a relatively new tool in teaching writing in the disciplines, is rapidly gaining adherents. Portfolios allow students to revise their writing, present their best work, and have their work in the course evaluated as a whole rather than in disparate pieces. Recognizing that some students excel at one kind of writing but not another, instructors use portfolio analysis to evaluate the various kinds of writing the academy demands within each discipline. A writing portfolio typically contains both formal and informal writing from the course. It might include journal entries, laboratory notes, field data, research papers, an annotated bibliography, a close analysis of a text or topic from the course, unrevised class notes (maybe from a date specified by the instructor or from a lecture outside of class), prewriting, drafts of a paper, vocabulary lists, formal writing from a variety of non-discipline-specific genres (e.g., description, analysis, argumentation), or imitations of other prose styles or writers. Pat Belanoff and Peter Elbow contend that portfolios allow for evaluation that "better reflect[s] the complexities of the writing process: with time for freewriting, planning, discussion with instructors and peers, revising, and copyediting. It lets students put these activities together in a way most productive for them" (14). Writing is a process that differs with each writer, and the portfolio model is one way to account for those differences. Burnham's description, in which a class uses portfolios as a "writing environment" rather than a "grading environment" (137), captures what is most beneficial about assigning portfolios. If students perceive each paper to be in the process of being finished, they will move away from the "one-draft wonders" they too frequently believe to be finished papers.

Representative sample portfolios

Representative sample portfolios allow students to showcase their best work, much as artists collect their finest work for presentation. Students select their best writing, revise it, and submit it in a portfolio for evaluation at the end of the semester. (As with traditional methods of evaluation, instructors determine an overall grade based on a collection of individual final products.) The representative sample portfolio may be particularly appropriate for courses in which students are not taught the writing process or are not encouraged to write more than two drafts. It is popular in disciplinary genre courses because it allows the instructor to evaluate how successfully students have learned to generate writing appropriate to the discipline. Assignments written at the beginning of the semester when the students were still learning the language of the discipline can be revised at the end to reveal how successful that learning process has been.

Many instructors list general categories from which students must select their writing, to ensure a cross-section of the kinds of writing required in the university or the discipline. Students are taught to select (and thus recognize) their best work and therefore do not suffer unduly for the paper or writing assignment that did not quite make the deadline in final form or the one to which they felt no particular commitment.

Developmental process portfolios

In a course focusing on writing as a developmental process (especially those using sequenced and multistaged assignments; see pages

110–114), developmental process portfolios allow instructors to read all the work produced prior to completing the finished paper in the sequence in which it was produced—much as a historian or literary critic might examine an author's drafts and notes to evaluate his or her development over time. Where representative sample portfolios include various assignments, a developmental process portfolio usually contains all of the formal and informal writing produced in response to a specific assignment, from notes to final product. It is particularly practical for courses with one major writing assignment. Like reviewing a student's working of a mathematical or scientific sequence, reviewing the writing process can reveal exactly where a student went wrong, which may explain otherwise mysteriously flawed final papers. Students are evaluated on the basis of what they tried to do as well as what they achieved. Instructors can see whether a "thin" paper is the result of a lack of research or an inability to process research material. Unresponsive interviewees, conflicting results, and errors of process can all lead to low-quality papers that, without the portfolio, might be taken to reflect a lack of work or comprehension on the part of the student. Proponents of portfolios observe that only this means of evaluation can fully reveal the factors that combine to produce strong or weak papers.

The presentation of portfolios

One of the elements that makes students take writing portfolios seriously is the way they are presented. Unlike papers slid tentatively under instructors' doors or buried in their mailboxes, portfolios have a performative or artistic element. It is standard practice to require a table of contents, partly to ensure that students don't omit anything, along with title and cover pages. Many instructors also require continuous pagination both for their own convenience and, again, to ensure that students don't omit any work. This "professional" presentation can produce an initially unexpected perfectionism in many students, which raises the overall quality of the portfolio. (Students may even become more concerned with proofreading it.) If the university print shop will bind copies for a reasonable fee, instructors can require bound portfolios rather than the manila or plastic folders generally used. Stressing that they must allow twenty-four hours for binding helps students to concentrate on finishing the work before the deadline, which in many cases further increases their organization. The care that must be taken simply to produce a table of contents has a positive effect, even without these other measures. It requires students to see the portfolio as a representation of the best work they can do and a record of what they have produced over the semester, and it prompts them to assert ownership of their writing.

Grading portfolios

Jeffrey Sommers observes that the type of portfolio assigned should be determined by the method of evaluation most appropriate for the objectives of the course, with careful consideration given to the degree of experience and the workload of the instructor. Sommers distinguishes three types of portfolio-based evaluation: individual paper grading, holistic grading, and progress grading. These categories work equally effectively with representative sample portfolios and with developmental process portfolios. While some methods may be a little more time-consuming than others, the real difference lies in their approach to grading and evaluating.

In *individual paper grading,* the instructor considers each piece of writing individually, assigns it a grade, and then averages the individual grades to determine the final portfolio grade. Both representative sample and developmental process portfolios can be evaluated this way, although individual paper grading is more commonly used for representative sample portfolios. Some instructors weigh certain assignments, giving more credit to a research paper, for example, than to a response paper. The advantage of grading each piece is that an exceptionally strong or weak first piece of writing does not influence the way one evaluates the entire portfolio, as Liz Hamp-Lyons and William Condon's research on holistic grading reveals is often the case (182).

In *holistic grading,* the instructor evaluates the writer's work as a whole rather than as a collection of individual pieces. This renders a complete picture of a student's work, rather as one might judge the entire oeuvre of a professional writer. Instead of comparing one piece with another, the instructor assesses overall writing ability, comprehension of course content, and ability to assimilate and apply materials and skills learned in the course. One piece of lower quality than the rest should not significantly damage the grade if the remainder of the work demonstrates a fairly consistent competency at a variety of different writing tasks. Hamp-Lyons and Condon's research suggests that holistically evaluated portfolios should contain only three or four papers, with at least one in-class writing assignment, and that comment sheets prompt instructors to place equal weight on early and later work (184).

Progress grading focuses on the progress each student has made from the beginning to the end of the semester. Students are, in effect, in competition with themselves alone. While designing the syllabus and determining goals for the course, the instructor must decide how to reward progress. Should the student who moved from "D" work to "B+" work receive a higher grade than a student whose work remained "B+" throughout the semester? Some instructors grade both the process and the product and award a grade averaged between the two. Some identify at the beginning of the semester certain discourse-specific or general writing skills that each student should develop and then award a final grade on the basis of the progress demonstrated in the portfolio and in the final assignment.

Some departments have adopted writing portfolios for multisection classes, often asking instructors to grade the portfolios from sections other than those they teach. Alternatively, they may establish a grading committee arranged so that instructors do not grade their own students or are not the only ones to grade them. Such a practice allows for greater objectivity and uniformity in grading—and often greater collegiality among the faculty involved. Because of the uniformity it provides, this method is especially popular in departments employing teaching assistants or adjuncts to teach courses. Proponents claim it is also considerably less labor-intensive than grading the portfolios of one's own students, because one must struggle much harder to achieve objectivity for students one knows, especially in the case of papers that both instructor and student have worked on throughout the semester. (See Ford and Larkin for a fuller discussion of this method.)

Checklist for grading student writing

DECIDING HOW TO GRADE PAPERS

_____ Decide whether to evaluate each paper in terms of the writer's progress over the course; the writer's purpose; or this paper in comparison to others in the class.

_____ Choose the method of grading (trait or holistic).

_____ List the writing skills that you have taught so far in the course as a basis for evaluation.

_____ Determine which types of features will be graded and which will not.

_____ Write a list of criteria by which grades will be assigned, and keep it in view while grading. (Consider giving the students a copy, too.)

_____ Write at least one sentence at the end of the paper explaining the grade and suggesting how the student may improve future papers.

DECIDING HOW TO HANDLE PLAGIARISM

_____ Try to differentiate between purchased papers; reproductions of extensive, unattributed passages of text; and patchwriting.

_____ Read the institution's published definition of and strictures against plagiarism.

_____ Avoid accusatory language in conversation with the student writer.

_____ Consult the department chair, the writing program director, or the person in charge of the campus judiciary system before deciding on a course of action.

_____ Consider a judicial response to a purchased paper and a pedagogical response to patchwriting.

_____ In making a pedagogical response to plagiarism, determine whether ignorance of citation conventions or unfamiliarity with vocabulary and concepts is at fault.

DEVELOPING A METHOD OF PORTFOLIO ANALYSIS

_____ Use representative sample portfolios for courses in which students are not taught the writing process or are not encouraged to write more than two drafts—especially useful for courses emphasizing disciplinary genres.

_____ Use developmental process portfolios if the course places emphasis on rewriting and the writing process in general—especially valuable for all forms of write-to-learn pedagogy.

_____ Use a combination of both forms of portfolios (two pieces of writing or more in each) to evaluate process and product.

_____ Decide whether to grade each piece of work in the portfolio independently and average the grades or to grade holistically. Developmental process portfolios can also be graded on writing progress.

_____ In multisection courses, discuss the possibility of collaborative portfolio grading among several or all instructors teaching the course.

For Further Reading

Assigning grades

Arnold, L. V. "Writer's Cramp and Eyestrain: Are They Paying Off?" *English Journal* 53 (1964): 10–15. Arnold reports that studies reveal no significant difference in the writing improvement between students whose teachers had marked every error and made extensive comments and those whose teachers had made only a few comments and error corrections.

Barnes, Linda Laube. "Gender Bias in Teachers' Written Comments." *Gender in the Classroom: Power and Pedagogy.* Ed. Susan L. Gabriel and Isaiah Smithson. Urbana: U of Illinois P, 1990. 140–59.

Bizzaro, Patrick. "Evaluating Student Poetry Writing: A Primary-Trait Scoring Model." *Teaching English in the Two-Year College* 17 (Feb. 1990): 54–61. In the model Bizzaro describes, grades are assigned according to revision of specific traits in each poem.

Butler, J. F. "Remedial Writers: The Teacher's Job as Corrector of Papers." *College Composition and Communication* 31 (1980): 270–77. Butler reports that by limiting their comments and corrections to grammar, instructors encourage students simply to "fix" grammar but not work on any other aspect of the paper during revision.

Connors, Robert J., and Andrea A. Lunsford. "Teachers' Rhetorical Comments on Student Papers." *College Composition and Communication* 44 (1993): 200–23.

Edwards, Renee. "Sensitivity to Feedback and the Development of Self." *Communication Quarterly* 38 (1990): 101–11.

Elbow, Peter. "Ranking, Evaluating, and Liking: Sorting Out Three Forms of Judgment." *College English* 55 (1993): 187–206.

Hairston, Maxine. "On Not Being a Composition Slave." *Training the New Teacher of Composition.* Ed. Charles W. Bridges. Urbana: NCTE, 1986. 117–24. Hairston summarizes the scholarship on how and why students do not learn from copious marginal comments and suggests nine ways to provide them with "quality feedback rather than overwhelming them with more advice than they can absorb and more criticism than they can tolerate."

Hamp-Lyons, Liz. *Holistic Writing Assessment of LEP Students.* Denver: Center for Research in Applied Language, U of Colorado at Denver, 1991.

Harris, Muriel. "Evaluation: The Process for Revision." *Journal of Basic Writing* 1.4 (1978): 82–90. Harris's research reveals that above a certain "minimal level," students learn from marginal comments "in inverse proportion to the amount of instructor notation on the page."

Haswell, Richard H. "Minimal Marking." *College English* 45 (1983): 600–04.

Lloyd-Jones, Richard. "Primary Trait Scoring." *Evaluating Writing: Describing, Measuring, Judging.* Ed. Charles Cooper and Lee Odell. Urbana: NCTE, 1977. 33–66.

MacAllister, Joyce. "Responding to Student Writing." *Teaching Writing in All Disciplines.* Ed. C. Williams Griffin. San Francisco: Jossey-Bass, 1982. 59–66.

Rankin, Libby. "An Anatomy of Awkwardness." *Journal of Teaching Writing* 9 (1990): 45–57. Rankin discusses the many uses, interpretations, and perceptions of the marginal notation "AWK."

Rothgery, David. "'So What Do We Do Now?': Necessary Directionality as the Writing Teacher's Response to Racist, Sexist, Homophobic Papers." *College Composition and Communication* 44 (1993): 241–47.

Sommers, Nancy. "Responding to Student Writing." *College Composition and Communication* 33 (1982): 148–56.

Zak, Frances. "Exclusively Positive Responses to Student Writing." *Journal of Basic Writing* 9.2 (1990): 40–53.

Zorn, Jeff. "How Numbers Numb: 1.325 Case Studies." *California English* 26 (March–April 1990): 8–26. Zorn's research indicates that numerical evaluations of writing are not more objective than other methods, despite their appearance.

Plagiarism

Bond, Harold L. *Sources, Their Use, and Acknowledgement.* Hanover: Dartmouth College, 1972.

Drum, Alice. "Responding to Plagiarism." *College Composition and Communication* 37 (1986): 241–43. Rpt. in *Background Readings for Instructors Using* The Bedford Handbook for Writers. 4th ed. Ed. Glenn Blalock. Boston: Bedford, 1994. 335–37.

Galles, Gary M. "Professors Are Woefully Ignorant of a Well-Organized Market Inimical to Learning: The Big Business in Research Papers." *Chronicle of Higher Education* 28 Oct. 1987: B1, B3.

Howard, Rebecca Moore. "A Plagiarism *Pentimento.*" *Journal of Teaching Writing* (Summer 1993): 233–46.

Kantz, Margaret. "Helping Students Use Textual Sources Persuasively." *College English* 52 (January 1990): 74–91. Rpt. in *Background Readings for Instructors Using* The Bedford Handbook for Writers. 4th ed. Ed. Glenn Blalock. Boston: Bedford, 1994. 320–35.

Kibler, William L., Elizabeth M. Nuss, Brent G. Paterson, and Gary Pavela. *Academic Integrity and Student Development: Legal Issues and Policy Perspectives.* Asheville, NC: College Administration Publications, 1988.

Mawdsley, Ralph D. *Legal Aspects of Plagiarism.* Topeka: National Organization on Legal Problems of Education, 1985.

McLeod, Susan H. "Responding to Plagiarism: The Role of the WPA." *WPA: Writing Program Administration* 15.3 (Spring 1992): 7–16.

Miller, Keith D. "Redefining Plagiarism: Martin Luther King's Use of an Oral Tradition." *Chronicle of Higher Education* 20 Jan. 1993: A60.

Murphy, Richard. "Anorexia: The Cheating Disorder." *College English* 52 (1990): 898–903.

Whitaker, Elaine E. "A Pedagogy to Address Plagiarism." *College Composition and Communication* 44 (1993): 509–14.

Portfolios

Belanoff, Pat, and Peter Elbow. "Using Portfolios to Increase Collaboration and Community in a Writing Program." *WPA: Writing Program Administration* 9 (Spring 1986): 27–39.

Belanoff, Pat, Peter Elbow, and Marcia Dickson. *Portfolios: Process and Product.* Portsmouth, NH: Boynton/Cook, 1991. Twenty-three essays discuss a range of possible uses, problems, and benefits of writing portfolios in a range of academic environments. Essays describe specific programs; discuss the benefits and potential problems of collaborative evaluation, holistic evaluation, and developmental evaluation; suggest establishing a department-wide portfolio review system; and discuss the benefits of portfolios in the assessment of writing in the disciplines.

Burnham, Christopher. "Portfolio Evaluation: Room to Breathe and Grow." *Training the New Teacher of College Composition.* Ed. Charles Bridges. Urbana: NCTE, 1986. 125–38. Burnham describes one method of portfolio assignment at New Mexico State University, the rationale behind it, and benefits for students and faculty. Although designed to help train new teaching assistants and overcome problems of evaluation, this method could be modified for individual courses across the disciplines. Students who have satisfactorily completed the writing assignments for the course may elect either to receive a "C" or to compile a portfolio of their best work, including a discussion of why they deem that work "good."

Courts, Patrick, and Kathleen H. McInerney. *Assessment in Higher Education: Politics, Pedagogy, and Portfolios.* Westport, CT: Praeger, 1993. The authors offer a useful survey of the history of portfolio assessment and types of portfolio evaluation, including a discussion of benefits and dangers and a checklist of things to avoid in using individual portfolio assessment.

Ford, James, and Gregory Larkin. "The Portfolio System: An End to Backsliding Writing Standards." *College English* 39 (1978): 950–55.

Hamp-Lyons, Liz, and William Condon. "Questioning Assumptions about Portfolio-Based Assessment." *College Composition and Communication* 44 (May 1993): 176–90. The authors explore the assumptions common to members of a holistic portfolio evaluation group in which instructors evaluate the portfolios of their own students and the same number from other sections. There must be some procedure to ensure that faculty consider the entire portfolio rather than reaching judgment after the first piece. They also found that faculty paid less attention to differences in genre than differences between drafts and thus suggest the inclusion of drafts as well as finished texts.

Larson, Richard. "Using Portfolios in the Assessment of Writing in the Academic Disciplines." *Portfolios: Process and Product.* Ed. Pat Belanoff and Marcia Dickson. Portsmouth, NH: Boynton/Cook, 1991. 137–50. One of the few discussions of the use of portfolios as part of large-scale curriculum development across the disciplines. Explains benefits of and strategies for using writing portfolios across the disciplines.

Sommers, Jeffrey. "Bringing Practice in Line with Theory: Using Portfolio Grading in the Composition Classroom." *Portfolios: Process and Product.* Ed. Pat Belanoff and Marcia Dickson. Portsmouth, NH: Boynton/Cook, 1991. 153–64. Focuses primarily on individual rather than collective assessment. Although, like most articles, the focus is on the composition class, the discussion and suggestions can be translated to other disciplines. Places portfolio theories within the context of broader composition and pedagogical theory.

CHAPTER 12

Teaching Advanced Reading Skills

In this chapter:

❏   The reading-writing connection

❏   Students' alternatives to reading

❏   Reading strategies for students

❏   Checklist for teaching advanced reading skills

❏   For further reading

The Reading-Writing Connection

The relationship of reading and writing

Reading and writing are interrelated. Many instructors who bemoan students' poor writing attribute it to young people's substitution of contemporary visual media for books: "They watch television instead." This commonplace observation would seem to impel those who teach writing to teach reading as well. Teaching reading includes teaching students to attend to the fine shades of meaning that can be imparted in print and to consider the various purposes and modes of reading (such as the informative and reflective modes identified by Judith Langer). Theorists in a variety of disciplines have explored the complex relationship between reading and writing. Bruce T. Peterson recognizes a "personal matrix at the heart of the reading and writing process [which] implies that reading and writing are connected thinking processes which derive from similar, if not identical, mental structures" (460). Composition theorist Charles Bazerman observes:

> It is within the art of writing to constrain potential meanings that might be imputed by readers from their likely frames of interests and interpretation to within the bounds desired by the writer. And it

is within the art of reading to reconstruct out of the reader's own cognitive resources a meaning that might plausibly account for the words handed over by the writer. (33)

Mary Crawford and Roger Chaffin explain that in the Platonic tradition the text determines meaning; similarly, in Locke's empiricism the mind is a passive receptor. From contemporary cognitive research, however, a new rationalist approach arises: Meaning derives from the conjunction of the text and the reader's prior understanding (Crawford and Chaffin 3). E. D. Hirsch calls this prior knowledge "cultural literacy" (2), asserting that it forms a schema that determines reading comprehension and advanced literacy skills, including academic writing (39ff). Whatever the precise relationship between reading and writing, it is clear from these and other studies that there *is* a relationship; therefore, instructors who teach writing are well advised to attend to advanced reading skills also. This need not absorb classroom time, however; Henry Steffens, teaching large lecture classes in history, encourages his students to keep reading journals. While they read assignments they note questions and insights; immediately upon completing the reading, they write a quick summary. This approach urges students away from the model of reading as the gathering of data and toward the model of reading as an interactive process.

The interplay of writing and reading

Because there are multiple theories about the precise nature of the relationship between reading and writing, various pedagogical strategies have evolved, and instructors develop their own models determined by their perception of the relationship. Perhaps the most successful pedagogy for weaving instruction in writing with instruction in reading considers the role of the reader in making meaning. Composition theorist Lynn Quitman Troyka says that college students who write at a precollege level may be too close to the texts they write, too lost in the word-by-word minutiae to make sense of the whole; or they may attempt to distance themselves from the text by writing quickly and then not rereading. They need to learn a sense of their own readers' needs, attending to the key question "Exactly how does my reader read, and, therefore, what must I do to help my reader function?" (190). To do so, they need to attend to their own reading processes. Troyka's analysis, though directed to the teaching of basic writing, offers important principles for any instructor who undertakes to make explicit the relationship between reading and writing and to encourage students to engage in more fruitful reading processes. Troyka suggests that the teacher of writing guide students to understand three principles of reading: (1) "Reading is a text-based activity," with meaning made by associating the text with "ideas already known to the reader" (190); (2) new information is learned by accessing prior information; and (3) reading is improved by predicting what comes next in the text, and the prediction need not be accurate.

Instructors who teach students to attend to style, structure, meaning, tone, word choice, and rhetorical strategies employed in their readings create more effective readers. They also help to shape more effective writers who have an array of rhetorical strategies open to them in addition to a finer sensitivity to language.

Students' Alternatives to Reading

Resistance to reading

Experienced, successful students do not always read all their assignments. When asked how they succeed without doing the reading, they sometimes say that they rely on a commercially prepared "study guide" such as Cliffs Notes, Monarch Notes, or Master Plots. Or they may say that they rely on class lectures as a substitute for reading the assignments.

The possible reasons for students' resistance to reading are plentiful. Teachers tend to assume that students who do not read are poor readers or lazy, indifferent students or that the students have been given excessively long or difficult assignments. Yet Joy S. Ritchie's discussion of Gerald Graff's theories points out other possibilities that instructors may not so readily consider: Students may choose not to read because they have a purely functional approach to reading (reading for informative purposes); because they view reading as an undesirable feminine activity; or because they resist the authority exercised by the instructor. They may also object to the "enforced passivity" of reading (122–23).

Students' reasons for not reading are worth their instructors' attention. So are their major alternatives, Cliffs Notes and class notes.

Strategies to avoid reading—Cliffs Notes and class notes

When asked about their use of Cliffs Notes, most advanced undergraduate students may immediately deny ever having used them. If they open up, however, they may say that they used commercial study guides in high school and when they first came to college but that they find them useless for advanced subjects. Yet they may very well remark that if they were English majors they would still be using them. They may also pass along the tale of the legendary English major "who graduated on them." The upshot of all this lore is the idea that Cliffs Notes are useful in courses for which they are available.

How students use them is yet another interesting question. Most students who admit to having used them will begin by saying that they used them as a "supplement" to reading; the Cliffs Notes helped them understand a difficult text that the instructor inadequately explained, or Cliffs Notes helped the insecure student appear knowledgeable in class. After more discussion, though, some students will admit that at least sometimes they used commercial study guides instead of reading some or all of an assigned text, and a few will say that they used Cliffs Notes to get ideas for writing papers.

The psychology instructor teaching an advanced course in theories of tests and measures need not concern himself or herself much with the possibility of Cliffs Notes replacing the assigned text, for Cliffs Notes are probably not available on the topic. The instructor should be concerned, though, with the possibility that students are relying on classroom lectures to the exclusion of assigned readings. Many successful advanced undergraduates report that class attendance and good note-taking skills are fine alternatives to reading assigned texts. Many of their instructors, they report, explain the readings in their lectures and also test students not on independent assigned reading but on the points covered in class. Students with good skills in listening, note taking, and analysis may therefore decide that reading is incidental to their academic success.

The challenge of bringing students to reading is therefore not a "remedial" issue but an issue of pedagogy at all levels. The instructor who is assigning reading that the students are not doing while they are nevertheless receiving good grades has a pedagogy that is not accomplishing its purpose.

Bringing students to reading

If reading is part of the pedagogical design—if it is the instructor's intention to engage students with printed texts—then the pedagogy must provide the means for that engagement. "Bringing students to reading" is best thought of in the positive terms of engagement with texts rather than the negative terms of preventing students' not reading. Otherwise, pedagogy becomes too much a guessing game and a power game, with the instructor and students trying to outwit each other, to enforce or thwart the instructor's will.

The positive alternative is to view pedagogy in dialogic terms, negotiating the needs and desires of both instructor and students. The instructor has the chief responsibility for ensuring the success of the negotiation. With that philosophy, the syllabus itself can be constructed to make students use both writing and talking as ways of conversing with themselves, one another, the instructor, and their texts. Response journals are a valuable means of furthering such dialogue (see Chapter 10), and summary writing promotes close attention to and comprehension of the text (see pages 237–240).

Reading Strategies for Students

Global reading

Whereas the research of Jeanne Fahnestock indicates that experienced readers sometimes read backward, understanding the first statement (e.g., a premise) only after reading the second (e.g., the concession), inexperienced readers may read in a nonrecursive, fixed linearity, trying to understand everything they are reading when they first read it. The result is a slow, laborious reading process, often with the reader using a highlighter pen to mark nearly every sentence. Even students in advanced courses may not realize that when they confront unfamiliar material, particularly in an unfamiliar discipline, it is often helpful to skim the text first, picking up key words and gaining a general sense of the subject under discussion. Then they are able to go back and read more slowly but with greater comprehension.

In the academic context, it is usually helpful for the instructor to give a "preview" of an assigned text. The preview might consist of a list of key words or the thesis of the article to help students achieve a global understanding of the text.

Instructors' previews can be accompanied by assignments based on the text. If the preview includes the thesis of the article, students may be asked to list and evaluate the evidence provided by the author. If the preview includes a list of key words, the students may be asked to define those words as they are used in the text. They may also be assigned to investigate standard discipline-specific reference works for definitions of key words from the reading assignment. Sending students to the standard reference works of the discipline weans them from *Webster's* as the sole arbiter of meaning while giving them a complex understanding of fundamental precepts of the discipline. Some instructors divide responsibility for defining a list of key words among the members of the class or assign the terms to designated groups, who then report on them at the beginning of the next class session.

Selective reading

Experienced readers develop a variety of strategies for selective reading, focusing on one or more subtopics in an essay. Readers engaged in selective reading look for those particular subtopics and pay only secondary attention to global understanding of the text. The selective approach helps scholars in the disciplines (and anyone doing research) read through a lot of material and focus on just the issues that are relevant to their purposes.

Again the instructor can be of great assistance by providing a preview. If the students are to read a text for specific issues rather

than for global understanding, the instructor can identify those issues in advance. Often selective reading is promoted through study
questions distributed when the reading assignment is made.

SAMPLE STUDY GUIDE (EXCERPTS)
Selective reading questions
Canadian Literature: Martha Dietz

ASSIGNMENT FOR FEBRUARY 14 (*FROM INK LAKE* GROUP C.)
R. Wiebe: "The Naming of Albert Johnson"
  1. Make a list of the events narrated in this story as they occurred
     in "real time" (chronological order).
  2. Why do you think the author chose to structure the narrative as
     he did?
  3. What is the significance of the title?

H. Hodd: "Ghosts at Jarry"
  1. How is the first sentence significant?
  2. Why is Mario's initial visit to the Olympic Stadium so unsatisfac-
     tory? (Find passages in the text to back up your observations.)
  3. How did he remember Jarry Park? What did he associate with
     going to games there?
  4. What's the significance of the title?

J. Hodgins: "Concert Stages of Europe"
M. Atwood: "The Man from Mars"
A. Munro: "Miles City, Montana"
A. Macleod: "The Closing Down of Summer"

> These four stories all narrate a particular event in the life of a
> character that in some way captures something about life with
> which we can all identify. The event seems very real (in some way
> honest) and also very specific to the character (with whom we
> most likely have very little in common) and yet on some level we
> can all identify with the feelings or the situation. Below I list a set
> of questions for the Hodgins story. Trying to answer those ques-
> tions I hope helps unlock the larger "story" within the narrative.

I'd like each of you to select one of the remaining three stories and
prepare a list of questions you think get at something special about
the story you have picked.

Professor Dietz's study
questions direct her
students to selective
reading of literature,
which is by its nature
experienced holistically
and responsively. The
study questions make
analysts of the stu-
dents, asking them to
figure out not only how
the components of the
text (chronology, title)
interact to build mean-
ing, but how the stu-
dents' own identifica-
tion with the narrated
events builds meaning.

Summary writing

For instructors who regard a text as containing a certain immutable
"meaning" that the astute reader must extract, summary writing is
academic drudgery. Those who regard summarizing as a means of

making the process of reading explicit find it a valuable tool of pedagogy. Summary writing can help students identify and articulate the meaning of the words on the page, differentiate them from the associations and ideas that the prose evokes in the reader, and discover the meaning made by the conjunction of the two. Many instructors regard summary writing as a means whereby both introductory and advanced students engage and manipulate the specialized vocabulary of the discipline (as Sandra Stotsky and Rebecca Moore Howard suggest).

For an introductory linguistics class, Professor Howard takes students through an exhaustive and, her students say, exhausting process of writing summaries. She guides her students through two revisions of the summary: the first for accuracy, completeness, and original language, the second for style and usage (not shown here). The students write three of these summaries during the semester and in the process master vocabulary and improve their ability to read texts closely. The syllabus for this course also assigns three response papers so that students learn not only to immerse themselves in their assigned texts but also to converse with them.

SAMPLE STUDY GUIDE (EXCERPTS)
Directions for summary writing
American English: Rebecca Moore Howard

THE SUMMARY

I. PURPOSE OF THE SUMMARY
   A. Internal: to reach a complete understanding of another's writing.
   B. External: to demonstrate that understanding to others, or to record it for yourself for future reference.

II. THE WRITING/LEARNING PROCESS
   This step-by-step process (derived from Behrens and Rosen, *Writing and Reading across the Curriculum,* 1994) assures your best work.
   A. *Read* the passage quickly. Avoid interruptions; aim for a general understanding of the piece.
   B. *Reread* carefully. Note the topic sentence (the main sentence) in each paragraph, and note key ideas. Continue to reread until you have mastered the material.
   C. On a separate sheet of paper, *write a one-sentence summary of each paragraph.* (If the piece is long, you will have to divide it into units larger than the paragraph—perhaps two or three paragraphs together.)
   D. Put away the book and all your notes, including your paragraph summaries. Now *write a thesis statement*—your own sentence that summarizes the entire passage. The author's main point should be captured in your thesis statement, but it should be expressed in your own words; that's why you must not look at the original while you compose this sentence. Behrens and Rosen specify, "In the case of persuasive passages, summarize in a sentence the author's conclusion. In the case of descriptive passages, indicate the subject of the description and its key feature(s)."
   E. With only your thesis statement, blank paper, and pen before you, close your books, put away your notes, and *write the first draft of your summary from memory alone.* Let the thesis statement be one of your first sentences. Of course you will leave

out some material; you may also find that you remember some incorrectly. Nevertheless, writing the first draft from memory alone will ensure that you express yourself *in your own words,* thus avoiding plagiarism.

    F. Compare your first draft with your notes and with the original text that you are summarizing. Check for any ideas that you may have remembered inaccurately, and check for any important concepts that you may have omitted.

III. FEATURES OF COMPLETED SUMMARY

    A. Introduction (usually one paragraph).

        1. Contains a one-sentence thesis statement that sums up the author's *point,* her *conclusion.*

        2. Also introduces the pieces to be summarized, giving title (use quotation marks to indicate titles of short pieces such as articles; underline titles of long pieces such as books— refer to *The Bedford Handbook for Writers,* sections 37d and 42a); author's name; and any pertinent background information about the author or his work.

    B. Summary (one or more paragraphs): paraphrases and condenses the original piece. In your summary, be sure that you—

        1. Include important data but omit minor points.

        2. Include one or more of the author's examples or illustrations; these will bring your summary to life.

        3. *Refrain from injecting your own ideas, illustrations, metaphors, or interpretations.*

Look upon yourself as a summarizing machine. The end! When you have finished summarizing the piece, you have completed your task. *Do not add your own concluding paragraph unless your professor directs you to do so.* The author's conclusion is your conclusion.

In-class summary serves as a good alternative to lecturing on assigned readings. In-class summary can be conducted in at least two different ways: small-group summary and whole-class summary. Students may spend the first five to fifteen minutes of class writing a summary of the most recently assigned reading, which the instructor then uses to stimulate class discussion. Or the instructor can ask the class to dictate a summary, which the instructor writes on the board. Requiring that the students keep their books closed during the exercise, the instructor asks a student, "What do you remember from the reading?" and writes the student's response on the board. Then he or she turns to another student: "What can you add to this?" The process continues until no one in the class can contribute anything further. Then they all open their books and look for major assertions or evidence that have been overlooked. Usually the passages not remembered are the most difficult ones, those that students did not understand as they read the assignment. In-class summary there-fore helps the instructor know what needs to be explained. A third method of in-class summary has the students form small groups and spend ten to twenty minutes summarizing the reading, with a designated scribe transcribing the final summary. (For tips on lead-ing class discussion and orchestrating small-group work in class, see Chapter 9.)

Close reading

For decades, a staple of literature curricula has been "close reading," in which students are taken through a text sentence by sentence to discover the fine shadings of meaning embedded in prose or poetry. Usually close reading is used in situations where the text is ap-proached for reflective rather than informative purposes. A feature of many other disciplines besides literature, close reading provides an apt counterpart to summary writing, which asks students to identify and replicate major points.

Scholars of textual studies warn instructors, however, to approach the pedagogy of close reading cautiously. As with any other sort of reading exercise, the danger exists that the instructor might believe in "only one" reading of the text or might believe that he or she is in possession of the "most important" points of the text. Close reading exercises then become games in which the students try to figure out what is in the instructor's head. Moreover, when close reading at-tends only to the text, taking into account neither reader nor writer, the meanings derived from the intersection of students' ideas and experiences with the text may be deemed "wrong." Writing teachers Glynda Hull and Mike Rose offer a case study in which a student's apparently "incorrect" reading of a text actually made meaning be-yond that which the instructor had decided was "correct," meaning derived from a set of assumptions different from those of the instruc-tor. Close reading, in other words, is best conducted as a transaction between readers and texts, not as a decoding of an immutable text.

Heather Murray points out that the customary pedagogy of close reading too readily engages the entire class in a dissection of the text with the erroneous assumption that the text is equally accessible to all. Linda Hutcheon concurs: Many theorists, she notes, propose that truth is not "a property of a text" but "something enacted or per-formed by a reader" (19). But, she emphasizes, it is not enough to say that truth is constructed by the community of readers, for the act of reading is also shaped by factors such as gender and culture. Just as truth is not unified, neither are readers (20). Again, the di-vergent reading habits and experiences that students bring to the classroom might best be made part of rather than marginal to the close reading exercise.

Checklist for teaching advanced reading skills

_____ Give reading a dialogic role so that students do not rely on commercial study guides or lecture notes instead of reading assigned texts.

_____ Assign response journals and response papers (dialogic reading) as a way of reducing resistance to reading.

_____ Make explicit some essential principles of reading: the role of the reader's prior information in making meaning from the text; the advantage of the reader's making predictions (even when incorrect) about what will come next in the text; the advantage of skimming unfamiliar material before reading closely; the need to read backward sometimes.

_____ Give reading previews such as key words and thesis statements to improve students' global understanding.

_____ Give reading previews such as study questions to improve students' selective reading.

_____ Assign students to interact with the reading previews as well as the texts (to define key words, list evidence for thesis statements, postulate answers to study questions).

_____ Assign summaries to engage students in the vocabulary and concepts of the discipline.

_____ Assign close reading as a way of engaging fine shades of meaning; temper close reading exercises with students' responses to readings.

_____ Consider how students' backgrounds and experiences shape their reading.

For Further Reading

Reading theories and pedagogies

Bazerman, Charles. "The Interpretation of Disciplinary Writing." *Writing the Social Text: Poetics and Politics in Social Science Discourse.* Ed. Richard Harvey Brown. New York: Aldine de Gruyter, 1992. 31–38.

Crawford, Mary, and Roger Chaffin. "The Reader's Construction of Meaning: Cognitive Research on Gender and Comprehension." *Gender and Reading.* Ed. Elizabeth A. Flynn and Patrocinio Schweickart. Baltimore: Johns Hopkins UP, 1986. 3–30.

Fahnestock, Jeanne. "Connection and Understanding." *Constructing Rhetorical Education.* Ed. Marie Secor and Davida Charney. Carbondale: Southern Illinois UP, 1992. 235–56.

Flitterman-King, Sharon. "The Role of the Response Journal in Active Reading." *The Quarterly of the National Writing Project and the Center for the Study of Writing* 10 (1988): 4–11.

Harvey, Sandra. "Cliff—Take Note!" *English Journal* 76 (1987): 46–47.

Hirsch, E. D. Jr. *Cultural Literacy: What Every American Needs to Know.* Boston: Houghton, 1987.

Hull, Glynda, and Mike Rose. "'This Wooden Shack Place': The Logic of an Unconventional Reading." *College Composition and Communication* 41 (1990): 287–98.

Hutcheon, Linda. "Response: Truth Telling." *Profession* (1992): 18–20.

Langer, Judith A. "The Process of Understanding: Reading for Literary and Informative Purposes." *Research in the Teaching of English* 24 (Oct. 1990): 229–60.

Murray, Heather. "Close Reading, Closed Writing." *College English* 53 (1991): 195–208.

Newkirk, Thomas, ed. *Only Connect: Uniting Reading and Writing.* Upper Montclair, NJ: Boynton/Cook, 1986.

Peterson, Bruce T. "Writing about Responses: A Unified Model of Reading, Interpretation, and Composition." *College English* 44 (1982): 459–68.

Ritchie, Joy S. "Resistance to Reading: Another View of the Minefield." *Journal of Advanced Composition* 12.1 (1992): 117–36.

Sims, Rudine. "Dialect and Reading: Toward Redefining the Issues." *Reader Meets Author/Bridging the Gap: A Psycholinguistic and Sociolinguistic Approach.* Ed. Judith A. Langer and M. Tricia Smith-Burke. Newark, DE: International Reading Association, 1982. 222–32.

Steffens, Henry. "Using Informal Writing in Large History Classes: Helping Students to Find Interest and Meaning in History." *Social Studies* 82 (1991): 107–09.

Troyka, Lynn Quitman. "Closeness to Text: A Delineation of Reading Processes as They Affect Composing." *Only Connect: Uniting Reading and Writing.* Ed. Thomas Newkirk. Upper Montclair, NJ: Boynton/Cook, 1986. 187–97.

Summary writing

Bartholomae, David. "Inventing the University." *When a Writer Can't Write: Studies in Writer's Block and Other Composing-Process Problems.* New York: Guilford, 1985. 134–65.

Bean, John C. "Summary Writing, Rogerian Listening, and Dialectic Thinking." *College Composition and Communication* 37 (1986): 343–45.

Behrens, Laurence, and Leonard J. Rosen. *Writing and Reading across the Curriculum.* 5th ed. New York: Harper, 1994.

Campbell, Cherry. *Writing with Others' Words: Native and Non-Native University Students' Use of Information from a Background Reading Text in Academic Compositions.* Washington: Office of Educational Research and Improvement, 1987. ERIC ED 287 315.

D'Angelo, Frank J. "The Art of Paraphrase." *College Composition and Communication* 30 (1979): 255–59.

Howard, Rebecca Moore. "A Plagiarism Pentimento." *Journal of Teaching Writing* (Summer 1993): 233–46.

Poe, Retta E. "A Strategy for Improving Literature Reviews in Psychology Courses." *Teaching of Psychology* 17 (Feb. 1990): 54.

Price, Derek W. W. "A Model for Reading and Writing about Primary Sources: The Case of Introductory Psychology." *Teaching of Psychology* 17 (Feb. 1990): 48–53.

Sherrard, Carol. "Summary Writing: A Topographical Study." *Written Communication* 3 (July 1986): 324–43.

Stotsky, Sandra. "Teaching the Vocabulary of Academic Discourse." *Journal of Basic Writing* 2 (1970): 15–39. Rpt. in *A Sourcebook for Basic Writing Teachers.* Ed. Theresa Enos. New York: Random, 1987. 328–47.

Appendix A:
A Bibliography of Discipline-Specific Sources for Teaching Writing

While some of the following sources explore the rhetoric of a discipline, most are studies of teaching writing in the disciplines. The lists are suggestive rather than exhaustive. Nearly every discipline has one or more journals devoted to pedagogy, and these frequently publish articles about teaching writing in the discipline. Barbara E. Fassler Walvoord also recommends that those who want to compile a discipline–specific bibliography of works on teaching writing should "search ERIC, using the descriptors 'Higher Education,' 'Writing,' 'Interdisciplinary Approach,' the name of your discipline, and inclusive dates" (*Helping Students Write Well*, 241).

Anthropology

Geertz, Clifford. *Works and Lives: The Anthropologist as Author.* Palo Alto: Stanford UP, 1988.

Hansen, Kristine. "Rhetoric and Epistemology in the Social Sciences: A Contrast of Two Representative Texts." *Writing in Academic Disciplines.* Vol. 2 of *Advances in Writing Research.* Ed. David A. Jolliffe. Norwood, NJ: Ablex, 1988. 167–210.

Herrington, Anne J. "Composing One's Self in a Discipline: Students' and Teachers' Negotiations." *Constructing Rhetorical Education.* Ed. Marie Secor and Davida Charney. Carbondale: Southern Illinois UP, 1992. 91–115.

Herrington, Anne J., and Deborah Cadman. "Peer Review and Revising in an Anthropology Course: Lessons for Learning." *College Composition and Communication* 4 (1991): 184–99.

Hess, David J. "Teaching Ethnographic Writing: A Review Essay." *Anthropology and Education Quarterly* 20 (1989): 163–76.

Pearce, W. Barnett, and Victoria Chen. "Ethnography as Sermonic: The Rhetorics of Clifford Geertz and James Clifford." *Rhetoric in the Human Sciences.* Ed. Herbert W. Simons. London: Sage, 1989. 119–32.

Art

Garfield, Eugene. "Is Information Retrieval in the Arts and Humanities Inherently Different from That in Science? The Effect That ISI's Citation Index for the Arts and Humanities Is Expected to Have on Future Scholarship." *Library Quarterly* 50 (1980): 40–57.

Astronomy

Beutler, Suzanne A. "Using Writing to Learn about Astronomy." *Reading Teacher* 41 (1988): 412–17.

Biology

Cannon, Robert E. "Experiments with Writing to Teach Microbiology." *American Biology Teacher* 52 (1990): 156–58.

Carter, Jack. "The Human Sciences Program and the Future." *American Biology Teacher* 44 (Oct. 1982): 427–28.

Flynn, Elizabeth A., George A. McCulley, and Ronald K. Gratz. "Writing in Biology: Effects of Peer Critiquing and Analysis of Models on the Quality of Biology Laboratory Reports." *Writing Across the Disciplines: Research into Practice.* Ed. Art Young and Toby Fulwiler. Upper Montclair, NJ: Boynton/Cook, 1986. 160–75.

Gragson, Gay, and Jack Selzer. "Fictionalizing the Readers of Scholarly Articles in Biology." *Written Communication* 7 (Jan. 1990): 25–58.

Halloran, S. Michael. "The Birth of Molecular Biology: An Essay in the Criticism of Scientific Discourse." *Rhetoric Review* 3.1 (1984): 70–83.

House, Ken. "Improving Student Writing in Biology." *American Biology Teacher* 45 (Summer 1983): 267–70.

Marsella, Joy, Thomas L. Hilgers, and Clemence McLaren. "How Students Handle Writing Assignments: A Study of Eighteen Responses in Six Disciplines." *Writing, Teaching, and Learning in the Disciplines.* Ed. Anne Herrington and Charles Moran. New York: MLA, 1992. 174–88.

Martin, Kathryn H. "Writing 'Microthemes' to Learn Human Biology." *Writing to Learn Mathematics and Science.* Ed. Paul Connolly and Teresa Vilardi. New York: Teachers College P, 1989. 113–21.

Myers, Greg. "The Social Construction of Two Biologists' Proposals." *Written Communication* 2 (1985): 219–45.

———. "Stories and Styles in Two Molecular Biology Review Articles." *Textual Dynamics of the Professions: Historical and Contemporary Studies of Writing in Professional Communities.* Ed. Charles Bazerman and J. Paradis. Madison: U of Wisconsin P, 1991. 45–75.

———. *Writing Biology: Texts in the Social Construction of Scientific Knowledge.* Science and Literature Series. Ed. G. Levine. Madison: U of Wisconsin P, 1990.

Spanier, Bonnie B. "Encountering the Biological Sciences: Ideology, Language, and Learning." *Writing, Teaching, and Learning in the Disciplines.* Ed. Anne Herrington and Charles Moran. New York: MLA, 1992. 193–212.

Trombulak, Steve. "The Real Value of Writing to Learn in Biology." *Journal of College Science Teaching* 18 (1989): 384–86.

Wilkinson, A. M. "A Freshman Writing Course in Parallel with a Science Course." *College Composition and Communication* 36 (1985): 160–65.

Zeakes, Samuel J. "Case Studies in Biology." *College Teaching* 37 (1989): 32–35.

Business

Broadhead, Glenn, and Richard C. Freed. *The Variables of Composition: Process and Product in a Business Setting.* Carbondale: Southern Illinois UP, 1985.

Bullock, Richard H. "Athens/Arts: Involving Students in Research on Their Community." *College Composition and Communication* 36 (1985): 237–39.

Krieger, Martin. "The Inner Game of Writing." *Journal of Policy Analysis and Management* 7 (1988): 408–16.

Shapiro, Michael J. *The Politics of Representation: Writing Practices in Biography, Photography, and Policy Analysis.* Madison: U of Wisconsin P, 1989.

Smart, Graham. "Writing to Discover and Structure Meaning in the World of Business." *Carleton Papers in Applied Language Studies* 2 (1985): 33–44.

Tebeaux, Elizabeth. "Redesigning Professional Writing Courses to Meet the Communication Needs of Writers in Business and Industry." *College Composition and Communication* 36 (1985): 419–28.

Chemistry

Cochran, John C. "A Novel Exam Format for Advanced Courses." *Journal of Chemical Education* 59 (1982): 217.

Meese, George. "Focused Learning in Chemistry Research: Suzanne's Journal." *The Journal Book.* Ed. Toby Fulwiler. Portsmouth, NH: Boynton/Cook, 1987. 337–47.

Powell, Alfred. "A Chemist's View of Writing, Reading, and Thinking Across the Curriculum." *College Composition and Communication* 36 (1985): 414–18.

Rymer, Jone. "Scientific Composing Processes: How Eminent Scientists Write Journal Articles." *Writing in Academic Disciplines.* Vol. 2 of *Advances in Writing Research.* Ed. David A. Jolliffe. Norwood, NJ: Ablex, 1988. 211–50.

Computer Science

Shibbi Abdullah. "Increasing Learning with Writing in Quantitative and Computer Courses." *College Teaching* 40 (1992): 123–27.

Economics

Burke, Kenneth. "Twelve Propositions by Kenneth Burke on the Relation between Economics and Psychology." *Science and Society* 2 (1938): 242–52.

Greco, J. "Teaching Intermediate Microeconomics by Adopting a Writing Strategy." *Journal of Business Education* 59 (1984): 254–56.

Henry, Louis H. "Clustering: Writing (and Learning) about Economics." *College Teaching* 34 (1986): 89–93.

McCloskey, Donald N. "The Literary Character of Economics." *Daedalus* 113 (1984): 97–119.

Education

Marsella, Joy, Thomas L. Hilgers, and Clemence McLaren. "How Students Handle Writing Assignments: A Study of Eighteen Responses in Six Disciplines." *Writing, Teaching, and Learning in the Disciplines.* Ed. Anne Herrington and Charles Moran. New York: MLA, 1992. 174–88.

Engineering

Barnum, Carol M. "Industrial Engineering Technology and English: Team Work on the Senate Project." *Writing Across the Curriculum* 3 (1985): 5.

Herrington, Anne. "Writing in Academic Settings: A Study of the Contexts for Writing in Two College Chemical Engineering Courses." *Research in the Teaching of English* 19 (1985): 331–61.

Hornbeck, David E. "Some Requirements of Technical Report Writing in Civil Engineering." *Writing Across the Curriculum* 1 (1984): 7.

Jones, Robert, and Joseph J. Comprone. "Where Do We Go Next in Writing across the Curriculum? *College Composition and Communication* 44 (1993): 59–68.

Kalmbach, James R. "The Laboratory Reports of Engineering Students: A Case Study." *Writing Across the Disciplines: Research into Practice.* Ed. Art Young and Toby Fulwiler. Upper Montclair, NJ: Boynton/Cook, 1986. 176–83.

Koen, Billy Vaughn. "Toward a Definition of the Engineering Method." *Engineering Education* 75 (1984): 150–55.

McCulley, George A., and Jon A. Soper. "Assessing the Writing Skills of Engineering Students: 1978–1983." *Writing Across the Disciplines: Research into Practice.* Ed. Art Young and Toby Fulwiler. Upper Montclair, NJ: Boynton/Cook, 1986. 109–36.

Miller, Carolyn R., and Jack Seltzer. "Special Topics of Argument in Engineering Reports." *Writing in Non-Academic Settings.* Ed. Lee Odell and Dixie Goswami. New York: Guilford, 1985. 309–41.

Selfe, Cynthia L., and Freydoon Arbabi. "Writing to Learn: Engineering Student Journals." *Writing Across the Disciplines: Research into Practice.* Ed. Art Young and Toby Fulwiler. Upper Montclair, NJ: Boynton/Cook, 1986. 184–91.

Seltzer, Jack. "The Composing Processes of an Engineer." *College Composition and Communication* 34 (1983): 174–87.

Winsor, Dorothy A. "What Counts as Writing? An Argument from Engineers' Practice." *Journal of Advanced Composition* 12 (1992): 337–48.

English

Marsella, Joy, Thomas L. Hilgers, and Clemence McLaren. "How Students Handle Writing Assignments: A Study of Eighteen Responses in Six Disciplines." *Writing, Teaching, and Learning in the Disciplines.* Ed. Anne Herrington and Charles Moran. New York: MLA, 1992. 174–88.

Moore, Leslie E., and Linda H. Peterson. "Convention as Connection: Linking the Composition Course to the English and College Curriculum." *College Composition and Communication* 37 (1986): 466–77.

Environmental Studies

Abrams, Kathleen. "Literature and Science: An Interdisciplinary Approach to Environmental Studies." *Current Review* 18 (1979): 302–04.

Film

Shapiro, Michael J. *The Politics of Representation: Writing Practices in Biography, Photography, and Policy Analysis.* Madison: U of Wisconsin P, 1989.

Folklore

Sweterlitsch, Richard. "The Honest Voice of Inquiry: Teaching Folklore through Writing." *The Journal Book.* Ed. Toby Fulwiler. Portsmouth, NH: Boynton/Cook, 1987. 239–45.

Foreign Languages

Sandler, Karen Wiley. "Letting Them Write When They Can't Even Talk? Writing as Discovery in the Foreign Language Classroom." *The Journal Book.* Ed. Toby Fulwiler. Portsmouth, NH: Boynton/Cook, 1987. 312–20.

Tabor, Kenneth. "Gaining Successful Writing in the Foreign Language Classroom." *Foreign Language Annals* 17 (1984): 123–24.

Geography

Baltensperger, Bradley H. "Journals in Economic Geography." *The Journal Book.* Ed. Toby Fulwiler. Portsmouth, NH: Boynton/Cook, 1987. 387–90.

Dunlap, Louise. "Advocacy and Neutrality: A Contradiction in the Discourse of Urban Planners." *Writing, Teaching, and Learning in the Disciplines.* Ed. Anne Herrington and Charles Moran. New York: MLA, 1992. 213–30.

Nightingale, Peggy. "Speaking of Student Writing. . . ." *Journal of Geography in Higher Education* 15 (1991): 3–13.

Geology

Beiersdorfer, Raymond E. "An Integrated Approach to Geologic Writing for Non-Science Majors Based on Study of California River." *Journal of Geologic Education* 39 (1991): 230–31.

History

Botein, Stephen, et al., eds. *Experiments in History Teaching.* Cambridge: Harvard U, Danforth Center, 1977.

Estus, Charles. "An Interdisciplinary Approach to Community Studies." *History Teacher* 13 (1979): 37–48.

Greene, Stuart. "The Role of Task in the Development of Academic Thinking through Reading and Writing in a College History Course." *Research in the Teaching of English* 27 (1993): 46–75.

Lorence, J. L. "The Critical Analysis of Documentary Evidence: Basic Skills in the History Classroom." *Teaching History: A Journal of Methods* 8 (1983): 77–84.

Mulholland, Bernadette Marie. "It's Not Just the Writing." *The Journal Book.* Ed. Toby Fulwiler. Portsmouth, NH: Boynton/Cook, 1987. 227–38.

Sherman, Sarah W. "Inventing an Elephant: History as Composition." *Only Connect: Uniting Reading and Writing.* Ed. Thomas Newkirk. Upper Montclair, NJ: Boynton/Cook, 1986. 211–26.

Simon, Linda. "De-Coding Writing Assignments." *History Teacher* 24 (1991): 149–55.

Steffens, Henry. "Designing History Writing Assignments for Student Success." *Social Studies* 80 (1989): 59–63.

———. "Helping Students Improve Their Own Writing: The Self-Conference Sheet." *History Teacher* 24 (1991): 239–41.

———. "Journals in the Teaching of History." *The Journal Book.* Ed. Toby Fulwiler. Portsmouth, NH: Boynton/Cook, 1987. 219–26.

———. "Using Informal Writing in Large History Classes: Helping Students to Find Interest and Meaning in History." *Social Studies* 82 (1991): 107–09.

Thieman, Gayle Y. "Using Fictional Journals to Study Underrepresented Groups in History." *Social Education* 56 (1992): 185–86.

Humanities

Garfield, Eugene. "Is Information Retrieval in the Arts and Humanities Inherently Different from That in Science? The Effect that ISI's Citation Index for the Arts and Humanities Is Expected to Have on Future Scholarship." *Library Quarterly* 50 (1980): 40–57.

Kelly, Kathleen. "Professional Writing in the Humanities Course." *College Composition and Communication* 36 (1985): 234–36.

Morgan, Bob. "Three Dreams of Language; Or, No Longer Immured in the Bastille of the Humanist Word." *College English* 49 (1987): 449–58.

Interdisciplinary Studies and General Education

Bean, John. "The Role of Writing-Across-the-Curriculum in General Education: A Guide for Administrators and Curriculum Planners." *Perspectives* 22 (1992): 138–59.

Hedley, Jane, and Jo Ellen Parker. "Writing Across the Curriculum: The Vantage of the Liberal Arts." *ADE Bulletin* 98 (Spring 1991): 22–28.

McCarthy, Lucille Parkinson, and Stephen M. Fishman. "Boundary Conversations: Conflicting Ways of Knowing in Philosophy and Interdisciplinary Research." *Research in the Teaching of English* 25 (1991): 419–68.

Thaiss, Christopher. "A Journal in the Arts." *The Journal Book.* Ed. Toby Fulwiler. Portsmouth, NH: Boynton/Cook, 1987. 246–53.

Law

Collins, Terence. "Further Notes on Legal Writing: Designing the Course for Legal Paraprofessionals." *College Composition and Communication* 31 (1980): 58–62.

Fuller, Steve. "Beyond the Rhetoric of Antitheory: Towards a Revisionist Interpretation of Critical Legal Studies." *Rhetoric in the Human Sciences.* Ed. Herbert W. Simons. London: Sage, 1989. 133–51.

Gopen, George D. "Rhyme and Reason: Why the Study of Poetry Is the Best Preparation for the Study of Law." *College English* 46 (1984): 333–47.

Liberal Arts

Bialostosky, Don H. "Liberal Education, Writing, and the Dialogic Self." *Contending with Words: Composition and Rhetoric in a Postmodern Age.* Ed. Patricia Harkin and John Schilb. New York: MLA, 1991. 11–22.

Bruffee, Kenneth A. "The Structure of Knowledge and the Future of Liberal Education." *Liberal Education* 67 (1981): 177–86.

Dubrow, Heather. "A World Elsewhere: Teaching in a Liberal Arts College." *ADE Bulletin* 103 (Winter 1992): 38–44.

Hedley, Jane, and Jo Ellen Parker. "Writing Across the Curriculum: The Vantage of the Liberal Arts." *ADE Bulletin* 98 (Spring 1991): 22–28.

Literature

Abrams, Kathleen. "Literature and Science: An Interdisciplinary Approach to Environmental Studies." *Current Review* 18 (1979): 302–04.

Deen, Rosemary. "An Interplay of Powers: Writing about Literature." *Only Connect: Uniting Reading and Writing.* Ed. Thomas Newkirk. Upper Montclair, NJ: Boynton/Cook, 1986. 174–86.

Fahnestock, Jeanne, et al. "The Stases in Scientific and Literary Argument." *Written Communication* 5 (1988): 427–43.

Flynn, Elizabeth A. "Composing Responses to Literary Texts: A Process Approach." *Writing Across the Disciplines: Research into Practice.* Ed. Art Young and Toby Fulwiler. Upper Montclair, NJ: Boynton/Cook, 1986. 208–14.

Fulwiler, Toby. "Writing and Learning American Literature." *Writing, Teaching, and Learning in the Disciplines.* Ed. Anne Herrington and Charles Moran. New York: MLA, 1992. 156–73.

Herrington, Anne J. "Teaching, Writing, and Learning: A Naturalistic Study of Writing in an Undergraduate Literature Course." *Writing in Academic Disciplines*. Vol. 2 of *Advances in Writing Research*. Ed. David A. Jolliffe. Norwood, NJ: Ablex, 1988. 133–66.

Livingston, Paisley. *Literary Knowledge: Humanistic Inquiry and the Philosophy of Science*. Ithaca: Cornell UP, 1988.

MacDonald, Susan Peck, and Charles R. Cooper. "Contributions of Academic and Dialogic Journals to Writing about Literature." *Writing, Teaching, and Learning in the Disciplines*. Ed. Anne Herrington and Charles Moran. New York: MLA, 1992. 137–55.

Marshall, James D. "The Effects of Writing on Students' Understanding of Literary Texts." *Research in the Teaching of English* 21 (1987): 30–63.

Shultz, Jean-Marie. "Writing Mode in the Articulation of Language and Literature Classes: Theory and Practice." *Modern Language Journal* 75 (1991): 411–17.

Sullivan, Patricia A. "Writing in the Graduate Curriculum: Literary Criticism as Composition." *Journal of Advanced Composition* 11 (1991): 283–300.

Mathematics

BeMiller, Stephen. "The Mathematics Workbook." *The Journal Book*. Ed. Toby Fulwiler. Portsmouth, NH: Boynton/Cook, 1987. 359–66.

Borasi, Raffaella. "Journal Writing and Mathematics Instruction." *Education Studies in Mathematics* 20 (1989): 347–65.

Connolly, Paul, and Teresa Vilardi. *Writing to Learn Mathematics and Science*. New York: Teachers College P, 1989.

Goldberg, D. "Integrating Writing into the Mathematics Curriculum." *Two-Year College Mathematics Journal* 14 (1983): 421–24.

Johnson, Marvin. "Writing in a Mathematics Class: A Valuable Tool for Learning." *Mathematics Teacher* 76 (1983): 117–19.

Marsella, Joy, Thomas L. Hilgers, and Clemence McLaren. "How Students Handle Writing Assignments: A Study of Eighteen Responses in Six Disciplines." *Writing, Teaching, and Learning in the Disciplines*. Ed. Anne Herrington and Charles Moran. New York: MLA, 1992. 174–88.

Miller, L. Diane. "Teacher Benefits from Using Impromptu Writing Prompts in Algebra Classes." *Journal for Research in Mathematics Education* 23 (1992): 329–40.

Selfe, Cynthia L., Bruce T. Petersen, and Cynthia L. Nahrgang. "Journal Writing in Mathematics." *Writing Across the Disciplines: Research into Practice*. Ed. Art Young and Toby Fulwiler. Upper Montclair, NJ: Boynton/Cook, 1986. 192–207.

Sterrett, Andrew, ed. *Using Writing to Teach Mathematics*. Washington: Mathematical Association of America, 1990.

Music

Ambrose, Jane. "Music Journals." *The Journal Book*. Ed. Toby Fulwiler. Portsmouth, NH: Boynton/Cook, 1987. 261–68.

Fulwiler, Toby. *Teaching with Writing*. Portsmouth, NH: Boynton/Cook, 1987. Chapter 8, "Writing and Testing."

Philosophy

Carella, Michael J. "Philosophy as Literacy: Teaching College Students to Read Critically and Write Cogently." *College Composition and Communication* 34 (1983): 57–61.

Cunningham, Frank J. "Writing Philosophy: Sequential Essays and Objective Tests." *College Composition and Communication* 31 (1985): 160–66.

Fulwiler, Toby. *Teaching with Writing*. Portsmouth, NH: Boynton/Cook, 1987. Chapter 8, "Writing and Testing."

Kent, O. T. "Student Journals and the Goals of Philosophy." *The Journal Book*. Ed. Toby Fulwiler. Portsmouth, NH: Boynton/Cook, 1987. 269–77.

McCarthy, Lucille Parkinson, and Stephen M. Fishman. "Boundary Conversations: Conflicting Ways of Knowing in Philosophy and Interdisciplinary Research." *Research in the Teaching of English* 25 (1991): 419–68.

Moulton, Janice. "A Paradigm of Philosophy: The Adversary Method." *Discovering Reality: Feminist Perspectives on Epistemology, Metaphysics, Methodology, and Philosophy of Science*. Ed. Sandra Harding and Merrill B. Hintikka. Boston: Reidel, 1983. 149–64.

North, Stephen M. "The Philosophical Journal: Three Case Studies." *The Journal Book*. Ed. Toby Fulwiler. Portsmouth, NH: Boynton/Cook, 1987. 278–88.

——. "Writing in a Philosophy Class: Three Case Studies." *Research in the Teaching of English* 20 (1986): 225–62.

Physical Education

Metcalf, James. "Teaching Writing in Physical Education and Recreation." *Journal of Physical Education and Recreation* 50 (1979): 38.

Physics

Chi, M. T. H., P. Feltovich, and R. Glaser. "Categorization and Representation of Physics Problems by Experts and Novices." *Cognitive Science* 5 (1981): 121–52.

Dee-Lucas, Diana, and Jill D. Larkin. "Novice Strategies for Processing Scientific Texts." *Discourse Processes* 9 (1986): 329–54.

Grumbacher, Judy. "How Writing Helps Physics Students Become Better Problem Solvers." *The Journal Book*. Ed. Toby Fulwiler. Portsmouth, NH: Boynton/Cook, 1987. 323–29.

Jensen, Verner. "Writing in College Physics." *The Journal Book*. Ed. Toby Fulwiler. Portsmouth, NH: Boynton/Cook, 1987. 330–36.

Kirkpatrick, Larry, and Adele Pittendrigh. "A Writing Teacher in a Physics Classroom." *Physics Teacher* 22 (1984): 59–64.

Larkin, J., J. McDermott, D. P. Simon, and H. Simon. "Expert and Novice Performance in Solving Physics Problems." *Science* 208 (1980): 1335–42.

Mullin, William J. "Writing in Physics." *Physics Teacher* 56 (1989): 70–73.

Political Science

Brodsky, David, and Eileen Meagher. "Journals and Political Science." *The Journal Book*. Ed. Toby Fulwiler. Portsmouth, NH: Boynton/Cook, 1987. 375–86.

Fulwiler, Toby. *Teaching with Writing*. Portsmouth, NH: Boynton/Cook, 1987. Chapter 8, "Writing and Testing."

Pittendrign, Adele S. "A Model for Teaching Writing in Large Introductory Political Science Classes." *Political Science Teacher* 2 (1991): 5–10.

Schall, James. "On the Teaching of Political Philosophy." *Perspectives on Political Science* 20 (1990): 353–58.

Voss, James F., et al. "Problem-Solving and Skill in the Social Sciences." *The Psychology of Learning and Motivation*. Vol. 17. Ed. G. H. Bower. New York: Academic, 1983. 165–213.

Psychology

Blevins-Knabe, B. "Writing to Learn while Learning to Write." *Teaching of Psychology* 14 (1987): 239–41.

Burke, Kenneth. "Twelve Propositions by Kenneth Burke on the Relation between Economics and Psychology." *Science and Society* 2 (1938): 242–52.

Friedrich, James. "Learning to View Psychology as a Science: Self-Persuasion through Writing." *Teaching of Psychology* 17 (1990): 23–26.

Gorman, Michael E., Margaret E. Gorman, and Art Young. "Poetic Writing in Psychology." *Writing Across the Disciplines: Research into Practice.* Ed. Art Young and Toby Fulwiler. Upper Montclair, NJ: Boynton/Cook, 1986. 139–59.

Hettich, Paul. "Journal Writing: Old Fare or Nouvelle Cuisine?" *Teaching of Psychology* 17 (1990): 36–39.

Jolley, Janina M., and Mark L. Mitchell. "Two Psychologists' Experiences with Journals." *Teaching of Psychology* 17 (1990): 40–41.

Journet, Debra. "Forms of Discourse and the Sciences of the Mind: Luria, Sacks, and the Role of Narrative in Neurological Case Histories." *Written Communication* 7 (1990): 171–99.

Leary, David E. "Communication, Persuasion, and the Establishment of Academic Disciplines: The Case of American Psychology." *Writing the Social Text: Poetics and Politics in Social Science Discourse.* Ed. Richard Harvey Brown. New York: Aldine de Gruyter, 1992. 73–90.

Levine, Judith R. "Using a Peer Tutor to Improve Writing in a Psychology Class: One Instructor's Experience." *Teaching of Psychology* 17 (1990): 57–58.

Madigan, Robert. "Improving the Writing Skills of Students in Introductory Psychology." *Teaching of Psychology* 17 (1990): 27–30.

Marsella, Joy, Thomas L. Hilgers, and Clemence McLaren. "How Students Handle Writing Assignments: A Study of Eighteen Responses in Six Disciplines." *Writing, Teaching, and Learning in the Disciplines.* Ed. Anne Herrington and Charles Moran. New York: MLA, 1992. 174–88.

Nadelman, Lorraine. "Learning to Think and Write as an Empirical Psychologist: The Laboratory Course in Developmental Psychology." *Teaching of Psychology* 17 (1990): 45–47.

Poe, Retta E. "A Strategy for Improving Literature Reviews in Psychology Courses." *Teaching of Psychology* 17 (1990): 54.

Price, Derek W. W. "A Model for Reading and Writing about Primary Sources: The Case of Introductory Psychology." *Teaching of Psychology* 17 (1990): 48–53.

Science

Bazerman, Charles. "Scientific Writing as a Social Act: A Review of the Literature of the Sociology of Science." *New Essays in Technical Communication: Research, Theory, Practice.* Ed. Paul V. Anderson, R. John Brockingham, and Carolyn Miller. Farmingdale, NY: Baywood, 1983.

———. *Shaping Written Knowledge: Genre and Activity of the Experimental Article in Science.* Madison: U of Wisconsin P, 1988.

———. "The Writing of Scientific Non-Fiction." *PRE/TEXT* 5 (1984): 39–74.

Fahnestock, Jeanne. "Accommodating Science: The Rhetorical Life of Scientific Facts." *Written Communication* 3 (1986): 275–96.

Fahnestock, Jeanne, et al. "The Stases in Scientific and Literary Argument." *Written Communication* 5 (1988): 427–43.

Gilbert, G. Nigel. "Referencing as Persuasion." *Social Studies of Science* 7 (1977): 113–22.

———. "The Transformation of Research Findings into Scientific Knowledge." *Social Studies of Science* 6 (1976): 262–306.

Gross, Alan G. "Discourse on Method: The Rhetorical Analysis of Scientific Texts." *Pre/Text* 9 (1988): 169–86.

———. "Does Rhetoric of Science Matter? The Case of the Floppy-Eared Rabbits." *College English* 53 (1991): 933–43.

———. *The Rhetoric of Science.* Cambridge: Harvard UP, 1990.

Hacking, Ian. "Styles of Scientific Reasoning." *Post-Analytic Philosophy.* Ed. John Rajchman and Cornel West. New York: Columbia UP, 1985. 145–65.

Harris, R. Allen. "Rhetoric of Science." *College English* 53 (1991): 282–307.

Jeske, Jeff. "Borrowing from the Sciences: A Model for the Freshman Research Paper." *The Writing Instructor* (1987).

Livingston, Paisley. *Literary Knowledge: Humanistic Inquiry and the Philosophy of Science.* Ithaca: Cornell UP, 1988.

Lynch, M. *Art and Artifacts in Laboratory Science: A Study of Shop Work and Shop Talk in a Research Laboratory.* London: Routledge, 1982.

Moulton, Janice. "A Paradigm of Philosophy: The Adversary Method." *Discovering Reality: Feminist Perspectives on Epistemology, Metaphysics, Methodology, and Philosophy of Science.* Ed. Sandra Harding and Merrill B. Hintikka. Boston: Reidel, 1983. 149–64.

Pickering, Andrew, ed. *Science as Practice and Culture.* Chicago: U of Chicago P, 1992.

Robbins, Martin. "Science Meets Style: Bridging the Two Cultures." *The Key Reporter* 40 (1975).

Rymer, Jone. "Scientific Composing Processes: How Eminent Scientists Write Journal Articles." *Writing in Academic Disciplines.* Vol. 2 of *Advances in Writing Research.* Ed. David A. Jolliffe. Norwood, NJ: Ablex, 1988. 211–50.

Zappen, James P. "Historical Perspectives on the Philosophy and the Rhetoric of Science: Sources for a Pluralistic Rhetoric." *Pre/Text* 6 (1985): 9–30.

Social Science

Bazerman, Charles. "Codifying the Social Scientific Style: *The APA Publication Manual* as Behaviorist Rhetoric." *The Rhetoric of the Human Sciences: Language and Argument in Scholarship in Public Affairs.* Ed. John S. Nelson, Allan Megill, and Donald N. McCloskey. Madison: U of Wisconsin P, 1987. 125–44.

Brown, Richard Harvey. *SA Poetic for Sociology: Toward a Logic of Discovery for the Human Sciences.* Chicago: U of Chicago P, 1989.

———, ed. *Writing the Social Text: Poetics and Politics in Social Science Discourse.* New York: Aldine de Gruyter, 1992.

Faigley, Lester, and Kristine Hanson. "Learning to Write in the Social Sciences." *College Composition and Communication* 36 (1985): 140–49.

Simon, Linda. "The Papers We Want to Read." *Social Studies* 81 (1990): 37–39.

Voss, James F., et al. "Problem-Solving and Skill in the Social Sciences." *The Psychology of Learning and Motivation.* Vol. 17. Ed. G. H. Bower. New York: Academic, 1983. 165–213.

White, Hayden. "The Real, the True, and the Figurative in the Human Sciences." *Profession* (1986): 15–17.

Sociology

Allen, Henry, and Lynn Fauth. "Academic Journals and the Sociological Imagination." *The Journal Book.* Ed. Toby Fulwiler. Portsmouth, NH: Boynton/Cook, 1987. 367–74.

Anderson, Leon. "Teaching Writing in Sociology: A Social Constructionist Approach." *Teaching Sociology* 18 (1991): 243–48.

Coker, Francis H. "Writing to Learn in Upper-Division Sociology Courses: Two Case Studies." *Teaching Sociology* 18 (1990): 218–22.

Cozzens, Susan. "Comparing the Sciences: Citation Context Analysis of Papers from Neuropharmacology and the Sociology of Science." *Social Studies of Science* 15 (1985): 127–53.

Day, Susan. "Producing Better Writers in Sociology Classes: A Test of the Writing Across the Curriculum Approach." *Teaching Sociology* 17 (1989): 458–64.

Hansen, Kristine. "Rhetoric and Epistemology in the Social Sciences: A Contrast of Two Representative Texts." *Writing in Academic Disciplines.* Vol. 2 of *Advances in Writing Research.* Ed. David A. Jolliffe. Norwood, NJ: Ablex, 1988. 167–210.

Marsella, Joy, Thomas L. Hilgers, and Clemence McLaren. "How Students Handle Writing Assignments: A Study of Eighteen Responses in Six Disciplines." *Writing, Teaching, and Learning in the Disciplines.* Ed. Anne Herrington and Charles Moran. New York: MLA, 1992. 174–88.

Stoddart, Kenneth. "Writing Sociologically: A Note on Teaching the Construction of a Qualitative Report." *Teaching Sociology* 19 (1991): 243–48.

Appendix B:
List of Samples Featured
in This Text by Discipline

African American Studies/English

Poetics of African American Women Writers
Sample response: Writing holistic comments
Jamieson, Sandra (Colgate University)
page 62

Anthropology

Ethnographic Writing: Describing and Interpreting Social Action
Sample syllabus (excerpt): Types of writing instruction in the
   course (write-to-learn and disciplinary genres)
Hess, David (Rensselaer Polytechnic Institute)
page 18

Ethnographic Writing: Describing and Interpreting Social Action
Sample handout (excerpt): Using a supplementary handout on
   discipline-specific writing
Hess, David (Rensselaer Polytechnic Institute)
page 33

Introduction to Cultural Anthropology
Sample writing assignment: Making the purpose clear
Hess, David (Rensselaer Polytechnic Institute)
page 96

Ethnographic Writing: Describing and Interpreting Social Action
Sample guidelines: Ethnographic writing
Hess, David (Rensselaer Polytechnic Institute)
page 138

*Cultural Diversity: An Introduction to Cultural Anthropology and
   Linguistics*
Sample instructions (excerpt): Drafting on a computer
Lefferts, Leedom (Drew University)
page 59

Political Anthropology: Conflict and Cooperation
Sample syllabus (excerpt): Types of writing assignments
Moran, Mary (Colgate University)
page 17

Women, Work, and Family
Sample guidelines: Writing a review of the literature (anthropology)
Moran, Mary (Colgate University)
page 123

Writing a Research Paper in the Social Sciences: Some Suggestions
    (excerpt from handout)
Sample guidelines: Documenting sources
Moran, Mary (Colgate University)
page 131

Women, Work, and Family
Sample guidelines (excerpt): Using interview data in field reports
Moran, Mary (Colgate University)
page 140

Art History

Art of India
Sample syllabus (excerpt): Assigning the research paper in stages
Kaimal, Padma (Colgate University)
page 23

Astronomy

Intelligent Life in the Universe
Sample syllabus (excerpt): Integrating the first assignment into
    the syllabus
Balonek, Thomas (Colgate University)
page 20

Biology

Reproductive Issues
Sample syllabus (excerpt): Assigning two research papers, with
    opportunity for revision
McMillan, Victoria E. (Colgate University)
page 23

Reproductive Issues
Sample writing assignment (excerpt): Writing in the discipline
McMillan, Victoria E. (Colgate University)
page 102

Reproductive Issues
Sample writing assignment: Expanding the range of the course
McMillan, Victoria E. (Colgate University)
page 107

Reproductive Issues
Sample guidelines: Writing a review of the literature (biology)
McMillan, Victoria E. (Colgate University)
page 124

Chemistry

Organic Chemistry
Sample syllabus (excerpt): Guidelines for writing (disciplinary genres)
Cochran, John, and Patricia Jue (Colgate University)
page 19

Organic Chemistry
Sample guidelines (excerpt): Analyzing purpose for laboratory reports
Cochran, John, and Patricia Jue (Colgate University)
page 48

Organic Chemistry
Sample guidelines (excerpt): Analyzing audience
Cochran, John, and Patricia Jue (Colgate University)
page 49

Organic Chemistry
Sample guidelines (excerpt): The purpose of keeping a laboratory notebook
Cochran, John, and Patricia Jue (Colgate University)
page 132

Organic Chemistry
Sample guidelines (excerpt): Defining the laboratory notebook
Cochran, John, and Patricia Jue (Colgate University)
page 133

Organic Chemistry
Sample guidelines: Procedures for keeping a laboratory notebook
Cochran, John, and Patricia Jue (Colgate University)
page 134

Organic Chemistry
Sample guidelines: Organizing laboratory reports
Cochran, John, and Patricia Jue (Colgate University)
page 136

Organic Chemistry
Sample guidelines: Presentation of a laboratory report
Cochran, John, and Patricia Jue (Colgate University)
page 140

Organic Chemistry
Sample essay exam question: Structuring students' answers
Cochran, John (Colgate University)
page 152

Classics

Latin Prose Authors
Sample assignment: Teaching style through imitation
Pinault, Jody Rubin (University of Pennsylvania)
page 88

The Art of Persuasion
Sample writing assignment: Writing beyond the course itself
Pinault, Jody Rubin (University of Pennsylvania)
page 104

Composition

Critical Reading and Writing
Sample guidelines: Feedback sheet for small-group workshops
Darby, Margaret Flanders (Colgate University)
page 187

Critical Reading and Writing
Sample handout: Using students' prose to teach editing
Howard, Rebecca Moore (Colgate University)
page 30

Prewriting and Essay Design
Sample handout (excerpt A): Generating ideas
Howard, Rebecca Moore (Colgate University)
page 50

Prewriting and Essay Design
Sample handout (excerpt B): Selecting the thesis
Howard, Rebecca Moore (Colgate University)
page 55

From "Writing the In-Class Draft of the Research Paper"
Sample guidelines (excerpt): In-class draft of a research paper
Howard, Rebecca Moore (Colgate University)
page 130

Prewriting and Essay Design
Sample handout: Analyzing assignments
Jamieson, Sandra (Colgate University)
page 47

Rhetoric
Sample assignment: Hierarchical and dialogic writing combined
Jamieson, Sandra (Colgate University)
page 175

Essay Organization and Development
Sample remarks: Commenting within the paper
Lautersack, Rebekah (student), and Rebecca Moore Howard
    (Colgate University)
page 65

Cultural Studies

Ethnicity and Identity in the U.S.
Sample assignment (excerpt): Writing an annotated bibliography
Jamieson, Sandra (Colgate University)
page 122

Cultural Literacy
Sample journal entry: Keeping a double-entry (dialectical) notebook
Jamieson, Sandra (Colgate University)
page 197

Ethnicity and Identity in the U.S.
Sample explanation of grades: Holistically graded papers
Jamieson, Sandra (Colgate University)
page 214

Cultural Literacy
Sample of student prewriting: Defining and developing the topic
Lowe, Ezra, for Sandra Jamieson (Colgate University)
page 52

Economics

Introduction to Economics
Sample writing assignment: Monitoring the course through writing
    assignments
Grapard, Ulla (Colgate University)
page 110

Introduction to Economics
Sample guidelines: Generating appropriate topics
Grapard, Ulla (Colgate University)
page 141

Economic Issues: Methods of Inquiry
Sample essay exam question: Testing for specific knowledge
Grapard, Ulla (Colgate University)
page 150

Education

Seminar in Curriculum Theory
Sample guidelines: Writing policy analysis
Osgood, Robert (Colgate University)
page 142

English

English I
Sample assignment (excerpt): Organizing a research proposal
Jamieson, Sandra (Drew University)
page 126

English I
Sample guidelines: Journal-writing
Jamieson, Sandra (Drew University)
page 198

English I
Sample grading sheet: Assigning grades to separate elements
    of a paper
Jamieson, Sandra (Drew University)
page 210

English I
Sample syllabus (excerpt): Guidelines regarding objection-
    able behavior
Jamieson, Sandra (Drew University)
page 222

Specialized Writing and Research Skills
Sample guidelines: Preparation for peer response workshops
Sotol, Katherine (Edinboro University)
page 188

From "Some Questions to Guide Editing"
Sample guidelines: Peer response, emphasizing introductions
   and conclusions
Steiner, Joan (Drew University)
page 186

Gender Studies

Language and Gender
Sample writing assignment: Fostering critical thinking
Jamieson, Sandra (Drew University)
page 105

Language and Gender
Sample assignment: Loosely defined research paper
Jamieson, Sandra (Drew University)
page 128

Language and Gender
Sample assignment: Tightly defined research paper
Jamieson, Sandra (Drew University)
page 129

General Education

Roots of Western Civilization
Sample writing assignment: Engaging in the discourse of
   the discipline
Howard, Tom (Colgate University)
page 103

Roots of Western Civilization
Sample instructor's response to an essay exam answer:
   Giving praise
Howard, Tom (Colgate University)
page 157

Roots of Western Civilization
Sample instructor's response to an essay exam answer:
   Commenting on errors
Howard, Tom (Colgate University)
page 158

Roots of Western Civilization
Sample essay exam question: Providing sufficient specificity
Jamieson, Sandra (Colgate University)
page 154

Roots of Western Civilization
Sample grading sheet: Using trait analysis
Jamieson, Sandra (Colgate University)
page 212

General Education/History

Talent, Society, and the State
Sample written student-to-student dialogue
Cardin, Kristin, for Tom Howard (Colgate University)
page 181

Geography

Introduction to Quantitative Social Research
Sample writing assignment: Applying course material
Elgie, Robert (Colgate University)
page 109

Introduction to Quantitative Social Research
Sample assignment (excerpt A): Establishing criteria for
    a research proposal
Elgie, Robert (Colgate University)
page 125

Introduction to Quantitative Social Research
Sample assignment (excerpt B): Explaining methodology for
    a research proposal
Elgie, Robert (Colgate University)
page 126

Introduction to Quantitative Social Research
Sample writing assignment (excerpt): Hierarchical
    collaborative writing
Elgie, Robert (Colgate University)
page 173

Geology

Dinosaur Extinctions
Sample syllabus (excerpts): Integrating writing into the course
    (write-to-learn genres)
Pinet, Paul R. (Colgate University)
page 15

From *"Ramblings and Notions about the Teaching of Critical Thinking"*
Sample writing assignment: Teaching critical thinking in the discipline
Pinet, Paul R. (Colgate University)
page 106

History

The Nation on Trial, 1787–1861
Sample syllabus guidelines (excerpt): Documenting sources
Hodges, Graham (Colgate University)
page 132

Racism, Sexism, and Social Darwinism
Sample assignment (excerpt): Including handbook references in assignments
Rampolla, Mary Lynn (Colgate University)
page 29

Racism, Sexism, and Social Darwinism
Sample writing assignment: Sequenced assignments
Rampolla, Mary Lynn (Colgate University)
page 112

Racism, Sexism, and Social Darwinism
Sample study questions (excerpt): Generating small-group discussion
Rampolla, Mary Lynn (Colgate University)
page 169

Racism, Sexism, and Social Darwinism
Sample guidelines: Using journals to incorporate class material
Rampolla, Mary Lynn (Colgate University)
page 194

Racism, Sexism, and Social Darwinism
Sample journal assignment: Exploring issues and generating paper topics
Rampolla, Mary Lynn (Colgate University)
page 195

Linguistics

American English
Sample assignment (excerpt): Listing traits for grading
Howard, Rebecca Moore (Colgate University)
page 213

American English
Sample study guide (excerpts): Directions for summary writing
Howard, Rebecca Moore (Colgate University)
page 238

Literature

Canadian Literature
Sample study guide (excerpts): Selective reading questions
Dietz, Martha (Colgate University)
page 237

World Literature
Sample essay exam question: Using quotations
Jacobsohn, Walter (Long Island University)
page 153

African American Literature
Sample writing assignment: An assignment that didn't work
Jamieson, Sandra (Colgate University)
page 98

Survey of British Literature
Sample handout (excerpt): Generating theses
Maurer, Margaret (Colgate University)
page 54

Mathematics

Critical and Qualitative Thinking
Sample initial response during reading (write-to-learn course)
Valente, Kenneth G. (Colgate University)
page 64

Critical and Qualitative Thinking
Sample essay exam question (excerpt)
Valente, Kenneth G. (Colgate University)
page 151

Natural Science

Juggling Science and Judeo-Christian Thought
Sample syllabus (excerpt): Calendar of assignments
Nolen, Ernest (Colgate University)
page 16

Political Science

Romance Languages and Literatures
Don Quixote: *Interpretation and Viewpoints*
Sample essay question (excerpt): Take-home exams
Hathaway, Robert (Colgate University)
page 149

Introduction to Political Science I
Sample course description: Explaining the role of writing in the
    course (disciplinary genres)
Johnston, Michael (Colgate University)
page 15

Introduction to Political Science I
Sample writing assignment (excerpt): Offering choices
Johnston, Michael (Colgate University)
page 99

Social Sciences

Writing from Sources in the Social Sciences
Sample writing assignment: Whole-class collaboration
Howard, Tom (Colgate University)
page 177

Sociolinguistics

Language and Race
Sample instructor's response to essay exam:
    Making holistic comments
Howard, Rebecca Moore (Colgate University)
page 160

Language and Race
Sample writing assignment: Procedures for an E-mail dialogue
Howard, Rebecca Moore (Colgate University)
page 184

Language and Race
Sample guidelines: Journal review procedure
Howard, Rebecca Moore (Colgate University)
page 201

Language and Race
Sample response to a student paper: Using trait analysis
Howard, Rebecca Moore (Colgate University)
page 217

Spanish

Intermediate Spanish
Sample handout (excerpt): Using a supplementary
    handout with stylistic suggestions
Johnson, Anita (Colgate University)
page 34

Women's Studies

Gendered Voices
Sample journal assignment: Generating personal
    responses and observations
Darby, Margaret Flanders (Colgate University)
page 195

Index

The ACS Style Guide: A Manual for Authors and Editors (ed., Dodd), 19, 134
American Anthropological Association (AAA) style, 130, 140
anthropology, 18, 59, 96, 137
  sample guidelines for, 18, 137–138
  sample writing assignment for, 96
  See also writing: ethnographic
anxiety, 59–60, 69–70, 97
arguments, 88, 122, 175, 185, 194, 222
assignments, writing, 95, 114
  analyzing, 47
  clarifying, 97–98
  in composition courses, 3, 112
  designing, 2, 5, 9, 13, 20, 95–100, 117, 213
  distribution of, 20
  evaluating, 99
  and literature reviews, 122
  mechanics of, 117
  multistaged, 110–111
  offering choices in, 99–100, 107
  order of, in syllabus, 21
  pedagogical uses of, 101–110, 117
  presenting, as part of course, 95
  sample, 15, 29, 96, 98, 99–100, 102, 103, 104, 105, 106, 107, 110
  scheduling, 101
  sequenced, 111–114
  types of, 13, 17, 25
  using, to monitor course, 109–110
  wording of, 96–97, 117
  See also handbooks; *under individual disciplines*

audience
  awareness of, in assignments, 47, 48, 103, 119, 122, 126, 132, 135
  revising for specific, 67–68
  and situational sequencing, 111, 112
audience, awareness of, 18, 47, 48, 67–68, 103, 111, 112, 119, 122, 126, 132, 135
  See also assignments, writing: sequenced

Bartholomae, David, 87
Bazerman, Charles, 3, 4, 232
The Bedford Handbook for Writers (Hacker), 29, 32, 48, 57, 239
Belanoff, Pat, and Peter Elbow, 224
Berthoff, Anne E., 196
bibliographies, annotated, 102, 111, 114, 120–121, 224
biology, 2, 4, 102, 107–108
book reviews
  vs. book reports, 122
  See also assignments, writing
Braddock, Richard, Richard Lloyd-Jones, and Lowell Schoer, 77
Bruffee, Kenneth, 6
Burnham, Christopher, 224

chemistry, 19, 48, 87, 109, 112, 131
  sample essay exam questions for, 153
  sample guidelines for, 49, 131, 133–134, 135–136, 139
citations, 111, 121, 145, 219, 230
  guidelines for, 139, 140
  and style of disciplines, 87, 120, 131

clustering and branching, 49, 51, 52
cognitive sequencing. *See* assignments, writing: sequenced
collaboration, 164–189, 192, 200
collaborative writing, 6, 13, 21, 22, 165–166, 172
  assigning, 172–179, 192
  dialogic, 172–177, 179, 180, 192
  grading, 180
  hierarchical, 172–175, 179–180, 192
  responding to, 178–180
  sample assignments in, 175–176, 177
  whole-class, 176–178
  and written dialogues, 180–189
comments of instructors, 2, 32, 75, 156, 208, 210
  and computer networks, 65–66
  at end of paper, 62, 85, 90, 179
  explaining grades, 216–217
  explaining specific errors, 157–158
  global, 211
  holistic, 62, 75, 160–161, 179, 216
  on journals, 200–201
  laudatory, 156–157
  marginal, 61, 63–64, 75, 81, 179, 216
  and marks in the text, 64–65
  sample, 157, 158, 160
computer networks, 63, 65, 66, 177, 183, 188
conferences, 43–44, 79, 111, 112
  electronic, 184
  one-on-one, 18, 35–36, 44, 84, 90, 93, 111

small-group, 18, 36–37, 44
timing of, 36
Connors, Robert J., and Andrea
    Lunsford, 216
Cooper, Charles, and Lee Odell,
    211
courses
    and assignments, 117, 191
    calendars for, 16, 25
    disciplinary, 4, 191
    expanding range of, 107–109
    sample descriptions of, 15,
        18
    texts for, 21
    traditional, 2–3, 4, 5
    write-to-learn, 3–4, 106, 120,
        192, 223, 231
    writing-intensive, 5
    See also syllabus; *individual
        disciplines*
Cox, Gerard H., 99, 101
critical thinking, 2, 3, 4, 6, 15,
    64, 223
    and journals, 196–197
    samples of questions for,
        105, 151
    stimulating, 104–106, 118
    teaching, in the discipline,
        106–107
critiques, 29, 113, 114, 128,
    166, 185
culture and language, 78, 84,
    93, 96, 197, 240

deadlines, 24, 69, 70, 101, 225
dialogues, student-to-student, 2,
    179–189, 192
    sample of E-mail, 184
    sample of written, 181
    See also collaborative writing;
        peer response
disciplines, 119
    writing in the, 4, 77
    writing styles of, 18–19
    See also writing-across-the-
        curriculum; *individual
        disciplines*
discourse communities, 4, 8–9,
    135, 139
documentation, 27, 33, 87, 130,
    213, 219, 221
    sample syllabus guidelines
        for, 130
drafting, 27, 28, 35, 39, 46, 50,
    53, 75

in-class, 128–129
teaching, 58–60
See also prewriting
drafts, 23, 33, 53, 111, 114,
    213, 225
    collaborative, 178–180
    final, 24, 63, 100
    first, 129, 175, 184
    handling multiple, 69–70
    in-class, 129
    outlining after first, 66–67
    second, 67

economics, 83, 95, 109, 110
    essay exams in, 147, 150
    sample guidelines for,
        140
    sample writing assignments
        for, 110
editing, 7, 28, 39, 46
Elbow, Peter, 65, 185, 213, 224
electronic mail (E-mail), 6, 63,
    97, 110, 180, 183–184
    and discussion groups, 183,
        188
    See also dialogues, student-
        to-student
electronic media, 85
electronic texts, 64, 65
endnotes, 59, 130
English
    nonstandard dialects of, 78,
        79, 84, 182–183, 209
    as a second language, 79–80,
        89–90, 209
    Standard, 8, 77, 78, 182
    Standard Written, 78–79, 93,
        209, 211
    teaching of, 4
ESL. *See* English: as a second
    language
essay, academic, 51, 110
essay development, 57
evaluation, 3, 98, 106, 122, 156,
    163, 226
    holistic, 214
    negative, 185
    self-, 202–203
    using writing portfolios for,
        223–227
evidence, 98, 111, 129, 131,
    133, 217, 223, 236
    and counterevidence, 98,
        111, 175, 217, 222
    vs. proof, 55–56, 57

examination questions
    answers to, 156–159, 163
    clarity in, 150–152
    distributed in advance, 147,
        160, 161
    key terms in, 152
    revision of, 154–155
    sample in-class, 150, 151,
        153, 154
    sample take-home, 149
    and study methods, 155
    using, to monitor course,
        156
    wording of, 152, 154, 163
    writing specific, 150, 163
examinations, essay, 5, 17, 21,
    22, 80, 146–161
    designing, for accurate
        evaluation, 150–155, 163
    grading, 159–161
    responding to, 156–159
    samples of, 149, 150, 151,
        157
    sequenced, 147, 163
    staged, 146–147, 163, 173
    take-home, 148–149, 150,
        163
    topics for, 150
    See also examination
        questions
exercises
    as supplements to hand-
        books, 32–33
    writing, 26

Fahnestock, Jeanne, 236
"Feminist Theory in the Class-
    room" (Dingwaney and
    Needham), 89
Flower, Linda, and John R.
    Hayes, 100
footnotes, 7, 18, 59, 130, 221
Freed, Alice F., 86
freetyping, 49
freewriting, 49, 129
Freire, Paulo, 101–102
Fulwiler, Toby, 204
    Teaching with Writing, 7

gender-neutral language. *See*
    language: sexist
genres
    disciplinary, 3–4, 8, 9, 15,
        18, 19, 27, 29, 133, 173,
        224, 230

traditional, 5
write-to-learn, 3–4, 6, 15, 18, 27, 29, 46, 104, 133, 174
geology, 2, 105
Gottschalk, Katherine K., 197
grading, 25, 32, 75, 93, 159–161, 189, 208–229, 230
  explanations of, 145, 216–217
  holistic, 160, 163, 211, 213–216, 224, 226, 230, 231
  individual paper, 226
  progress, 226–227
  sample, sheets, 210, 212
  sample assignment for, 213
  sample guide for, 214–216
Graff, Gerald, 234
grammar, 7–8, 18, 19, 64, 86
  comments of instructor on, 65–66, 211
  common problems of, 89
  grading papers for, 208, 209
  nonstandard, 182
  teaching, 77–78, 80, 81, 88–90, 93, 158–159, 186
  teaching, from writer's perspective, 76–77
  using handbooks for, 8, 26, 27, 29, 32
grammar checking, 58, 69
Grapard, Ulla, 111, 140, 150
Graybeal, Jean, 199–200
Guide to Writing Sociology Papers (Giarrusso et al.), 27

Hacker, Diana, 29, 32, 48, 57, 239
Hairston, Maxine, 61, 64, 208, 211
Hamp-Lyons, Liz, 211, 226
handbooks, 5, 25, 211, 218
  and assignments, 29, 32–33, 49, 75
  choosing, 13, 43
  for disciplinary genres, 27
  discipline-specific, 124, 130, 134, 138
  electronic, 27
  examination copies of, 26–27, 43
  and library research, 126
  on-line, 59
  and revision, 69
  teaching students to use, 8, 21, 28–33, 43, 62, 79, 81,

83, 89, 90, 93, 111, 113, 186
  use of, in class, 28–33, 43, 78
  for write-to-learn genres, 27
handouts, 18, 29, 117, 124, 125, 139, 140, 208
  sample, 30, 33–34, 47, 50, 54, 55, 129, 135, 137
  as supplement to handbooks, 27, 33–34, 75, 130, 145
Harris, Muriel, 61, 64, 79, 80, 111, 211
  Teaching One-to-One, 81
Heath, Shirley Brice, 79
heuristics. *See* prewriting
Hirsch, E. D., 233
history, 7, 18, 84, 103, 169, 233
Hjortshoj, Keith, 119
Howard, Rebecca Moore, 30–31, 184, 201–202
  on grading, 213, 217
  and instructor's comments, 65–66, 160
  on patchwriting, 219, 220
  on prewriting, 50, 55
  on summary writing, 238–239
  "Writing the In-Class Draft of the Research Paper," 129
Howard, Tom, 103, 157, 179, 181
Hull, Glynda, and Mike Rose, 240
humanities, 87, 120

ideas, 104, 109, 223, 238
  development of, 27, 33, 35, 46, 48–49, 57, 58, 60, 66, 77, 129, 209
  presentation of, 77, 82
  and prewriting, 50
imitation
  of academic prose, 87
  of rhetorical strategies, 7, 18
instructors, 5
  choices for, 21, 27
  and electronic discussion groups, 184
  leading class discussions, 167–169
  leading small-group discussions, 169–172
  learning from exams, 156
  multilingual, 79–80

one-on-one work with students, 57, 80
  and personal computers, 69
  role of, 2, 3, 50
  and sociolinguistic perspective, 78–79
  and students, 22, 35, 38–39, 50, 69, 117, 119–120, 130, 219
  See also collaboration; comments of instructors; tutors
interpretation, 119
  symbolic, 18
interviews, 140

Jamieson, Sandra
  on class behavior, 222–223
  on grading, 212, 214
  on holistic comments, 62–63
  on prewriting, 47
  sample assignments of, 98, 105, 121, 125–126, 127, 128, 154, 175–176, 197, 198–199, 210
Jolliffe, David A., and Ellen Brier, 8
journals, 2, 6, 13, 49, 102, 120, 223, 235
  academic, 135, 140, 193–198
  assigning and collecting, 21–22, 198, 207
  collaborative, 182, 199–200
  discipline-based, 223
  grading, 103, 204
  personal revelations in, 203–204, 207
  purposes of, 193–198
  responding to, 200–204, 207
  sample assignments for, 195–196, 198–199
  sample guidelines for using, 194
  sample review procedure, 201–203
  topics for, 207

Knoblauch, C. H., 6

Labov, William, 78
language
  Arabic, 79
  Asian, 79

and code-switching, 181–183
discipline-specific, 3, 9, 133,
    136, 217, 219, 220, 236,
    238
effect of, 84
and jargon, 84
Latin, 88
sexist, 85–86, 93
Spanish, 34, 79
use of, 3
See also English
learning disabilities, 80–81
libraries
    use of, 27, 113, 114, 119,
        124, 126–131, 141, 188,
        218
linguistics, 59, 213, 217, 238
literacy, 1
    computer, 184
    cultural, 233
    print, 85
    See also reading skills;
        writing skills
literature, 98, 103, 112, 146–
    147
    sample essay exam question
        for, 153
    sample study questions for,
        237
Lunsford, Andrea A., and Robert
    J. Connors, 216

MacAllister, Joyce, 211, 212,
    213
*A Manual for Writers of Term
    Papers, Theses, and
    Dissertations* (Turabian),
    131
manuscript preparation, 33
mathematics, 58, 64, 110
McKeachie, Wilbert, 150, 155–
    156, 158, 159
McLeod, Susan H., 3, 219, 220
McMillan, Victoria E., 23, 28,
    102, 107–108, 124

narrative, 18, 111
notebooks
    dialectical (double-entry),
        196–197
    dialogic, 6
    field, 131, 132, 196, 223
    laboratory, 131–133, 196,
        223

sample guidelines for
    keeping, 131, 132, 195
See also journals

outlines, 56, 57–58, 101, 111,
    174
    collaborative, 176
    post-draft, 66–67, 129
    and revision, 129
    sample, 57

papers, 2, 5
    assignment of, 16, 20, 122,
        145
    collaboratively written, 172
    failed, 70, 111
    formal, 102
    format for, 123
    instructor's response to, 69,
        75, 217
    late, 17, 20, 25, 59
    objectionable, 221–222
    purchased, 218, 221, 230
    research, 9, 13, 17, 22, 23–
        24, 67, 80, 110–111, 113,
        118–141, 145, 218, 221,
        224, 226
    response, 2, 6, 22, 87, 110,
        182, 226, 238, 243
    time frame for, 101
    See also assignments,
        writing; conferences
patchwriting, 129, 217, 220,
    230
    definition of, 220
peer response, 18, 30, 122, 123,
    128, 166, 184–189
    facilitating, 37, 69, 191
    guidelines for, 184–185, 186
    one-on-one, 185
    small-group, 6, 49, 69, 77,
        80, 93, 164, 187–188
    and whole-class workshops,
        188–189
    See also papers: response
Perry, William, 101, 112, 154,
    160
personal computers (PCs)
    drafting on, 58–59, 64
    revising on, 68–69, 133
    use of, by instructors, 65–66
Pflanze, Otto, 7
plagiarism, 129, 166, 213
    accidental, 133, 219

coping with, 217–221, 230
deterring, 219, 220–221
identifying, 143, 217–218
responding to, 218–220
Pocket Style Manual (Hacker), 27
point of view, 82, 83, 138, 146
policy analysis, 139–141
political science, 15, 99, 100,
    109, 140
portfolios, writing, 223–227
    developmental process, 224–
        225, 226, 231
    grading, 226–227, 231
    presentation of, 225
    representative sample, 224,
        226, 230, 231
prewriting, 45, 46–58, 60, 75,
    114, 129, 141, 147, 224
proofreading, 63, 225
prose
    of engineers vs. philosophers,
        87
    formal vs. informal, 84
    paragraph development in,
        82
    parallel structure in, 82–83,
        86, 217
    passive vs. active construc-
        tions in, 81, 82
    repetition in, 82
    responding to awkward, 81–
        83, 93
    stilted, 81–82
    and women's voices, 88
    wordiness in, 82
psychology, 235
punctuation, 18, 26, 27, 217
    grading papers for, 208
    teaching, 8, 30–31, 60, 61,
        64, 77–78, 90, 93
    teaching, from writer's
        perspective, 76–77

qualitative thinking, 64, 151
questions, asking, 49, 50, 51
quotations, 18, 62, 221

Rampolla, Mary Lynn, 29, 112–
    114, 169, 194, 195
reading
    bringing students to, 235
    close, 240, 243
    critical, 15
    global, 236

relationship with writing, 232–234
resistance to, 234, 243
selective, 236–237, 243
strategies to avoid, 234
students' alternatives to, 234–235
summarizing, 102, 233, 237–240
teaching, 232
three principles of, 233–234, 243
See also writing
reading skills, 7, 106, 120
advanced, 13, 232–240, 243
reports, 119–120
field, 137–138, 140
introductions to, 136, 188
laboratory, 13, 19, 48, 120, 132, 134–136, 139
oral, 128, 175
titles of, 135
research
ethnographic, 27, 137
laboratory, 119, 131–139
library, 27, 113, 114, 119, 120, 124, 126–131
quantitative, 27
social science, 120
tools for, 28
transition to college-level, 118–120
See also papers: research
research paper industry, commercial, 218
research proposals, 123–126
methodology for, 124, 145
sample assignments for, 124, 125–126
revision, 36, 39, 53, 58, 84, 238
fear of, 60, 69–70
global, 62–63, 67
grading, 23, 32, 210, 213, 214, 216
and handbooks, 27, 28, 29, 30, 32, 33, 81
leaving time for, 75, 158–159
student responsibility for, 64, 189
through interaction with readers, 69
See also drafting; prewriting
Rose, Mike, and Glynda Hall, 240

science, 58, 87, 131, 166, 169, 173
See also individual sciences
Selfe, Cynthia L., 183
sentence structure, 62, 81
and variety, 83–84
Shaugnessy, Mina, 78
A Short Guide to Writing about Biology (Pechenik), 134
Shuman, R. Baird, 61, 64, 65, 208, 211
situational sequencing. *See* assignments, writing: sequenced
situational writing. *See* assignments, writing: sequenced
social research, 108, 124, 125
social sciences, 7, 18, 112, 138, 166, 173, 177
sample guidelines for research in, 129
See also individual social sciences
Sommers, Jeffrey, 70, 226
Sommers, Nancy, 216
sources, 22, 119, 120, 121, 129, 220
primary vs. secondary, 126
special education. *See* learning disabilities
spell checking, 58, 63, 69
spelling, 18, 19, 60, 80, 213
Standard Written English. *See* English
students
conferring with, 35–37
differences in, 109
distribution of writing in class, 30, 54, 160, 163
learning-disabled (LD), 80–81, 209, 218
relevant knowledge of, 102
study guides, commercial, 234–235, 243
style, 5, 8, 18, 217
and audience, 111
and handbooks, 26, 27
and ideas, 77
teaching, 13, 19, 33, 77–78, 80, 81–88, 93, 137, 138, 158
teaching, from writer's perspective, 76–77
teaching of, through imitation, 86–88

summaries, 29, 112–113, 114, 133, 235, 237–240, 243
of arguments, 122
collaborative, 178
in-class, 239–240
syllabus, 235
description of course in, 13, 17–18
potential components of, 25
preparing the, 14–24
and purpose of course, 14–15, 25
and reference to handbooks, 28
samples of, 15, 16, 17, 18, 19, 20, 23, 222
and writing guidelines, 18–19, 25

tagmemics. *See* prewriting
teaching writing
See also grammar, teaching; punctuation, teaching; plagiarism, deterring; English (language);
See also genres, disciplinary and write-to-learn
terms
describing vs. explaining, 151
textbooks, 26
textual analysis, 27, 154
thesis, 111, 217, 236
development of, 18, 37, 46, 60
and revision, 67–68
stating the, 51–53, 55, 56–57, 62–63, 98, 121, 128, 129, 141, 185, 238, 243
and using sources, 120
vs. topic, 51, 53, 54
writing the, 54, 114
See also evidence; outlines
topic
changes in, 60
choice of, 99–100, 107–108, 111, 117, 119, 124, 140–141, 195
controversial, 175
development into thesis, 51, 53, 60, 129
and grading, 214
loosely defined research, 127
narrowing the, 52, 100, 113, 114, 127, 145
research, 127

tightly defined research, 128
vs. thesis, 51, 53, 54
trait analysis, 65, 85, 158, 209,
211–213, 216, 217, 230
transitions, 62, 82
Trimbur, John, 163
Troyka, Lynn Quitman, 231
tutors, 5, 18, 101, 156
benefits of, 37–38
multidisciplinary, 37
referring students to, 37–39,
44, 75, 79, 80, 81, 109
typing skills, 58

usage, 5, 13, 29, 64, 77, 208,
209, 211

WAC. See writing-across-the-
curriculum
words
meaning of, 238, 243
in reading and writing vs. in
speech, 85
slang, 84
unnecessary, 82
use of, 3, 77, 84, 85, 182,
236
write-to-learn. See genres
Writer's Guide: Political Science
(Biddle and Holland), 140

Writer's Guide: Psychology (Bond
and Magistrale), 134
writers' workshops. See peer
groups
writing
academic, 46, 81, 84, 86–87,
107, 113, 233
assignments. See assign-
ments, writing
bias in, 223
"business," 112
coalition, 88
"college," 112
as conversation, 6, 7
discipline-specific, 33, 46,
75, 77, 81, 86–88, 93,
102–104, 117, 124, 174
ethnographic, 18, 33–34,
137–138
evaluation of, 18
as form of critical thinking, 6,
64
guidelines for, 18, 19, 47–48
interactive, 6
mechanics of, 7, 19, 27, 64,
158, 208, 209
as performance, 5, 6
as personal expression, 5–6
"private," 112
"public," 112
role of, in academic life, 3
scientific, 102

summary, 237–240
teaching of, 233–234, 240
thinking–in–, 196
See also collaborative writing;
reading
writing, teaching of, 1
by assigning writing, 4–5
in context, 1, 95
traditional models of, 2–3
writing-across-the-curriculum
(WAC), 1, 2, 3, 4, 5, 6
checklist for, 13
first-stage, 3
second-stage, 4
writing centers, 5, 37–38, 69
referrals to, 38–39, 81, 90,
156
Writing Papers in the Biological
Sciences (McMillan), 28
writing process, 13
explaining the, 75
general tips on teaching, 75
reasons for teaching, 45–46
writing skills, 18, 46, 64, 70,
112, 127, 213, 230
and critical thinking skills, 3,
4, 104
and reading skills, 7, 232–
233
"Writing the Laboratory Notebook" (Kanare), 132